ASSESSING FOR LEARNING

ASSESSING FOR LEARNING

Building a Sustainable Commitment
Across the Institution

PEGGY L. MAKI

STERLING, VIRGINIA

AMERICAN ASSOCIATION
for HIGHER EDUCATION™

First published in 2004 by

Stylus Publishing, LLC
22883 Quicksilver Drive
Sterling, Virginia 20166

Library of Congress Cataloging-in-Publication Data

Maki, Peggy.
    Assessing for learning : building a sustainable
commitment across the institution / Peggy L.
Maki.—1st ed.
        p. cm.
"Published in association with the American
Association for Higher Education."
Includes bibliographical references.
ISBN 1-57922-087-8 (hard : alk. paper)
ISBN 1-57922-088-6 (pbk. : alk. paper)
1. Universities and colleges—United States—
Examinations. 2. Education, Higher—United
States—Evaluation. I. Title.
LB2366.2.M35 2004
378.1'67'1—dc22   2004001285

First edition, © 2004
ISBN: hardcover 1-57922-087-8
        paperback 1-57922-088-6

Printed in the United States of America
All first editions printed on acid-free paper

To my husband for his enduring patience and support

CONTENTS

ACKNOWLEDGMENTS

Breathing life into this book are examples of assessment practices from institutions across the United States. Not only do I acknowledge the individuals who contributed those examples, but I hereby also celebrate their work and their institutions' work in advancing educational assessment as a core institutional process. Thank you to the following individuals for committing to this important process in higher education and for allowing me to make public your campus practices throughout the book:

Alverno College: Kathy Lake, Georgine Loacker, Glen Rogers

Azusa Pacific University: Connie Austin, D. Vicky Bowden, Julie Jantzi, Shila Wiebe

California State University Monterey Bay: Amy Driscoll

Florida Community College at Jacksonville: Janice Terrell

Guam Community College: John Rider, Ray Somera

Hampden-Sydney College: Robert Herdegen III

Indiana University–Purdue University Indiana: Trudy W. Banta

Keystone College: Judith Keats, David Porter, William Tersteeg

Marion College: Carleen VandeZande

Mesa Community College: Andrea Greene, Elizabeth Hunt Larson, Gail Mee

New Jersey City University: Grace Bulaong, William Craven, John Egan, Marilyn Ettinger, Richard Fabris, Shimshon Kinory, Patricia McGuire, Robert Matthews, Leonard Nass, Barbara O'Neal, Jeanette Ramos-Alexander, Richard Riggs, Afaf Shalaby, Joseph Stern, Susan Williams, Rosalyn Young

North Carolina State University: James Anderson, Jo Allen, Sarah Ash, Marilee Bresciani, Patti Clayton, Marian McCord, Joni Spurlin, and Carrie Zelna

Portland State University: Terrel Rhodes, Devorah Lieberman

Providence College: Brian Bartolini, Raymond Sickinger

Rochester Community and Technical College: Anne High, Tammy Lee

Rocky Mountain College of Art & Design: Neal King, Julie Steward-Pollack

Rose-Hulman Institute of Technology: Gloria Rogers

Simmons College: Peter Hernon

Stonehill College: Kathryne Drezek, Elizabeth Newman, Susan Mooney, Karen Talentino

United States Naval Academy: Peter Gray

University of Michigan: Matt Mayhew

University of Portland: Mark Eifler, Terrence Favero, Becky Houck, Ken Kleszynski, Marlene Moore, Elayne Shapiro

University of South Florida: Teresa Flateby

University of Washington: Richard Roth and members of the Geography Department faculty

University of Wisconsin–River Falls: Virginia Coombs

Washington State University: Diane Kelly-Riley

This book draws its inspiration from the recent research on learning presented through the work of the National Research Council and other researchers cited throughout the chapters. Their work challenges educators to draw upon research on learning to inform the design of educational practices, as well as the design of assessment methods. I thank those researchers for laying important groundwork for this book.

I express deep appreciation to the National Center for Higher Education's librarians, Jill Bogard and Cynthia Powell, whose commitment to assisting authors deserves special mention.

The author and publisher also wish to thank the following for permission to reproduce their copyrighted material:

Elsevier Publishing for Figure 1.1, Figure 1.2, and Figure 1.3 in Chapter 1, originally published in the *Journal of Academic Librarianship, 28,* 2002, pp. 8–13, from the article by Peggy Maki entitled "Developing an Assessment Plan to Learn About Student Learning."

Anne M. High, RDH, MS, Director of Dental Hygiene/Co-Coordinator of Assessment, and Tammy J. Lee, MBA, EdD, Business Instructor and Co-Coordinator of Assessment, both at Rochester Community and Technical College, for Exercise 4, Chapter 4.

Marilee J. Bresciani, James A. Anderson and Jo Allen, North Carolina State University, for the institutional example (Box 1.2) in Exercise 3, Chapter 1.

Marlene Moore, Dean, College of the Arts and Sciences and the University of Portland 2002 AAHE Summer Academy Team, for the University of Portland institutional example (Box 1.1) in Chapter 1.

The Business Administration faculty (William Craven, John Egan, Marilyn Ettinger, Richard Fabris, Shimshon Kinory, Patricia McGuire, Robert Matthews, Leonard Nass, Barbara O'Neal, Jeanette Ramos-Alexander, Afaf Shalaby, Joseph Stern, Susan Williams, and Rosalyn Young), New Jersey City University, for the curriculum map, in Appendix 2.1 of Chapter 2.

Gloria M. Rogers, Rose-Hulman Institute of Technology, for the curriculum map in Figure 2.4 of Chapter 2.

Sarah Ash and Patti Clayton, North Carolina State University, for Appendix 3.2, Chapter 3; the institutional example (Box 4.3) in Chapter 4; and the institutional example (Box 5.2) in Chapter 5.

The Australian Council for Educational Research for the introductory quotation in Chapter 3 from "Towards a Theory of Quality in Higher Education" by Ference Marton, p. 84, from *Teaching and Learning in Higher Education,* edited by Dart and Boulton-Lewis, 1998.

The California State University Monterey Bay for its University Learning Requirements, 2002, in the institutional example (Box 3.1) in Chapter 3.

Richard Roth and members of the faculty, Department of Geography, University of Washington for Figure 3.1 and the "Department of Geography's Learning Outcome Project" in Appendix 3.1: University of Washington, Department of Geography's Learning Outcome Project, both in Chapter 3.

Dr. Karen Talentino, Dr. Susan Mooney, Elizabeth Newman, and Kathryne Drezek of Stonehill College for the "Stonehill College Draft 2015 Long-Range Plan Vision" in the institutional example (Box 3.3) in Chapter 3.

Joni E. Spurlin, Marian McCord, and the engineering faculty at North Carolina State University for Figure 3.3, Chapter 3.

The undergraduate nursing department at Azusa Pacific University under the leadership of Professor Shila Wiebe, Program Director; D. Vicky Bowden, Curriculum Committee Chair; Professor Connie Austin, e-Portfolio Program Director; and Julie Jantzi, Director of Institutional Assessment Planning, for Appendix 3.3, Chapter 3.

Matthew Mayhew, Center for the Study of Higher and Postsecondary Education, University of Michigan, for the institutional example (Box 4.2) in Chapter 4.

Marilee Bresciani and Jo Allen of North Carolina State University for "Academic Integrity, Student Learning, and Campus Culture" in the exercises in Chapter 4.

Georgine Loacker, Senior Assessment Scholar and Professor of English, Alverno College, for the institutional example (Box 4.4) in Chapter 4.

Carleen VandeZande, Marian College, for the institutional example (Box 4.5) in Chapter 4.

Digital Images: David Porter, Judith L. Keats, and William Tersteeg of Keystone College for the institutional example (Box 4.6) in Chapter 4.

Mentkowski & Associates, 2000, for material contributed for Box 4.7 by Glen Rogers, Senior Research Associate, Educational Research and Evaluation, and Kathy Lake, Professor of

Education, Alverno College, with citations from: Alverno College Faculty. (1979/1994). *Student assessment-as-learning at Alverno College.* Milwaukee, WI: Alverno College Institute. Original work published 1979, revised 1985 and 1994; and Mentkowski, M., & Associates. (2000). *Learning That Lasts: Integrating Learning, Development, and Performance in College and Beyond.* San Francisco: Jossey-Bass.

Peter Hernon, Professor, Simmons College, Graduate School of Library and Information Science, Boston, Massachusetts, and Robert E. Dugan, Director, Mildred F. Sawyer Library, Suffolk University, Boston, Massachusetts, for the exercise in Chapter 4.

Jo Allen, Carrie Zelna, and Marilee Bresciani, North Carolina State University, for use in the exercises in Chapter 4 of Allen, J., & Zelna, C. L. (2002, February). "Academic integrity at NC State University: Creating a culture of honor." *Emphasis: Teaching and Learning, 11*, 3.

The Modern Languages Association for the quotation in Chapter 4 from E. White et al., *Assessment of Writing: Politics, Politics, Practices,* New York: MLA, 1996.

Sarah Ash and Patti Clayton, North Carolina State University, for the institutional example (Box 5.2) in Chapter 5.

Richard Riggs, Professor and Chairperson, Mathematics Department, New Jersey City University, for Appendix 5.1, Chapter 5.

G. Bulaong, Library Director; Dr. H. Hoch, Chair, Biology; Prof. R. Matthews, Business Administration; New Jersey City University for the rubric reproduced as Appendix 5.2, Chapter 5, and originally published in the Association of College and Research Libraries (2000), *Information Literacy Competency Standards for Higher Education.* Chicago, IL: ACRL.

Julie Steward-Pollack, Rocky Mountain College of Art & Design, for "Interior Design Studio Final Project Criteria" and the "Freshman Year Portfolio Review" rubrics in Appendix 5.3 in Chapter 5.

Robert T. Herdegen III, Hampden-Sydney College, for Appendix 5.4, Chapter 5, "Primary Trait Scoring Sheet for Senior Thesis" and "Senior Thesis Primary Trait Analysis—Scoring Sheet."

The Perseus Books Group for permission to reproduce the opening quotation of Chapter 6 from John Gardner, *The Unschooled Mind: How Children Think and How Schools Should Teach,* 1991, New York: Basic Books.

Teresa L. Flateby, University of South Florida, for the institutional example (Box 6.2) in Chapter 6.

Mesa Community College for the institutional example (Box 6.3) in Chapter 6.

Florida Community College at Jacksonville for Figure 6.1 in Chapter 6, "Cohort Approach to Assessing Student Learning."

Brian J. Bartolini and Raymond L. Sickinger, Providence College, for the institutional example (Box 6.4) in Chapter 6.

HarperCollins Publishers for permission to reprint the quotation that opens Chapter 7 from Jim Collins' *From Good to Great: Why Some Companies Make the Leap and Others Don't.* Copyright © 2001 by Jim Collins.

The Faculty Assessment Committee, University of Wisconsin–River Falls, and Michael Middleton, Chair, for the institutional example Box 7.5 in Chapter 7.

Diane Kelly-Riley, Washington State University Critical Thinking Project, for the consent form in Appendix 7.2, Chapter 7.

The United States Naval Academy for the mission statement reproduced as Figure 7.1 in Chapter 7.

Trudy W. Banta, Vice Chancellor for Planning and Institutional Improvement, IUPUI, for Figure 7.2, Chapter 7.

Peter J. Gray, Director, Academic Assessment, United States Naval Academy for description of the Academy's assessment infrastructure and Figure 1, Chapter 7, Assessment Structure and Process at the United States Naval Academy.

Ray Somera, Associate Dean and Chair, Committee on College Assessment, and John R. Rider, Vice President, Academic Affairs, Guam Community College, for Figure 7.3, Chapter 7.

Finally, I express an author's gratitude to John von Knorring, President and Publisher, Stylus Publishing, LLC, whose early commitment to this book sustained its development.

PREFACE

Assessing for learning is a systematic and systemic process of inquiry into what and how well students learn over the progression of their studies and is driven by intellectual curiosity about the efficacy of collective educational practices. That professional context anchors assessment as a core institutional process guided by questions about how well students learn what we expect them to learn—based on pedagogy; the design of curricula, co-curricula, and instruction; and other educational opportunities. Through examining students' work, texts, performances, research, responses, and behaviors across the continuum of their learning, we gain knowledge about the efficacy of our work.

This book is designed to assist colleges and universities build a sustainable commitment to assessing student learning at both the institution and program levels. This collective inquiry among faculty, staff, administrators, and students seeks evidence of students' abilities to integrate, apply, and transfer learning, as well as to construct their own meaning. Thus, this book focuses on the "bigger picture" of student learning—the kind of learning that students will draw and build upon as they move into the workplace, their local communities, and an increasingly global community. To that end, assessment is a process of ascertaining how well students achieve higher education's complex expectations through the multiple experiences and avenues inside and outside of the classroom. This process that is embedded in our professional commitment to develop undergraduate and graduate students' knowledge, understanding, abilities, habits of mind, ways of thinking, knowing, and behaving then becomes the collective responsibility of all educators in our higher-education institutions. It brings constituencies together from across a campus or across a program, as well as external constituencies who contribute to our students' education through internships, practica, and community-based projects.

PROGRESSION OF THE BOOK

Moving often in fits and starts, assessment is not initially a linear start-up process or even necessarily sequential. Institutions develop their own processes. For that reason this book does not take a prescriptive or formulaic approach to building this commitment. What it does present is a framework, processes, strategies, and structures that assist faculty, staff, administrators, and campus leaders to develop a sustainable and shared core institutional process. This process enables institutions and programs to determine the fit between agreed-upon expectations for learning and students' representation or demonstration of that learning at points along their educational careers.

Each chapter pauses to explore nested sets of decisions, tasks, and interdependent kinds of discourse that characterize collective inquiry. Institutional examples punctuate the text to illustrate how colleges and universities have developed or are developing practices that embed assessment into institutional life. Additional Resources, listed at the end of each chapter, including meta-sites to larger sets of resources, enable you to pursue particular foci to deepen your institution's or your program's efforts. In addition, each chapter ends with Worksheets, Guides, and Exercises designed to build collaborative ownership of assessment. The chapters progress as follows.

Chapter 1 provides an overview of institution- and program-level assessment as a systemic and systematic process of collective inquiry anchored in institutional and professional values and collective principles of commitment. It also presents an anatomy of the assessment process that unfolds in succeeding chapters. The Worksheets, Guides, and Exercises at the end of this chapter are designed to deepen, strengthen, or initiate a collective commitment to assessing for learning that is anchored in (1) intellectual curiosity about student learning, (2) institutional principles of commitment, and (3) meaningful beginnings.

Chapter 2 describes the coordinating role of institution- and program-level assessment committees in initiating, orchestrating, and sustaining a core institutional process rooted in dialogue about teaching and learning. A first phase of their work centers on identifying shared expectations for student learning and verifying the curricular and co-curricular coherence that contributes to these expectations. The Worksheets, Guides, and Exercises at the end of the chapter are designed to (1) establish collaboration as a principle that underlies the work of institution- and program-level assessment committees; (2) promote institution- and program-level dialogue about teaching and learning as the context for embedding assessment; and (3) guide the development of visual representations that document where and how students learn what an educational community values.

Chapter 3 presents strategies for translating collective institution- and program-level expectations for student learning into learning outcome statements—sentences that describe what students should be able to demonstrate or represent as a result of how and what they learn. The Worksheets, Guides, and Exercises at the end of this chapter are designed to (1) foster collaborative authorship of learning outcome statements; (2) foster collective review and approval of these statements; and (3) orient students to institution- and program-level learning outcomes.

Chapter 4 focuses on engaging core working groups in identifying or designing formative and summative assessment methods that align with students' learning histories and the ways they have represented and received feedback on their learning. The Worksheets, Guides, and Exercises at the end of this chapter, together with the Inventory of Direct and Indirect Assessment Methods in Appendix 4.2, are designed to deepen discussions leading to the selection or design of methods. Specifically, they focus on the (1) parameters of decision making that lead to choices; (2) properties of methods that make them fit for use; and (3) the range of direct and indirect methods that capture the dimensions of learning.

Chapter 5 describes how observers or raters interpret student work, projects, or assignments in response to methods of assessment. Developing criteria and quality standards of judgment—such as scoring rubrics—provides a means to document and interpret patterns of student achievement. The Worksheets, Guides, and Exercises at the end of this chapter are designed to assist core working groups as they (1) develop scoring rubrics; (2) pilot test scoring rubrics; and (3) develop interrater reliability among scorers as they apply these criteria to samples of student work.

Chapter 6 presents strategies for collecting evidence of student learning; scoring student responses; and analyzing, representing, and interpreting results to make decisions about educational practices. The Worksheets, Guides, and Exercises at the end of the chapter are designed to (1) move an institution or a program through a complete cycle of inquiry and (2) develop the habit of documenting this work and its results to build institution- and program-level knowledge about teaching and learning.

Chapter 7 identifies the ways in which an initial commitment becomes embedded into institutional life through structures, processes, decisions, channels and forms of communication, resources, and institutional practices. The Worksheets, Guides, and Exercises at the end of this chapter are designed to (1) promote institutional self-reflection about current institutional commitment to assessment and (2) stimulate collective discussion about ways to deepen or expand this core process.

Institutions at the early stages of launching a commitment to assessment may wish to follow the processes and strategies as they unfold in each chapter, beginning by embedding assessment into dialogue about teaching and learning. Institutions that already have developed an institutional commitment may benefit from delving into chapters that deepen or refine their assessment practices. For example, they may develop maps or inventories to help visualize curricular coherence (Chapter 2), or draw upon strategies for identifying collectively agreed-upon outcome statements (Chapter 3) to further root assessment into professional values.

Educators are by nature curious: they observe and analyze from multiple perspectives. Learning more about how well students translate our intentions into their own work extends that curiosity into the profession of teaching. What we learn promotes programmatic and institutional self-reflection about our practices. This self-reflection, in turn, stimulates innovations, reform, modification, revisions, or rethinking of educational practices to improve or strengthen student learning.

As institutions develop systemic and systematic core processes of inquiry, they will also increasingly be able to represent their students' achievement to external audiences in ways that reflect educational practices, institutional values, and the diverse ways in which students represent and demonstrate their learning. The significant learning outcomes of our colleges and universities are not discrete abilities; they are complex. And they are understood through multiple methods of assessment that capture integrated learning.

Chapter 1

DEVELOPING A COLLECTIVE INSTITUTIONAL COMMITMENT

If we wish to discover the truth about an educational system, we must look into its assessment procedures. What student qualities and achievements are actively valued and rewarded by the system? How are its purposes and intentions realized? To what extent are the hopes and ideals, aims and objectives professed by the system ever truly perceived, valued, and striven for by those who make their way within it? The answers to such questions are to be found in what the system requires students to do in order to survive and prosper. The spirit and style of student assessment defines the de facto curriculum.

—Derek Rowntree, 1987

> **OVERVIEW:** Driven by intellectual curiosity about the efficacy of collective educational practices, assessment of student learning pursues questions about teaching and learning. This chapter provides an overview of institution- and program-level assessment as a systemic and systematic process of inquiry along the continuum of students' learning to determine what, how, and how well students learn over time. In addition, it presents an anatomy of the process that unfolds more specifically through succeeding chapters. To anchor assessment within professional and institutional values, it also focuses on developing collective principles of commitment. The Worksheets, Guides, and Exercises at the end of this chapter are designed to deepen, strengthen, or initiate a collective commitment to assessing for learning that is anchored in (1) intellectual curiosity about student learning, (2) institutional principles of commitment, and (3) meaningful beginnings.

A CULTURE OF INQUIRY

How humans learn is complex. Ask a group of people to identify strategies, contexts, and conditions for how they learn. That list will likely include some of the following responses: repetition; practice in multiple contexts; time; feedback from peers, colleagues, or trusted others; self-reflection; motivation; risk taking; modeling behavior against that of another; observation; preference for learning a certain way to ground new learning, such as the need to visualize; and even the instructiveness of failure. More than a process of ingesting information, learning is a multidimensional process of making meaning. This process differs from human being to human being and may even vary within each of our own selves depending on the nature of the task we face. What is easy for one person to learn may be difficult for another.

Insert the complexity of learning into the complexity of what we expect our students to achieve while studying at our colleges and universities. At the undergraduate level we aim to develop complex, higher-order thinking abilities that, in turn, inform or shape behaviors, values, attitudes, and dispositions. We educate individuals to respond to environmental, social, technological, scientific, and international developments, as well as to work with diverse perspectives to solve interdisciplinary problems. We develop students' communication abilities so that they are versatile in their ability to represent their thoughts in written, oral, and visual forms for different audiences and purposes. We prepare students to develop lifelong learning habits of mind and ways of knowing that contribute to their personal and professional development. In addition, we educate our students to become morally and socially responsible citizens who contribute to their local and even global communities, cognizant of the ethical dimensions of their work, decisions, and actions. We also expect students to understand and practice the conventions, behaviors, disciplinary logic, and problem-solving strategies of their major field of study, as they become our future biologists, chemists, accountants, artists, journalists, physicians, researchers, and public figures.

At the graduate level we educate people to become experts who explore new territories in their fields or professions and question findings or challenge claims that lead to new directions in research and lines of inquiry. We educate them to work effectively in teams, to cross disciplinary boundaries, to become "scholar-citizens who connect their work to the needs of society" and understand "ethical conduct as researchers, teachers, and professionals, including issues of intellectual property" (Nyquist, 2002, p. 19).

How well do we achieve our educational intentions? How do we know? Therein lies the wellspring of an institutional commitment to assessment—intellectual curiosity about what and how well our students learn. Assessment is the means of answering those questions of curiosity about our work as educators. A systemic and systematic process of examining student work against our standards of judgment, it enables us to determine the fit between what we expect our students to be able to demonstrate or represent and what they actually do demonstrate or represent at points along their educational careers. Beyond its role of ascertaining

what students learn in individual courses, assessment, as a collective institutional process of inquiry, examines students' learning over time. It explores multiple sources of evidence that enable us to draw inferences about how students make meaning based on our educational practices.

This book presents a framework, processes, strategies, illustrative campus practices, key resources, guides, worksheets, and exercises that assist institutions in developing a sustainable culture of inquiry about students' learning. This inquiry builds on the successful practices of classroom-based assessment to explore students' cumulative learning at various points in their educational careers represented in their "texts," that is, their behaviors, interactions, reactions, reflections, and their visual or written products or performances. Specifically, this book focuses on assessing how well students achieve at two levels:

1. The program level (department, division, school, or service within an institution)

2. The institution level, based on a college's or university's mission statement, educational philosophy, or educational objectives

At these two levels of assessment, collective questions such as the following initiate inquiry into student learning:

• How well do students transfer and apply concepts, principles, ways of knowing, and problem solving across their major program of study?

• How well do students integrate their core curriculum, general studies, or liberal studies into their major program or field of study?

• How well do students develop understanding, behaviors, attitudes, values, and dispositions that the institution asserts it develops?

This book also presents inquiry into student learning as a systemic and systematic core process of institutional learning—a way of knowing about our work—to improve educational practices and, thus, student learning. Becoming learning organizations themselves, higher-education institutions deepen understanding of their educational effectiveness by examining the various ways in which students make their learning visible. Each chapter explores ways to position this inquiry into program- and institution-level processes, decisions, structures, practices, forms of dialogue and channels of communication. Some campuses may embed or weave this institutional commitment into existing institutional structures and practices. Others may develop new ways of behaving that accommodate the depth and breadth of this commitment.

DIALOGUE ABOUT TEACHING AND LEARNING ACROSS THE INSTITUTION

Driven by compelling questions about how students translate what they have learned into their own set of practices, assessment promotes sustained institutional dialogue about teaching and learning. A complex process, learning occurs over time inside and outside of the classroom but not at the same time for all learners or under the same set of educational practices or experiences. Compatible with the intellectual curiosity that characterizes educators—a desire to explore and question issues from multiple perspectives—assessment channels intellectual curiosity into investigating students' learning. This investigation occurs through the multiple lenses of individuals who contribute to students' learning: faculty, staff, administrators, graduate and undergraduate students, local community leaders, alumni, and mentors.

Building a collective commitment to assessing student learning also involves establishing new or different kinds of relationships and opportunities for dialogue. Some of these relationships involve deepening or transforming working relationships that already exist, such as among faculty in a department, program, or division, or among professional staff in a service. Other relationships involve crossing boundaries to create lasting new partnerships, such as among academic affairs, student affairs, student services, and those in library and information resources. Still other relationships require breaking new ground to build an organic and systematic focus on learning and improving learning. Establishing learning circles or inquiry groups that track student learning over time to understand how students construct meaning along different dimensions of their educational experiences is one kind of groundbreaking relationship. Developing communication structures and processes that channel assessment results into program- and institution-level planning, budgeting, and decision making is yet another kind of new relationship. These kinds of relationships characterize a culture of inquiry that relies on evidence of student learning to inform institutional actions, decisions, and long- and short-term planning focused on improving student achievement.

Learning as defined in this book encompasses not only knowledge leading to understanding but also abilities, habits of mind, ways of knowing, attitudes, values, and other dispositions that an institution and its programs and services assert they develop. Identifying patterns of student performance represented in various kinds of student "texts"—written, visual, oral, and interactive—provides robust evidence of how well undergraduate and graduate students progress toward and achieve our expectations for their learning. Exploring reasons why students are not achieving our expectations stimulates specific discussion about ways to improve the following sets of educational practices:

- Pedagogy
- Instructional design
- Curricular and co-curricular design
- Institutional programs and services that support, complement, and advance student learning
- Educational resources and tools
- Educational opportunities, such as internships or study abroad
- Advising

Situated within our sets of educational practices, assessment becomes integral to teaching and learning. Within this context we become more aware of how well we translate our intentions into multiple, varied, and frequent opportunities for students to learn. What an institution and its programs and services learn through students' work promotes programmatic and institutional dialogue and self-reflection about the processes of teaching and learning and their relationship to levels of student achievement. Dialogue and self-reflection, in turn, stimulate innovation, reform, modification, change, and revision or rethinking of educational practices and pedagogy to improve or strengthen student achievement.

ANATOMY OF THE COLLABORATIVE PROCESS

Providing a global view of assessment at this point in the book illustrates the dimensions of this internally driven commitment. As you read the following chapters, you will be able to flesh out the process for your institution and its programs and services. If you already have a process in place, the remaining chapters may help to refine or deepen it.

The collaborative process has no universal model that fits all institutions. Rather, individual institutions embed or evolve practices that enable them to sustain a culture of inquiry. (Internet resources for assessment glossaries and online institutional handbooks, listed under "Additional Resources" at the end of this chapter, illustrate campus approaches.) Further, assessment is an iterative process—moving forward is often dependent on exploring or unearthing information that shapes a decision or on establishing new procedures or lines of communication that advance the process (Maki, 2000a). Assessment is also a process of nested discussions, decisions, and actions. Two examples illustrate this point:

- Developing institution- or program-level *outcome statements,* sentences that describe what students should be able to demonstrate during

or at the end of their undergraduate or graduate careers, is not simply a matter of wordmanship. Authoring them depends upon reaching consensus among educators about how, when, and where they address these outcomes. Clear outcome statements emerge from this kind of collaborative work.

- Determining a schedule to assess students' cognitive development in a discipline rests on discussions among faculty and others who contribute to students' learning about how they design their courses, curriculum, and educational experiences to advance students' cognitive development. How students track and monitor their own development might also be a part of this discussion. Agreement about collective intentionality, then, becomes the backbone of a schedule to assess student learning.

Figure 1.1, Figure 1.2, and Figure 1.3 provide an anatomy of the collaborative assessment process.

A. State Expected Outcomes at the Appropriate Level	B. Identify Where Expected Outcomes Are Addressed	C. Determine Methods and Criteria to Assess Outcomes	D. State Institution's or Program's Level of Expected Performance	E. Identify and Collect Baseline Information
For example: • Derive supportable inferences from statistical and graphical data. • Analyze a social problem from interdisciplinary perspectives. • Evaluate proposed solutions to a community issue.	*For example, in:* • Courses • Programs • Services • Internships • Community service projects • Work experiences • Independent studies	*Examples:* • Test • In-class writing sample • In-class analysis of a problem • In-class collaborative problem-solving project • Portfolio • Performance • Simulation • Focus group	*Examples:* • Numerical score on a national examination • Numerical score on a licensure examination • Holistic score on ability to solve a mathematical problem • Mastery-level score on a culminating project • Mastery-level score on writing samples	*By means of:* • Standardized tests • Locally designed tests or other instruments • In-class writing exercise • In-class case study • Portfolio • Performance

FIGURE 1.1 Determining Your Expectations at the Institution and Program Levels

A. Determine Whom You Will Assess	**B. Establish a Schedule for Assessment**	**C. Determine Who Will Interpret Results**
For example:	*For example:*	*For example:*

• All students
• Student cohorts, such as
  • At-risk students
  • Historically underrepresented students
  • Students with SATs over 1200
  • Traditional-aged students
  • Certificate-seeking students
  • International students
  • First-generation immigrant students
	• Upon matriculation
	• At the end of a specific semester
	• At the completion of a required set of courses
	• Upon completion of a certain number of credits
	• Upon program completion
	• Upon graduation
	• Upon employment
	• A number of years after graduation
		• Outside evaluators:
		  • Representatives from agencies
		  • Faculty at neighboring institutions
		  • Employers
		  • Alumni
		• Inside evaluators:
		  • Librarian on team for natural science majors
		  • Student affairs representative on team to assess general education portfolio
		  • Interdisciplinary team
		  • Assessment committee
		  • Writing center
		  • Academic support center
		  • Student affairs office

FIGURE 1.2   Determining Timing, Identifying Cohort(s), and Assigning Responsibility

A. Interpret How Results Will Inform Teaching/Learning and Decision Making	**B. Determine How and with Whom You Will Share Interpretations**	**C. Decide How Your Institution Will Follow Up on Implemented Changes**
For example:	*For example:*	Repeat the assessment cycle after you have implemented changes or innovations:
• Revise pedagogy, curricula, or sequence of courses. • Ensure collective reinforcement of knowledge, abilities, habits of mind by establishing, for example, quantitative reasoning across the curriculum. • Design more effective student orientation. • Describe expected outcomes more effectively. • Increase connections between in-class and out-of-class learning. • Shape institutional decision making, planning, and allocation of resources.	• General education subcommittee of the curriculum committee through an annual report • Departments through a periodic report • Students through portfolio review day • College planning/budgeting groups through periodic reports • Board of trustees through periodic reports • Accreditors through self-studies	**Assessment Cycle** 

FIGURE 1.3   Interpreting and Sharing Results to Enhance Institutional Effectiveness

These figures are not designed to prescribe a lock-step institution- or program-level strategy. Rather, they identify major tasks that occur in a sustainable process. Chapter 2 through Chapter 7 will elaborate on these major tasks, describe various strategies for carrying them out, and incorporate institutional examples that illustrate representative campus practices.

Figure 1.1 focuses on the collective tasks and decisions involved in describing major program- and institution-level outcomes, on developing methods to assess those outcomes, and on developing criteria and standards of judgment to assess student work. Figure 1.2 focuses on collective tasks and decisions related to identifying when to assess students' work to ascertain how well they are achieving or have achieved program- or institution-level outcomes. Two kinds of assessment are important for this process:

1. *Formative,* designed to capture students' progress toward institution- or program-level outcomes based on criteria and standards of judgment
2. *Summative,* designed to capture students' achievement at the end of their program of study and their undergraduate or graduate education based on criteria and standards of judgment

Figure 1.3 focuses on collective tasks and decisions related to interpreting and using the results of assessment methods to verify students' achievement or to identify patterns of weakness in their achievement. It also focuses on the importance of implementing changes to improve learning, an action that stimulates anew the inquiry process. Consisting of more than isolated cells of activity, assessment becomes an institutional way of behaving, an institutional rhythm involving educators within and outside of the institution in examining evidence of student learning at significant points in students' undergraduate and graduate programs.

A SHARED COMMITMENT: ROLES AND RESPONSIBILITIES

This commitment involves several constituencies. These are discussed in the following sections.

Presidents, Chancellors, and System Heads

Communicating the value of assessing student learning within an institution—learning about the efficacy of our work through our students' work, for example—is a primary responsibility of presidents, chancellors, and system heads (see A Collaborative Beginning: Principles of Commitment later in this chapter). Situating assessment within an institution or system as a core process is also primarily an executive leader's responsibility. This responsibility also includes making sure that assessment is structured into the institution or system and that assessment results are channeled and embedded in institutional self-reflection, decision making, budgeting, and long- and short-range planning. Incorporating assessment results into institutional decisions and actions demonstrates institutional commitment to improving programs and services and to advancing student learning. Achieving this goal requires integrating interpretations and decisions based on assessment results into an institution's planning and decision-making timetables. Currently, this process remains a challenge to most colleges and universities because often institutional decision-making and planning calendars do not match those of assessment reporting cycles.

Finally, an executive leader's ability to create a neutral zone on a campus or across a system is essential for building an institutional commitment. Formal and informal times to share institution- and program-level results, good news and not-so-good news; to collectively reflect on results; and to propose innovations in practice or modifications in current practices define this neutral zone. Collective dialogue about how members of an academic community might address patterns of weakness in student learning, such as developing a progression of experiential opportunities within the co-curriculum that intentionally complement or build upon the progression of learning in a program, marks an institutional commitment to assessment.

Boards of Trustees

Learning about student achievement is a responsibility of boards of trustees. Beyond being fiscally responsible, board members are also champions of our colleges and universities, their educational quality, and students' achievement. Establishing structures and channels to learn about assessment results and interpretations, in collaboration with the chief executive officer, faculty, staff, administrators, and student representatives, assures that board members remain informed about students' achievement. Through these relationships, assessment results can inform and shape board deliberations and decisions about institutional priorities, commitment of resources, allocation or reallocation of resources, fund-raising priorities, and strategic planning. Student learning becomes, then, a focus at the level of institutional decision making and planning, a focus that marks a serious commitment to improving programs and the quality of education.

Campus Leaders

Establishing structures, processes, and channels of communication at the institution and program levels is the responsibility of campus leaders—provosts, vice presidents, deans, chairs, and department heads. Provosts and vice presidents facilitate the establishment of an institution-level process and a central committee, such as an assessment committee, that consists of representatives from across an institution This committee sets a timetable for receiving institution-level and program-level reports that present findings and interpretations based on cycles of assessing student learning. Results of these reports shape a chief academic officer's budgets and academic plans to improve student learning. Similarly, provosts, deans, chairs, and department heads assure that each of their schools, divisions, departments, programs, and services establishes an assessment process and cycles of inquiry. Results and interpretations of program-level assessment shape annual budgets, priorities, and plans to improve student learning.

Two other major responsibilities fall within the role of campus leaders in collaboration with faculty and staff:

1. Determining how an institution will value a commitment to assessing student learning as a core institutional process:
   • How will an institution recognize and reward this professional work?
   • Will such work be valued in promotion, tenure, and renewal processes as a form of scholarship? If so, under what criteria?
   • Will it also be valued in periodic reviews of staff?
   • How does this commitment translate into the ways in which people spend their professional time?

2. Identifying, establishing, or making available support and resources that initiate, build, and sustain this commitment as a core institutional process:
   • What kinds of human, financial, or technological resources will build and sustain program- and institution-level capacity?

Responses to these questions vary from institution to institution. The framework presented in this book, including the institutional examples, offers campus leaders a range of approaches to determine how they will develop, design, support, and sustain assessment as a core institutional process.

Faculty, Administrators, Staff, and Other Contributors to Student Learning, Including Students

Those who teach and those who learn form the fabric of the actual process of assessment. Thus, a collective institutional commitment to assessing student learning engages all who contribute to the educational process, including students themselves. Faculty, administrators, and staff design the curriculum, co-curriculum, sets of educational experiences and opportunities, and support services to provide multiple ways of learning. Individuals in local communities educate students as they participate in internships, service learning programs, and other experiential opportunities, thus extending learning opportunities beyond a campus environment. Teaching assistants and tutors bring fresh perspectives to the assessment process as both teachers and observers of student learning. Involving student representatives in institution- and program-level assessment brings learners' perspectives into this collective effort and encourages students to take responsibility for their learning. Beyond an act imposed on students, assessment is a process of learning about how students make meaning. Opportunities to engage students in this collective process abound: seeking their contributions to identifying or designing relevant assessment methods or developing criteria and standards to assess student work. Sharing and discussing results with them offer an opportunity to integrate students into institution- and program-level learning processes. Expanding the range of contributors brings different lenses to assessing student learning that broaden interpretations of student achievement.

A COLLABORATIVE BEGINNING: PRINCIPLES OF COMMITMENT

Establishing the principles of a collective commitment to assessment is a necessary foundation to signaling its institutional value within the context of a college or university. Identifying the purposefulness of this commitment also serves to engage individuals because they see the place of this work within their profession. Involving representatives from across an institution or system—as well as representatives from external stakeholders such as community leaders, legislators, or policy makers—signals the collaborative nature of this work at the outset. The following list identifies those who might work together to draft and circulate principles of commitment that provide an institutional context for this work:

- President, chancellor, or system head
- Board of trustees' representative
- Faculty, including those involved in governance
- Administrators
- Staff from student affairs, support services, and library and information resources
- Undergraduate and graduate students
- Alumni
- Employers
- Local community leaders
- Parents
- Other interested parties

ANCHORS FOR DEVELOPING INSTITUTIONAL PRINCIPLES OF COMMITMENT

Establishing assessment as a core institutional process that extends across a campus calls for a collaborative beginning. Drawing members of an educational community together to develop a statement of institutional principles of commitment signals the collaborative nature of assessment. Through collaborative authorship, a college's or university's principles of commitment statement anchors assessment within the mission, purposes, and values of an institution and, thereby, provides an institutionally meaningful context for this work. Eventually, the language of an institution's vision and mission statements may also contain these principles, indicating campus ownership of assessment as

a way of knowing, learning, and evolving. The following contexts may serve as anchors that ground, shape, and contribute to the language of an institution's principles of commitment.

The Science of Learning

Research on the complexity of learning is increasingly challenging educators to examine the assumptions underlying teaching and learning, as well as those underlying methods of assessment. Halpern and Hakel (2002) make the compelling case that it is, indeed, the business of educators to engage in research on teaching to promote students' long-term retention and recall or, at least, to draw upon existing research to inform educational practices. In *Applying the Science of Learning to University Teaching and Beyond,* they explore the effects of various pedagogies on long-term retention. Integral to this arena of work is assessment, a means to ascertain the effectiveness of different kinds of pedagogy or instructional tools in fostering desired learning.

Over the last several years, the National Research Council's publications on research on learning have stimulated deeper thinking about how we design for learning. That is, how do we design pedagogy, curricula, and learning environments; or how do we integrate educational practices or resources that foster what we intend our students to learn? How we assess our students is inextricably related to the answer to that question. If we layer assessment methods onto students as afterthoughts, as opposed to designing them based on dialogue about our educational philosophies, practices, and intentions, then we cannot learn about the efficacy of our designs, nor determine how to improve them. It is reasonable, then, that the National Research Council (2001, p. 3) calls for "a richer and more coherent set of assessment practices" that align with what and how students learn. Engaging in research on learning or drawing upon research on learning in the design of pedagogy, curricula, educational experiences, and methods of assessment may serve as a professional underpinning for an institutional commitment to assessment.

The Scholarship of Teaching and Learning

Since Ernest Boyer's 1990 landmark reconsideration of scholarship as four interrelated priorities for the professoriate—discovery, integration, application, and teaching—inquiry into teaching and learning has become an avenue for scholarship (Boyer, 1990). In that inquiry, assessment, a means of providing evidence about the effectiveness of teaching practices, has received scholarly status as well. Shulman (1998) contributes to this status by describing the scholarship of teaching as entailing

> a public account of some or all of the full act of teaching—vision, design, enactment, outcomes, and analysis—in a manner susceptible to critical review by the teacher's professional peers and amenable to productive employment in future work by members of that same community. (p. 6)

A year later in their *Change* article, "The Scholarship of Teaching: New Elaborations, New Developments," Hutchings and Shulman (1999) describe the stance that characterizes the Carnegie Academy for the Scholarship of Teaching and Learning's (CASTL) approach to teaching:

> It requires a kind of "going meta," in which faculty frame and systematically investigate questions related to student learning—the conditions under which it occurs, what it looks like, how to deepen it, and so forth—and to do so with an eye not only to improving their own classroom but to advancing practice beyond it. (p. 13)

More recently, a 2002 collection of CASTL scholars' essays notably advances dialogue about and inquiry into the scholarship of teaching and learning through ten disciplinary perspectives. Discussions of disciplinary styles of teaching necessarily raise questions about the relationship between methods of teaching and methods of assessing disciplinary learning. For example, among the pedagogical disciplinary questions Calder, Cutler, and Kelly raise in "Historians and the Scholarship of Teaching and Learning" are ones focused on identifying the "best ways to help students develop historical knowledge" and on identifying the kinds of assessment that "count as evidence for the understanding" they hope to build (Huber & Morreale, 2002, pp. 59–60).

Litterst and Tompkins' (2001) article, "Assessment as a Scholarship of Teaching," and Banta and Associates' (2002) *Building a Scholarship of Assessment* represent two recent publications that make a compelling case for viewing assessment as scholarship. For Litterst and Tompkins, assessment "belongs to the scholarship of teaching" because it is a systematic study of "situated teaching practices . . . using particular forms of research and knowledge" (p. 10). Banta and Associates' book, the most exhaustive collection of writings to date dedicated to exploring assessment as scholarship, draws together the writings of scholars, researchers, and practitioners that provide different disciplinary rationales for and perspectives on this approach to assessment, including the scholarly assessment of student development. For institutions that make the case that they value or intend to value a commitment to assessment as a form of scholarship, Banta and Associates' book provides a rich resource on procedures and methods that define the scholarly parameters of this work.

Disciplinary and Professional Organizations' Focus on Student Learning

Disciplinary and professional organizations are also advancing assessment as a means of upholding educational quality, as well as improving teaching and learning. In 1995 the National Council of Teachers of English, through its Conference on College Composition and Communication, developed a position statement on writing assessment that articulates principles of effective assessment design in relation to the pedagogy of teaching writing (www.ncte.org/about/over/positions/category/write/107610.htm). This position is particularly significant because it is rooted in research on writing as a process that led to developments in pedagogy on the teaching of writing. Thus, this public position on assessment practices is congruent with current pedagogy. The Council of Writing Program Administrators has also developed an "Outcomes Statement for First-Year Composition" that describes the "common knowledge, skills, and attitudes sought by first-year composition programs in American postsecondary education." This statement also reflects research on how students learn to write, as well as reflects current practices in the teaching of writing (www.ilstu.edu/~ddhesse/wpa/positions/outcomes.htm).

Science, technology, engineering, and mathematics have demonstrated an impressive staying power in their commitment to advancing assessment as integral to teaching and learning. Project Kaleidoscope, an informal national alliance working to build learning environments for undergraduate students in mathematics, engineering, and various fields of science, has maintained a focus on assessing learning through its workshops, seminars, and publications (www.pkal.org). Over the last decade, the Mathematical Association of America has consistently focused on assessing undergraduates' quantitative reasoning, best represented in *Quantitative Reasoning for College Graduates: A Complement to the Standards* (Sons, 1996).

Maintaining a consistently high profile in the advancement of teaching, learning, and assessment in the sciences, engineering, and medicine are the National Academies whose recent publications represent the Academies' commitment to improving education for future scientists and to promoting assessment as integral to teaching and learning (National Research Council, 2002a, 2002b, 2003). Sustained focus on assessment is also evident in funding opportunities supported by the National Science Foundation. Its Assessment of Student Achievement in Undergraduate Education supports the development of new assessment methods, adaptation of practices that have proven effective, and dissemination of effective assessment practices (www.ehr.nsf.gov/ehr/DUE/programs/asa).

The American Psychological Association (APA) has taken a leadership role in assessment in two ways:

1. It has developed undergraduate learning goals and outcomes for undergraduate psychology majors
   (www.apa.org/monitor/julaug02/psychmajors .html? CFID=2855600&CFTOKEN=20065970).

2. It has developed a robust resource Web site, a CyberGuide, to advance assessment methods in psychology programs
   (www.apa.org/ed/ guide_outline.html).

Focus on assessment of graduate student learning is also receiving attention. Specifically, the Woodrow Wilson National Fellowship Foundation under its Responsive Ph.D. Program has developed a Ph.D. Professional Development Assessment Project that directs attention to "program assessment at the graduate level" (www.woodrow.org/responsivephd/activities.html).

The Carnegie Initiative on the Doctorate focuses on discipline-based conceptual work and design experiments in doctoral education in chemistry, education, English, history, mathematics, and neuroscience (www.carnegiefoundation.org/CID/index.htm). (Other representative national projects focusing on assessment are listed in the "Additional Resources" at the end of this chapter.)

The Book of Professional Standards for Higher Education in its "Standards Contextual Statement" describes the role of outcomes assessment and program evaluation for student affairs, student services, and student development programs (Miller, 2003). Included in this statement is a focus on the importance of "assessing individual and collective outcomes of programs and services" and "assessing the developmental impact of individual programs and the total collegiate experience" (p. 239). Among its recent publications, the National Association of Student Personnel Administrators (NASPA) lists several assessment resources that advance assessment practices in the co-curriculum (www.naspa.org/publications/index.cfm).

Institutional Focus on Learning-Centeredness

Increasingly, institutions across the country are characterizing themselves as learning-centered or student-centered, a term that appears in many college and university mission and purpose statements. Learning-centered institutions view students as active learners, creators of or contributors to knowledge and understanding, while at the same time reflecting on how well they are learning. Students are shaped by the contexts of their learning inside and outside of the classroom, just as they shape their own learning. Learning-centered institutions shift away from being what Barr and Tagg (1995, pp. 12–25) describe as providers of instruction to providers of learning. Faculty become designers of environments and tasks that foster student discovery and construction of meaning rather than predominantly transmitters of knowledge. Under this paradigm, the learning environment expands beyond the classroom to include, for example, face-to-face and online learning, interactive distance education, virtual studio classrooms, simulations accessed over the Internet, self-paced learning, peer-to-peer learning, cooperative learning, and service learning.

Learning-centered institutions also focus on how programs and services outside of the formal curriculum contribute to, support, and complement the curriculum and, thereby, achieve institutional mission and purposes. How do the programs and services of librarians and information resource staff, student affairs staff, learning support staff, and other professional staff or administrators contribute to student achievement? An institution that asserts it develops ethical decision making or civic responsibility would wish to explore not only how these dispositions develop in the classroom but also how they develop or manifest themselves in residence life, athletics, governance, and work on and off campus. Students' participation in multiple social contexts or in communities within and outside of the academy offers opportunities for them to learn and opportunities for us to learn about the efficacy of our teaching or educational practices and experiences. Within this expanded learning environment, faculty, staff, administrators, students, teaching assistants, graduate assistants, alumni, community members, and community leaders contribute to student learning.

Exploring how different complementary relationships contribute to learning, as illustrated in Figure 1.4, enables an institution to understand the efficacy of these relationships in contributing to its students' education (Maki, 2002b). In this figure, the learner transfers, deepens, or affirms learning in social contexts with people in various roles and responsibilities. Relationships with one or more individuals contribute to students' learning in the following ways:

- Advancing, challenging, and building on new or previous learning

- Providing feedback that corrects misunderstandings

- Extending contexts for learning that illustrate the relevance or usefulness of new or previous learning

- Providing models of a particular behavior or ability

Faculty, staff, peers, mentors, advisors, administrators, internship supervisors, and community leaders, for example, assume teaching roles, offering diverse opportunities for students to apply or transfer knowledge, understanding, ways of knowing, and behaving. Consider the power of the following contexts in enabling students to deepen understanding:

- Observing how another peer or teaching assistant solves a chemistry problem

- Applying business principles to a student-run organization

- Applying principles of effective writing in preparing a proposal to undertake an independent study

- Serving as a resident assistant in a dormitory and wrestling with the ethical dimensions of a student complaint

- Challenging a decision made in a committee or group meeting that demonstrates a bias or violates agreed-upon working principles

- Applying principles of design to a community-based public art project

Directing professional energy and curiosity into what and how students learn, then, is an essential process in a learning-centered institution. Questioning how students develop understanding, professional, or disciplinary habits of mind; how they recall, use, and transfer what they have learned into new contexts; and how they move beyond long-held misconceptions to develop new understanding represents a challenging avenue of exploration in learning-centered institutions. What specific intellectual capacities or ways of understanding, for example, do problem-based collaborative projects, learning communities, and service learning experiences promote that other educational experiences may not? How different pedagogies or learning experiences contribute to students' behaviors or values represents still another line of inquiry.

Institutional Focus on Organizational Learning

The development of a collective commitment is an essential step in an institution's evolution toward becoming a learning organization. This commitment is reflected in the kinds of institutional structures, processes, and practices that evolve to answer and reflect on such questions about student learning as:

- How do institutions learn about research on the science of learning?

- How is this knowledge applied or translated into educational practices?

- How does an institution gather, store, and provide easy access to information about student learning that contributes to greater understanding about the efficacy of educational practices and experiences for cohorts of students?

- How do students, alumni, faculty, other campus professionals, and members of the surrounding community contribute to institutional discourse on teaching and learning?

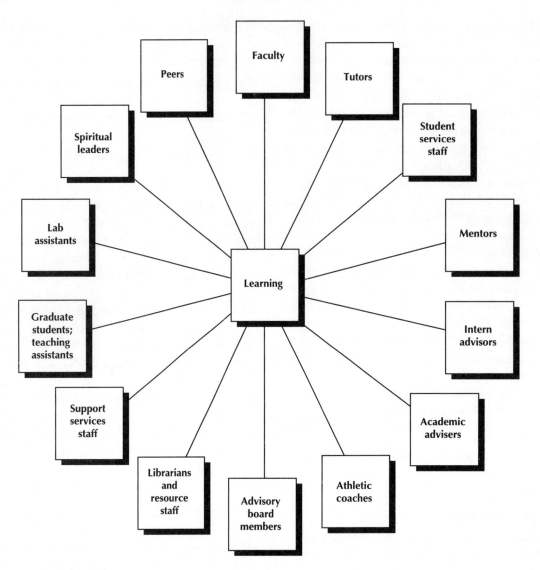

FIGURE 1.4   Some Contributors to Student Learning. *Source:* Adapted from P. Maki, *Learning contexts inside and outside of the academy* (AAHE Special Report). www.aahe.org/specialreports/part2.htm. Reproduced with permission.

Individuals and groups working across traditional boundaries to focus on student learning from multiple perspectives are indicative of a new behavior that defines an institution's commitment to learn about its work. In their learner-centered paradigm, Barr and Tagg (1995) envision the "institution itself as a learner—over time, it continuously learns how to produce more learning with each graduating class, each entering student" (p. 14). An institution may ground its principles of commitment within the context of becoming a learning organization dedicated to continuously exploring its educational effectiveness. Institutions may in this way decide to

view themselves as learners, shaped by what they learn from and about their students.

Accountability

Responding to federal, state, and regional calls for accountability provides another kind of impetus for an institution's commitment, especially when such demands have funding or accreditation implications. More than ever, accreditors, legislators, and policy makers are seeking evidence of student learning. New educational delivery systems, the heterogeneity of our student populations, and the learning histories they bring with them challenge us to focus on our educational practices. Exploring students' learning within our educational practices—such as combinations of synchronous and asynchronous learning, the use of technology, self-paced learning, and accelerated learning courses and programs—provides an institution and higher education with evidence about the efficacy of these practices.

Given the heterogeneity of our students, how well do our diverse populations learn what we assert we teach? What do we know about our traditional- and nontraditional-aged students, historically underrepresented students, first generation students, international students, commuter students, transfer students, students who drop out and then return to higher education, working students, and students who weave together their education from several institutions? Johnstone, Ewell, and Paulson (2002) view students' ability to demonstrate their learning through assessment as a "new approach to 'accounting for' student achievement." Assessing student learning becomes an objective "academic currency" for evaluating contemporary education's impact on diverse student populations (p. 13).

Though legislators, policy makers, and accreditors become external drivers of an institutional commitment to assessment, it is important to shift from an externally driven process to an internally driven one. It is vital to position assessment as integral to our professional work and to a commitment to teaching and learning that is responsive to our students' needs. Developing a sustainable internally driven core process of inquiry to improve student learning, as opposed to an externally driven periodic activity, is, in fact, what accreditors aim to promote in higher education. Regional accreditors seek evidence of an institution's ability to build a systemic process from the inside out. National and specialized accreditors seek the same process with a focus at the level of a program or service. A few examples from several recently revised regional accrediting standards illustrate accreditors' focus on assessment as an institutionwide responsibility:

- Standard 2 of the standards of the Accrediting Commission for Community and Junior Colleges of the Western Association of Schools and Colleges, "Student Learning Programs and Services," requires that an institution demonstrate how instructional programs, as well as student development and

support services and learning support services, facilitate the achievement of an institution's stated student learning outcomes. Results need to become a part of "institution wide dialogue" focused on how well a campus achieves its mission and purposes (www.accjc.org/).

- Standard 4 of the standards of the Accrediting Commission for Senior Colleges and Universities of the Western Association of Schools and Colleges, "Creating an Organization Committed to Learning and Improvement," asks institutions to present evidence of their commitment to develop a climate of inquiry to learn about and improve student learning (wascweb.org/senior/handbook.pdf).

- Standard 7 of the standards of the Commission on Higher Education of the Middle States Association calls for faculty and administrators to "work together to implement a sound, institution wide program of outcomes assessment" to improve the overall educational quality and enhance the effectiveness of teaching and learning (www.msache.org/).

- Criterion 3, "Student Learning and Effective Teaching," under the accreditation standards of the Higher Learning Commission of the North Central Association of Schools and Colleges, calls for patterns of evidence documenting that "Faculty and administrators routinely review the effectiveness of the organization's programs to assess student learning" (www.ncahigher learningcommission.org/restructuring).

Specialized and national accrediting bodies, as well, seek evidence of a sustained commitment to assessment at the program or service level—an indicator of program quality and a commitment to improving student learning. Some specialized accreditors, such as the Accrediting Board for Engineering and Technology (ABET), hold programs responsible for assessing learning outcomes that the institution values as well (www.abet.org/images/).

MEANINGFUL BEGINNINGS

Where and how an institution and its programs and services initially position an institutional commitment to assessing for learning are dependent on its

---

BOX 1.1   INSTITUTIONAL EXAMPLE: *University of Portland*

The University of Portland has anchored its institutional commitment in its definition of scholarly teaching. The following statement and descriptors provide the context within which assessment takes place. Significant are the ways in which the descriptors embed assessment within the broader scope of teaching and improving student learning:

> Scholarly teaching is an intellectual activity designed to bring about documented improvements in student learning. Scholarly teaching reflects a thoughtful engagement and integration of ideas, examples, and resources, coupled with pedagogically informed strategies of course design and implementation to bring about more effective teaching and learning. Scholarly teaching documents the effectiveness of student learning in a manner that models or reflects disciplinary methods and values.

THE SCHOLARLY TEACHER

- exhibits curiosity about his/her students, student learning, and students' learning environments;
- identifies issues/questions (problems) related to some aspect of student learning;
- develops, plans, and implements strategies designed to address/enhance student learning;
- documents the outcomes of his/her strategies using methodology common to the discipline;
- reflects upon and shares with others his/her ideas, designs and strategies, and outcomes of his/her work;
- consistently and continually builds upon his/her work and that of others (i.e., process is iterative).

The desire to create a new core curriculum at the University of Portland became the opportunity to initiate an institutional commitment to assessing student learning. As faculty, staff, administrators, and students created the new core and articulated learning outcomes, they also simultaneously designed an assessment program. A governing body oversees the implementation of the core, as well as the assessment program that cuts across disciplines to ascertain how well students are able to address seven questions common to this curriculum.

Source: Statement developed by the University of Portland 2002 AAHE Summer Academy Team and contributed by Marlene Moore, Dean, College of Arts and Sciences. Reproduced with permission.

current context. There are no absolute places to start, but there are contexts, issues, or institutional developments that become opportunities to initiate the effort. (See Box 1.1.) The following occasions may initiate your institution's commitment:

- Developing a new mission statement or educational philosophy for the institution, an academic department, school, program, or service
- Embarking on institutional strategic planning
- Re-conceptualizing or revising faculty and staff roles and rewards
- Designing a new core curriculum or revising a core curriculum at the undergraduate or graduate level
- Developing new programs or services

- Selecting a new institutional leader
- Responding to voiced dissatisfaction about student learning, such as perceived weaknesses in quantitative reasoning or critical thinking
- Recognizing achievements in classroom-based assessment as a foundation for institution- and program-level assessment
- Preparing documentation to respond to legislators, accreditors, policy makers, or other public audiences.

HIGHER EDUCATION'S OWNERSHIP

How we situate assessment as a process of collective inquiry matters. Driven solely by external forces, such as legislators or accreditors, assessment typically resides on the margins of our institutions, eliciting periodic attention. This peripheral location divorces us from our institutional missions, values, and the educational practices that translate our intentions into multiple contexts for learning. Driven by internal curiosity about the nature of our work, assessment becomes a core institutional process, embedded into definable processes, decisions, structures, practices, forms of dialogue, channels of communication, and rewards.

By taking ownership of assessment and developing an internally driven core process, colleges and universities can profile their students' learning within institutional educational practices and intentions. Moreover, within this context, assessment becomes an institution's means to examine its educational intentions on its own terms within the complex ways that humans learn and within the populations an institution serves. Undertaken systematically, assessment can provide longitudinal documentation or profiles of student learning for external bodies, such as accreditors or legislators, demonstrating patterns of students' performance over time, as opposed to one point in time.

A dialogue that focuses on teaching and learning is a sign that the assessment process is developing and maturing. As you will read in the following chapters, this focus and collaboration are essential to establish and sustain a collective commitment to

- developing sustained dialogue about teaching and learning;
- identifying shared expectations for student learning;
- developing or designing methods to assess those expectations;
- developing criteria and standards of judgment to assess student work;
- analyzing and interpreting students' demonstration or representation of learning;
- modifying, changing, or designing educational practices to improve student learning based on analysis and collective interpretations of results.

Without a focus on teaching and learning, assessment runs the risk of remaining or becoming marginalized. Worse yet, it remains an empty and intellectually unfulfilling activity.

WORKS CITED

Accrediting Board for Engineering and Technology: *www.abet.org.*

Accrediting Commission for Community and Junior Colleges of the Western Association of Schools and Colleges: *www.accjc.org/default.html.*

Accrediting Commission for Senior Colleges and Universities of the Western Association of Schools and Colleges: *www.wascweb.org/senior.*

American Council on Education: *www.acenet.edu.*

American Psychological Association: *www.apa.org/monitor/julaug02/psychmajors.html?CFID=2855600&CFTOKEN=20065970.*

Banta, T. W., & Associates. (2002). *Building a scholarship of assessment.* San Francisco: Jossey-Bass.

Barr, R. B., & Tagg, J. (1995, November–December). From teaching to learning: A new paradigm for undergraduate education. *Change, 27,* 13–25.

Boyer, E. L. (1990). *Scholarship reconsidered: Priorities of the professoriate.* Princeton, NJ: Carnegie Foundation for the Advancement of Teaching.

Carnegie Foundation for the Advancement of Teaching. *Carnegie initiative on the doctorate: carnegiefoundation.org/CID/partners_allies.htm.*

Commission on Higher Education of the Middle States Association: *www.msache.org.*

Council of Writing Program Administrators: *www.ilstu.edu/~ddhesse/wpa/positions/outcomes/htm.*

Halpern, D., & Hakel, M. (2002, Spring). *Applying the science of learning to university teaching and beyond.* New Directions for Teaching and Learning, 89. San Francisco: Jossey-Bass.

Higher Learning Commission of the North Central Association of Schools and Colleges: *www.ncahigherlearningcommission.org.*

Huber, M. T., & Morreale, S. P. (Eds.). (2002). *Disciplinary styles in the scholarship of teaching and learning: Exploring common ground* (A Collaboration of the Carnegie Foundation for the Advancement of Teaching and the American Association for Higher Education). Washington, DC: American Association for Higher Education.

Hutchings, P., & Shulman, L. S. (1999). The scholarship of teaching: New elaborations, new developments. *Change, 31,* 11–15.

Johnstone, S. M., Ewell, P., & Paulson, K. (2002). *Student learning as academic currency* (Fourth in a Series: Distributed Education: Challenges, Choices, and a New Environment). Washington, DC: American Council on Education Center for Policy Analysis.

Litterst, J. K., & Tompkins, P. (2001, January). Assessment as a scholarship of teaching. *Journal of the Association for Communication Administration*, 1–12.

Maki, P. (2002a, January/February). Developing an assessment plan to learn about student learning. *Journal of Academic Librarianship*, 28, 8–13.

Maki, P. (2002b, October). *Learning contexts inside and outside of the academy* (AAHE Special Report): *www.aahe.org/specialreports/part2.htm*.

Miller, T. K. (Ed.). (2003). *The book of professional standards for higher education*. Washington, DC: Council for the Advancement of Standards in Higher Education.

National Association of Student Personnel Administrators (NASPA): *www.naspa.org/publications/index.cfm?pcID=5*.

National Council of Teachers of English. (Writing Assessment: A Position Statement): *www.ncte.org/about/over/positions/category/write/107610.html*.

National Research Council. (2001). *Knowing what students know: The science and design of educational assessment*. Washington, DC: National Academy Press. *www.nap.org*.

National Research Council. (2002a). BIO2010: *Transforming undergraduate education for future research biologists*. Washington, DC: National Academies Press.

National Research Council. (2002b). BIO2010: *Undergraduate education to prepare biomedical research scientists*. Washington, DC: National Academies Press.

National Research Council. (2003). *Evaluating and improving undergraduate teaching in science, technology, engineering, and mathematics*. Washington, DC: National Academies Press.

National Science Foundation. *Assessment of student achievement in undergraduate education*: *www.ehr.nsf.gov/ehr/DUE/programs/asa*.

Nyquist, J. D. (2002, November/December). The Ph.D.: A tapestry of change for the 21st century. *Change*, 34, 13–20.

Project Kaleidoscope: *www.pkal.org*.

Rowntree, D. (1987). *Assessing students: How shall we know them?* (2nd ed.). London: Kogan Page.

Shulman, L. S. (1998). *The course portfolio*. Washington, DC: American Association for Higher Education.

Sons, L. (Ed.). (1996). *Quantitative reasoning for college graduates: A complement to the standards*. Washington, DC: The Mathematical Association of America.

Woodrow Wilson National Fellowship Foundation. (Responsive Ph.D. Program): *www.woodrow.org/responsivephd/activities.html*.

ADDITIONAL RESOURCES

Assessment Glossaries and Handbooks Online

American Association for Higher Education: *www.aahe.org/assessment/web.htm#Assessment glossaries*.

James Madison University (Dictionary of Student Outcome Assessment): *people.jmu.edu/yangsx*.

Northern Illinois University Glossary: *www.niu.edu/assessment/_resourc/gloss.shtml*.

Schechter, E., Testa, A., & Eder, D. (2002, May–June). Assessment handbooks online. *Assessment Update*, 14(3) 13–14. Lists institutional Web sites with online handbooks for faculty and administrators involved in assessment.

Learning-Centeredness

Angelo, T. A. (1997). The campus as learning community: Seven promising shifts and seven powerful levers. AAHE *Bulletin*, 49, 3–6.

Boggs, G. R. (1999, January). What the learning paradigm means for faculty. AAHE *Bulletin*, 51, 3–5.

Doherty, A., Riordan, T., & Roth, J. (Eds.). (2002). *Student learning: A central focus for institutions of higher education: A report and collection of institutional practices of the student learning initiative*. Milwaukee, WI: Alverno College Institute.

Huba, M. E., & Freed, J. E. (2000). *Learner-centered assessment on college campuses: Shifting the focus from teaching to learning*. Needham Heights, MA: Allyn & Bacon.

McClenney, K. M. (2003, Spring). The learning-centered institution: Key characteristics. I*nquiry & Action*, 1, 2–6. Washington, DC: American Association for Higher Education: *www.aahe.org/pubs/IASpring2003.pdf*.

McMillin, L., & Berberet, J. (Eds.). (2002). A *new academic compact: Revisioning the relationship between faculty and their institutions*. Bolton, MA: Anker.

O'Banion, T. (1997). A *learning college for the 21st century*. Washington, DC: American Association of Community Colleges (AACC), American Council on Education Series on Higher Education, Oryx Press.

O'Banion, T. (1997). *Creating more learning-centered community colleges*. Mission Viejo, CA: League for Innovation.

Tagg, J. (2003). *The learning paradigm college*. Bolton, MA: Anker.

Learning Organizations

Ewell, P. T. (1997). Organizing for learning: A new imperative. AAHE *Bulletin*, 50, 10–12.

Senge, P. M. (1990). *The fifth discipline. The art and practice of the learning organization*. New York: Doubleday.

Tinto, V. (1997). Universities as learning organizations. *About Campus*, 1, 2–4.

National, Regional, and Specialized Accreditors

To locate regional, national, and specialized accreditors' standards and criteria for assessing student learning, search through the Council of Higher Education Association's (CHEA) directories Web site: *www.chea.org/Directories/index.cfm*.

Representative Professional and Disciplinary Organizations Focusing on Assessment

American Association for Higher Education (AAHE): *www.aahe.org*.

American Council on Education (ACE): *www.acenet.edu/programs/international/current.cfm*.

American Educational Research Association (AERA): *www.aera.net/about/about.html*.

American Psychological Association (APA): *www.apa.org*.

Association of American Colleges and Universities (AAC&U): *www.aacu.org*.

Association of College and Research Libraries (ACRL): *www.ala.org/acrl/ilcomstan.html*.

Association for Institutional Research (AIR): *airweb.org*.

Association for the Study of Higher Education (ASHE): *www.ashe.ws*.

The Carnegie Foundation for the Advancement of Teaching: *www.carnegiefoundation.org/ourwork/index.htm*.

Higher Education Research Institute (HERI): *www.gseis.ucla.edu/heri/heri.html*.

LibQUAL+: *www.libqual.org*.

The National Academies: *www4.nas.edu/webcr.nsf/projectsearch/?searchview&query=assessment*.

National Association of Student Personnel Administrators (NASPA): *www.naspa.org*.

National Council of Teachers of English (NCTE): *www.ncte.org*.

National Learning Infrastructure Initiative (NLII) of Educause: *www.educause.edu/nlii*.

National Science Foundation (NSF): *www.nsf.gov*.

Project Kaleidoscope (PKAL): *www.pkal.org*.

Scholarship of Teaching and Learning

Angelo, T. A. (Ed.). (1998). *Classroom assessment and research: An update on uses, approaches, and research findings*. San Francisco: Jossey-Bass.

Angelo, T. A., & Cross, K. P. (1993). *Classroom assessment techniques: A handbook for college teachers* (2nd ed.). San Francisco: Jossey-Bass.

Biggs, J. (1999). *Teaching for quality learning at university*. Birmingham, Great Britain: The Society for Research into Higher Education and Open University Press.

Cross, K. P., & Steadman, M. H. (1996). *Classroom research: Implementing the scholarship of teaching*. San Francisco: Jossey-Bass.

Glassick, C. E., Huber, M. T., & Maeroff, G. I. (1997). *Scholarship assessed: Evaluation of the professoriate*. San Francisco: Jossey-Bass.

Hutchings, P., & Bjork, C. (1999). *An annotated bibliography of the scholarship of teaching and learning in higher education*. Carnegie Foundation: *http://search.atomz.com/search/?sp-q=annotated+bibliography&sp-a=sp03265f00&sp-f=iso-8859-1&image.x=24&image.y=1*.

McKeachie, W. J. (1994). *Teaching tips: Strategies, research, and theory for college and university teachers* (11th ed.). Boston: Houghton Mifflin.

Menges, R. J. (1996). *Teaching on solid ground: Using scholarship to improve practice*. San Francisco: Jossey-Bass.

Rice, E. (1991). The new American scholar: Scholarship and the purposes of the university. *Metropolitan Universities*, 4, 7–18.

Shulman, L. S. (1999). Taking learning seriously. *Change*, 31, 10–17.

Meta-sites on the Scholarship of Teaching and Learning

The American Association for Higher Education's Fields of Inquiry, Partners in Learning, Learning about Learning, Organizing for Learning, and Assessing for Learning, provide information about and access to research on and practices in teaching and learning, as well as information about current projects focused on teaching and learning. AAHE's Fields of Inquiry are available at: *aahe.org/newdirections/fieldsofinquiry.htm*.

The Carnegie Center for the Advancement of Teaching offers a rich collection of print and online publications focused on the scholarship of teaching and learning:

1. Its elibrary contains downloadable and printable articles that may well serve to jumpstart dialogue about the philosophies, assumptions, theories, research or practices that underlie teaching in a discipline or that underlie how curricula are structured for learning. The elibrary is available at: *www.carnegiefoundation.org/ elibrary/index.htm.*

2. Its publication archive is available at: *www.carnegiefoundation.org/publications/ publication_archive.htm.*

3. Recent Carnegie publications on the scholarship of teaching and learning are available at: *www.carnegiefoundation.org/ Publications/index.htm.*

Science of Learning

Bereiter, C., & Scardamalia, M. (1989). Intentional learning as a goal of instruction. In L. Resnick (Ed.), *Knowing, learning, and instruction: Essays in honor of Robert Glaser*, Hillsdale, NJ: Lawrence Erlbaum. (pp. 361–392).

Leamnson, R. (1999). *Thinking about teaching and learning: Developing habits of learning with first year college and university students*. Sterling, VA: Stylus.

Leamnson, R. (2000, November/December). Learning as biological brain change. *Change, 32*, 34–40.

Magolda, M. B. (1992). *Knowing and reasoning in college: Gender-related patterns in students' intellectual development*. San Francisco: Jossey-Bass.

Magolda, M. B., & Terenzini, P. T. (n.d.). Learning and teaching in the 21st century: Trends and implications for practice. In C. S. Johnson & H. E. Cheatham (Eds.), *Higher education trends for the next century: A research agenda for student success*. American College Personnel Association: *www.acpa.nche.edu/seniorscholars/trends/trends4.htm.*

Mentkowski, M., & Associates. (2000). *Learning that lasts: Integrating learning, development, and performance in college and beyond*. San Francisco: Jossey-Bass.

Merrill, M. D., Zhongmin, L., & Jones, M. K. (1990, December). ID2 and constructivist theory. *Educational Technology*, 52–55.

National Research Council. (2000). *How people learn: Brain, mind, experience, and school* (Expanded ed.) Washington, DC: National Academy Press.

National Research Council. (1999). *How people learn: Bridging research and practice*. Washington, DC: National Academy Press.

Oxford Centre for Staff Development. (1992). *Improving student learning*. Oxford, UK: Author, Oxford Brookes University.

Svinicki, M. D. (Ed.). (1999, November). *Teaching and learning on the edge of the millennium: Building on what we have learned*. New Directions for Teaching and Learning, 80. San Francisco: Jossey-Bass.

21st Century Learning Initiative. (1997). *A transnational program to synthesize the best of research and development into the nature of human learning, and to examine its implications for education, work, and the development of communities worldwide: A work in progress*. Washington, DC: Author.

Wiske, M. S. (Ed.) (1998). *Teaching for understanding: Linking research with practice*. San Francisco: Jossey-Bass.

Zull, J. E. (2002). *The art of changing the brain: Enriching teaching by exploring the biology of learning*. Sterling, VA: Stylus.

Some Meta-sites on the Science of Learning

Halpern, D. Halpern's site is dedicated to sharing research, publications, and other resources on developments in the science of learning and research on learning through assessment. An annotated bibliography and abstracts from current research are available on this frequently updated Web site: *berger.research.claremontmckenna.edu/asl/tp.asp.*

Huitt, B. Huitt's Homepage, Educational Psychology Interactive at Valdosta State University, provides a wealth of readings, Internet resources, articles, and books focused on teaching and learning, problem solving and decision making, systems theory applied to human behavior, and theories of learning: *chiron.valdosta.edu/whuitt.*

A Representative List of National Projects Focused on Assessing Student Learning

American Council on Education. Under its International Initiatives Program, the American Council on Education (ACE) is working on several funded projects that integrate assessment of student learning to advance educational practices in international programs: *www.acenet.edu/programs/international/current.cfm.*

American Association for Higher Education Projects.

1. The Building Engagement and Attainment of Minority Students (BEAMS) project, a partnership between AAHE and the National Survey of Student Engagement (NSSE) Institute, with support from the Lumina Foundation for Education, is a five-year initiative fostering ways in which Historically Black, Hispanic-serving, and Tribal colleges and universities can use

NSSE data for institutional improvement. This project serves up to 150 four-year colleges and universities from the Alliance for Equity in Higher Education. Each institution commits to analyzing the scope and character of its students' engagement in learning and to implementing well-designed action plans for improvement of engagement, learning, persistence, and success: *www.aahe.org*/BEAMS.

(See also Center for Postsecondary Research and Planning, Indiana University Bloomington.)

2. AAHE and the National Survey of Student Engagement (NSSE) Institute, with support from the *Lumina Foundation for Education*, are collaborating in the Documenting Effective Educational Practices (DEEP) project to explore ways in which campuses use NSSE data for institutional improvement. (See also Center for Postsecondary Research and Planning, Indiana University Bloomington.)

3. The Carnegie Academy Campus Program Clusters, representing institutions from across the United States, are focusing on specific themes in the scholarship of teaching and learning, such as active pedagogies. Though still in their first phase of planning, several of these clusters will be focusing on assessing student learning: *webcenter.aahe.org*.

Association of American Colleges and Universities' Projects.

1. The Association of American Colleges and Universities' Collaborative Project with the Carnegie Foundation for the Advancement of Teaching, Integrative Learning: Opportunities to Connect, is designed to engage campuses in developing comprehensive approaches aimed at providing students with "purposeful, progressively more challenging, integrated educational experiences." For information about this project, go to the following Web site: *www.aacu.org/integrativelearning/index.cfm*.

   A background paper for this project, Huber, M., & Hutchings, P. "Integrative Learning: Mapping the Terrain," focuses on deliberate promotion of integrated learning in students' undergraduate studies. This background paper is available at: *www.carnegiefoundation.org/ LiberalEducation/Mapping_Terrain.pdf*.

   To trace developments in its commitment to general education initiatives, go to: *www.aacu.org/issues/generaleducation*.

2. The Association's Project on Accreditation and Assessment, a component of the Association's national initiative, Greater Expectations: The Commitment to Quality as A Nation Goes to

College, focuses on identifying and assessing the outcomes of liberal education. Specifically, this project aims to develop a "shared understanding of the desired outcomes of a liberal education"; to identify "the curricular design principles that help students reach these outcomes"; and to identify the "criteria for 'good practice' in assessing liberal education as collaborative and integrative": *www.aacu-edu.org/paa/index.cfm*.

Center for Postsecondary Research and Planning, Indiana University Bloomington.

1. The National Survey of Student Engagement (NSSE) and the Community College Survey on Student Engagement (CCSSE) ask students to respond to their college and university experiences under five benchmarks of effective educational practices that foster student learning: level of academic challenge, active and collaborative learning, student-faculty interaction, enriching educational experiences, and supportive campus environment: *www.iub.edu/~nsse*.

   The importance of relating these results to other sources of student performance is discussed in Kuh, G. W. (2003, March/April). What we're learning about student engagement from NSSE: Benchmarks for effective educational practices. *Change*, 24–32. See, especially, page 31.

2. The NSSE Institute for Effective Educational Practice brings together faculty, administrators, and others to identify and link information about student experiences to efforts to improve academic programs and support services. One of these efforts is the DEEP Project, Documenting Effective Educational Practices. In collaboration with AAHE, this project is identifying promising practices at 20 colleges and universities that have higher-than-predicted scores on the NSSE benchmarks and higher-than-predicted graduation rates: *www.iub.edu/~nsse/html/ deep/main.htm*; *www.aahe.org/DEEP*.

3. The NSSE Institute is also working with AAHE and the Alliance for Equity in Higher Education on the Beams Project (*www.aahe.org/BEAMS*; *www.iub.edu/~nsse/html/beams_feature.htm*), designed to reduce the national gap in educational attainment for African-Americans, Hispanics, and Native Americans by increasing the number of these students who earn bachelor's degrees.

Council on Social Work Education. The Quality in Social Work Education Committee of this council is inviting bachelor of social work and masters of social work programs to conduct a systematic empirical study of the effectiveness of their students with clients. The purpose of this study is to determine the feasibility of implementing such an evaluation plan within the context of social work practice, and to undertake a preliminary appraisal of the actual outcomes of practice conducted by social work students: *www.cswe.org*.

First College Year Project. Some two hundred institutions are collaborating to establish aspirational models for the first year of college that are appropriate for various sectors of higher education. The Hallmarks of Excellence in the First Year of College Project, funded by the Lumina Foundation for Education and The Atlantic Philanthropies, is producing research-based statements of what constitutes excellence in first-year programs and how institutions could measure their own accomplishment of these hallmarks: *www.brevard.edu/fyfoundations*.

The Mathematical Association of America. Supporting Assessment in Undergraduate Mathematics (SAUM) is an association project supported by a grant from the National Science Foundation. This project is designed to help departments effectively assess one or more goals common to undergraduate mathematics departments in the major, in preparing future teachers, in college placement programs, in mathematics-intensive programs, and in general education courses: *www.maa.org/features/fourAs.html*.

Quality in Undergraduate Education. With support from the Education Program of the Pew Charitable Trusts, the Quality in Undergraduate Education (QUE) program has brought together two- and four-year institutions to develop learning outcomes and performance level descriptors in five disciplines: biology, chemistry, English, history, and mathematics. In addition, those involved will develop methods of assessment the results of which will be used to help students achieve agreed upon standards: *www.pewundergradforum.org/project9.html*.

Visible Knowledge Project. This five-year project is aimed "at improving the quality of college and university teaching through a focus on both student learning and faculty development in technology-enhanced environments." The project involves over 70 faculty from 21 campuses nationwide. Assessment of student learning in technology-enhanced environments is built into many of these projects: *crossroads.georgetown.edu/vkp*.

Washington State University. With funding from the Fund for Innovation in Quality Undergraduate Education, in 1999 Washington State University developed a critical thinking rubric to assess students' higher-order thinking skills and use those results to inform educational practices. More recently it has received a grant from the U.S. Department of Education FIPSE Comprehensive Program to integrate assessment with instruction in general education to promote higher-order thinking. This project will be in collaboration with two- and four-year institutions in the State of Washington: *wsuctproject.wsu.edu/ph.htm*.

For a list of other national projects, go to the project list found under the Pew Forum: *www.pewundergradforum.org/project_list.html*.

A Representative List of Research Projects that Integrate Assessment

Research on teaching and learning is contributing to our understanding of the effectiveness of pedagogy, educational tools, and practices in developing disciplinary habits of mind and problem-solving abilities. Some representative projects that are incorporating assessment are the following:

Center for Innovative Learning Technologies. Founded in 1997 with a grant from the National Science Foundation, this center focuses its work on developing and studying technology-enabled solutions to teaching science, mathematics, engineering, and technology in K–14. In its commitment to assessing for learning, CILT develops methods of assessment that enable educators to "see qualities of student achievement that are invisible on traditional, standardized tests": *www.cilt.org/themes/assessments.html*.

Knowledge Media Lab of the Carnegie Foundation for the Advancement of Teaching. Focused on advancing teaching and learning through the use of media and new technologies, this lab shares faculty research on teaching. Assessment is providing evidence of the effects and limitations of these educational practices: *kml2.carnegiefoundation.org/html/gallery.php*.

Massachusetts Institute of Technology. A part of the Office of the Dean for Undergraduate Education, Massachusetts Institute of Technology's (MIT) Teaching and Learning Laboratory (TLL) increases campus understanding about the process of learning in science and engineering. It achieves this goal by conducting research that can be applied to the classroom and by developing innovative educational curricula, pedagogy, technologies, and methods of assessment. Allied with several programs and centers across the institution, the laboratory disseminates its work on campus as well as nationally and internationally: *web.mit.edu/tll/ about_tll.htm.*

Vanderbilt University, Northwestern University, the University of Texas at Austin, and the Health Science and Technology Program of Harvard and MIT. Bioengineering and learning sciences faculties from these institutions, with support from the National Science Foundation, have established a center to conduct research on bioengineering educational technologies within the various domains of this science. In conjunction with developing new learning materials that relate to the structure of knowledge in bioengineering domains, the center is developing assessment methods to determine the effectiveness of these new materials: *www.vanth.org.*

WORKSHEETS, GUIDES, AND EXERCISES

The following worksheets, guides, and exercises are designed to anchor assessing for learning as a core institutional process.

1. *Principles of Commitment.* Developing a principles of commitment statement positions assessment within an institution or system and establishes a context for collective engagement. As an institutional or system leader, draw from the following list of possible individuals who might work together to draft that document within the context of your institution's or system's mission, purposes, and values:

   ❏ Administrators

   ❏ Alumni

   ❏ Board of trustees members

   ❏ Faculty—full- and part-time

   ❏ Librarians and information resource staff

   ❏ Local community members, including advisory committee members

   ❏ Other staff

   ❏ Parents

   ❏ Representative employers

   ❏ Representatives from professions or professional organizations

   ❏ Students

   ❏ Student affairs and support staff

   ❏ Other stakeholders inside or outside of the institution

2. *Principles of Commitment.* As an institutional or system leader, once you have identified a cross-representation of individuals to draft a principles of commitment document, you may want to ask the authoring group to read one of more of the following documents before they collaboratively draft a statement and then send it out for wider review. Focused on principles of learning and assessment, these documents may inform your institution's or system's discussion and resulting statement.

a. Chickering, A. W., & Gamson, Z. F. (1987). Seven principles of good practice in undergraduate education. *AAHE Bulletin, 39*(7), 3–7. These principles appear in summary on numerous institutional Web sites, such as the following: www.rochester.edu/ITS/edtech/documentation/Pedagogy/7principles.pdf.

b. The American Association for Higher Education's "9 Principles of Good Practice for Assessing Student Learning," which follows:

American Association for Higher Education

9 Principles of Good Practice for Assessing Student Learning

1. **The assessment of student learning begins with educational values.** Assessment is not an end in itself but a vehicle for educational improvement. Its effective practice, then, begins with and enacts a vision of the kinds of learning we most value for students and strive to help them achieve. Educational values should drive not only *what* we choose to assess but also *how* we do so. Where questions about educational mission and values are skipped over, assessment threatens to be an exercise in measuring what's easy, rather than a process of improving what we really care about.

2. **Assessment is most effective when it reflects an understanding of learning as multidimensional, integrated, and revealed in performance over time.** Learning is a complex process. It entails not only what students know but what they can do with what they know; it involves not only knowledge and abilities but values, attitudes, and habits of mind that affect both academic success and performance beyond the classroom. Assessment should reflect these understandings by employing a diverse array of methods, including those that call for actual performance, using them over time so as to reveal change, growth, and increasing degrees of integration. Such an approach aims for a more complete and accurate picture of learning and, therefore, firmer bases for improving our students' educational experience.

3. **Assessment works best when the programs it seeks to improve have clear, explicitly stated purposes.** Assessment is a goal-oriented process. It entails comparing educational performance with educational purposes and expectations—those derived from the institution's mission, from faculty intentions in program and course design, and from knowledge of students' own goals. Where program purposes lack specificity or agreement, assessment as a process pushes a campus toward clarity about where to aim and what standards to apply; assessment also prompts attention to where and how program goals will be taught and learned. Clear, shared, implementable goals are the cornerstone for assessment that is focused and useful.

4. **Assessment requires attention to outcomes but also and equally to the experiences that lead to those outcomes.** Information about outcomes is of high importance; where students "end up" matters greatly. But to improve outcomes, we need to know about student experience along the way—about the curricula, teaching, and kind of student effort that lead to particular outcomes. Assessment can help us understand which students learn best under what conditions; with such knowledge comes the capacity to improve the whole of their learning.

5. **Assessment works best when it is ongoing, not episodic.** Assessment is a process whose power is cumulative. Though isolated, "one-shot" assessment can be better than none, improvement is best fostered when assessment entails a linked series of activities undertaken over time. This may mean tracking the process of individual students or of cohorts of students; it may mean collecting the same examples of student performance or using the same instrument semester after semester. The point is to monitor progress toward intended goals in a spirit of continuous improvement. Along the way, the assessment process itself should be evaluated and refined in light of emerging insights.

6. **Assessment fosters wider improvement when representatives from across the educational community are involved.** Student learning is a campus-wide responsibility, and assessment is a way of enacting that responsibility. Thus, while assessment efforts may start small, the aim over time is to involve people from across the educational community. Faculty play an especially important role, but assessment's questions can't be fully addressed without participation by student-affairs educators, librarians, administrators, and students. Assessment may also involve individuals from beyond the campus (alumni, trustees, employers) whose experience can enrich the sense of appropriate aims and standards for learning. Thus understood, assessment is not a task for small groups of experts but a collaborative activity; its aim is wider, better-informed attention to student learning by all parties with a stake in its improvement.

7. **Assessment makes a difference when it begins with issues of use and illuminates questions that people really care about.** Assessment recognizes the value of information in the process of improvement. But to be useful, information must be connected to issues or questions that people really care about. This implies assessment approaches that produce evidence that relevant parties will find credible, suggestive, and applicable to decisions that need to be made. It means thinking in advance about how the information will be used, and by whom. The point of assessment is not to gather data and return "results"; it is a process that starts with the questions of decision makers, that involves them in the gathering and interpreting of data, and that informs and helps guide continuous improvement.

8. **Assessment is most likely to lead to improvement when it is part of a larger set of conditions that promote change.** Assessment alone changes little. Its greatest contribution comes on campuses where the quality of teaching and learning is visibly valued and worked at. On such campuses, the push to improve educational performance is a visible and primary goal of leadership; improving the quality of undergraduate education is central to the institution's planning, budgeting, and personnel decisions. On such campuses, information about learning outcomes is seen as an integral part of decision making and is avidly sought.

9. **Through assessment, educators meet responsibilities to students and to the public.** There is a compelling public stake in education. As educators, we have a responsibility to the publics that support or depend on us to provide information about the ways in which our students meet goals and expectations. But that responsibility goes beyond the reporting of such information; our deeper obligation—to ourselves, our students, and society—is to improve. Those to whom educators are accountable have a corresponding obligation to support such attempts at improvement.

Authors: Alexander W. Astin; Trudy W. Banta; K. Patricia Cross; Elaine El-Khawas; Peter T. Ewell; Pat Hutchings; Theodore J. Marchese; Kay M. McClenney; Marcia Mentkowski; Margaret A. Miller; E. Thomas Moran; & Barbara D. Wright. 1992.

This document was developed under the auspices of the AAHE Assessment Forum with support from the Fund for the Improvement of Postsecondary Education with additional support for publication and dissemination from the Exxon Education Foundation. Copies may be made without restriction.

c. The collaborative document, "Powerful Partnerships: A Shared Responsibility for Learning," written by a joint task force consisting of representatives from the American Association for Higher Education, the American College Personnel Association, and the National Association of Student Personnel Administrators, June 1998: www.aahe.org/teaching/tsk_frce.htm.
This document presents ten principles for learning drawn from research and practice. Two other American College Personnel Association documents, "The Student Learning Imperative: Implications for Student Affairs" (www.acpa.nche.edu/sli/sli.htm) (1996), and "Principles of Good Practice for Student Affairs" (www.acpa.nche.edu/pgp/principle.htm) focus on principles and practices to promote discussion about ways to intentionally enhance student learning, including collaborating with others across a campus.

d. Angelo, T. (1999, May). Doing assessment as if learning matters most. *AAHE Bulletin:* www.aahebulletin.com/public/archive/angelomay99.asp.

e. Maki, P. (2002, May). Moving from paperwork to pedagogy: Channeling intellectual curiosity into a commitment to assessment. *AAHE Bulletin:* aahebulletin.com/public/archive/paperwork.asp.

3. *Principles of Commitment.* Another way to draft a principles of commitment statement is to ask representatives from across your institution to identify institutional anchors that link assessment to mission, values, and vision. North Carolina State University has anchored its commitment to assessment within four contexts. Read the summary of the university's approach in Box 1.2.

To address institution- or program-level readiness for a collective commitment to assessing student learning, ask individuals to explain how one or more of the following principles might anchor your institution's shared commitment to assessing student learning. Ask individuals to fill out the following chart as a way to stimulate discussion leading to a draft.

Possible Anchors for an Institutional Commitment

Research on learning or the integration of research on learning into educational practices	
Scholarship of teaching and learning	
Responsiveness to developments in disciplinary and professional organizations' work focused on assessment	
Focus on learning-centeredness	
Focus on organizational learning	
Responsiveness to accountability	
Other	

4. *Meaningful Beginnings*. Having authored a draft principles of commitment statement, ask individuals of that authoring group to list meaningful ways in which the institution (or a program) can launch a shared commitment to assessing student learning. Use the scenario in Box 1.3 from Rochester Community and Technical College as a way to think about how your institution will initiate a meaningful and shared commitment.

BOX 1.2   INSTITUTIONAL EXAMPLE: *North Carolina State University*

North Carolina State University, a premier research-extensive institution, has anchored its commitment to assessment in four ways: (1) responsiveness to professional and public accountability, including its primary constituents: students; (2) clarity about its institutional descriptors, "high quality programming," "institutional excellence," and "effectiveness," and its status as a premier research-extensive institution focused on learner-centeredness; (3) desire to provide evidence of student learning to better inform decision makers and planners as they direct and allocate resources that support the institution's work; (4) desire to promote dialogue across the institution about student learning. The meaningful beginning point for the university has been its decision to focus annually on student outcomes within programs across the institution and to integrate this work as part of program review. Thus, assessment at the program level is a continuous process of raising and answering a significant question or questions about student learning that each program chooses to assess each year. Program review, then, characterizes the university's meaningful beginning.

Source: Contributed by Jo Allen, James A. Anderson, and Marilee J. Bresciani, North Carolina State University. Reproduced with permission.

BOX 1.3   INSTITUTIONAL EXAMPLE: *Rochester Community and Technical College*

Rochester Community and Technical College (RCTC), the oldest of the community colleges in Minnesota, established in 1915, began its institutional commitment to assessing student learning by linking institution wide planning, a commitment to assuring quality throughout the institution, and accreditation. It has realigned its mission and vision for the 21st century, identified design criteria and academic performance indicators to determine points of reference for assessing quality performance, and has begun to implement comprehensive assessment of student learning. The college's focus on performance indicators at all levels of its work has provided an institutional context within which the community now works. RCTC established a college wide assessment committee consisting of representatives from across the institution that has established broad commitment. The college launched its initial commitment to assessment through pilot projects in general education and in certain programs, including connecting its work to a larger statewide system office project that is piloting a data software program designed to track student learning results. Key to the institution's sustained commitment was the president's recognition that a budget line needed to be established in the institutional budget, a clear recognition that this work is recognized and valued. An institutional Web site provides descriptions of assessment work in departments and programs, highlights work faculty are undertaking, provides resources on assessment, and provides committee meeting minutes (*www.acd.roch.edu/asl*).

Source: Contributed by Anne M. High, RDH, MS, Director of Dental Hygiene, Co-coordinator of Assessment, and Tammy J. Lee, MBA, EdD., Business Instructor, Co-coordinator of Assessment, Rochester Community and Technical College. Reproduced with permission.

5. *Meaningful Beginnings.* Another way to develop a meaningful beginning is to reach consensus with representatives across the campus about ways to initiate institution- and program-level assessment. Ask members of this group to discuss the possibilities listed in the following chart or to generate other approaches that may be more appropriate for your institutional context.

Meaningful Beginnings

Development of a new mission statement or educational philosophy for the institution, an academic department, school, program, or service	
Initiation of strategic planning	
Re-conceptualization or revision of faculty and staff roles and rewards	
Design or revision of a core curriculum	
Development of a new program or service	
Selection of a new institutional leader	
Response to voiced dissatisfaction about student learning	
Recognition of classroom-based assessment as a foundation for institution- and program-level assessment focus	
Preparation of documentation to respond to legislators, accreditors, policy makers, or other public audiences	

6. *Relationships to Explore Compelling Questions.* As institution- and program-level groups begin to identify collective questions that initiate inquiry, such as those listed on page 2, identify constituencies within and outside of your institution who contribute to students' learning, using the figure that follows. Determine how representatives from some of these constituencies might become involved in assessing institution- or program-level compelling questions. For example, if your institution or program wants to inquire into how well students integrate interdisciplinary perspectives into problem solving, which of those constituencies might become involved in exploring how and how well students develop these perspectives over the continuum of their studies? What new kinds of working relationships might you develop to assess the development of this kind of perspective taking?

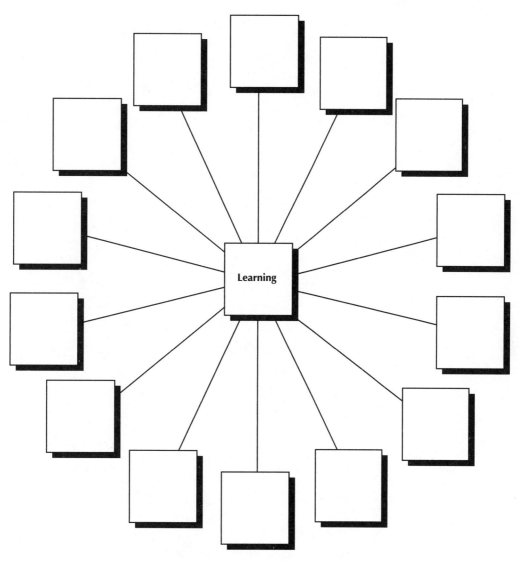

Contributors to Student Learning

Chapter 2

BEGINNING WITH DIALOGUE ABOUT TEACHING AND LEARNING

It is essential for any organization, academic or not, to assess the extent to which individual work contributes to collective needs and priorities. No organization can function effectively as a collection of autonomous individuals in which everyone pursues personal priorities and the overall achievements consist, in essence, of a casual, nonoptimal aggregate of activities. If universities are to have the resilience and adaptability they will need in the decades to come, they must find better ways to make individual faculty members' work contribute to common organizational needs, priorities, and goals.

—Ernest Lynton, 1998

OVERVIEW: This chapter focuses on the coordinating role of institution- and program-level assessment committees that initiate, orchestrate, and sustain cycles of inquiry into student learning. To root assessment practices into teaching and learning, these committees initiate rounds of dialogue that lead to consensus about shared expectations for student learning, followed by collaborative strategies that explore the curricular and co-curricular coherence that contributes to these expectations. Institution- and program-level representations of the landscape of students' learning opportunities become the bedrock upon which assessment methods and practices are shaped. The Worksheets, Guides, and Exercises at the end of this chapter are designed to (1) establish collaboration as a principle that underlies the work of assessment committees and their relationship with members of the academic community; (2) promote institution- and program-level dialogue about teaching and learning as the context for embedding assessment; and (3) guide the development of visual representations that document where and how students learn what an educational community values.

THE CONTINUUM OF LEARNING: BEYOND AN AGGREGATION OF COURSES, CREDITS, AND SEAT TIME

With the exception of a small percentage of institutions in the United States that provide narrative transcripts of students' achievement, providing contexts for students' learning, typically colleges and universities record student achievement through a system of numbers and grades. Number of courses, number of credit hours, and grades document student learning. For example, somewhere in the range of 120 to 135 credits equal an undergraduate degree that is, in turn, divided into credits and courses delineating majors, minors, concentrations, electives, and general education. At both the graduate and the undergraduate levels a certain number of courses or credits certifies a focus of learning—an area of specialization in graduate school, for example, or a minor in undergraduate school. This number-grade system is based on the assumption that students progressively transfer and build upon previous learning as they advance through courses.

More than an aggregation of courses and credits, learning is a process of constructing meaning, framing issues, drawing upon strategies and abilities honed over time, reconceptualizing understanding, repositioning oneself in relation to a problem or issue, and connecting thinking and knowing to action. Institution- and program-level assessment extends inquiry about student learning beyond students' achievement in individual courses to their achievement over time. This chapter describes structures and strategies for institution- and program-level tasks focused on

1. identifying collective expectations for student learning;

2. verifying how well pedagogy, the design of curriculum, co-curriculum, instruction, and other educational experiences or practices intentionally contribute to students' achievement of these expectations.

The tasks described in this chapter are essential for embedding assessment into the processes of teaching and learning. Further, the initial ways in which members of an academic community work together to identify shared expectations for student learning pave the way for the collective dialogue, tasks, and decisions that characterize assessment as a core institutional process.

A FOCUS ON INTEGRATION

A focus on institution- and program-level learning moves beyond students' achievement in single courses to their achievement over time. This focus, then, examines the integration, rather than the separation, of the three domains of learning identified by Bloom and collaborators (1956); later extended by Krathwohl, Bloom, and Masia (1964); and more recently revised by Anderson and Krathwohl (2001):

1. The *cognitive domain,* involving the development of intellectual abilities: knowledge, comprehension, application, analysis, synthesis, and evaluation, such as a medical student's knowledge of anatomy, a graduate linguistic student's abilities to select and apply a method of discourse analysis to a text, or an undergraduate business students' evaluation of multiple solutions to a problem in a case study

2. The *psychomotor domain,* involving the development of physical movement, coordination, and sets of skills, such as the intricately timed movements of a dancer, the precision of a neurosurgeon, or the task-centered procedures involved in human-computer interactions

3. The *affective domain,* involving the development of values, attitudes, commitments, and ways of responding, such as valuing others' perspectives, responding to situations that disadvantage a group of people, exercising tenacity in practicing an ability to improve it over time, or demonstrating a passion for learning

The integration of these three domains, represented in the area of overlap in Figure 2.1, illustrates the focus of institution- and program-level assessment: students' construction of meaning represented or demonstrated through their interactions, responses, commitments, creations, projects, products, research, interpretations, and chronological self-reflection.

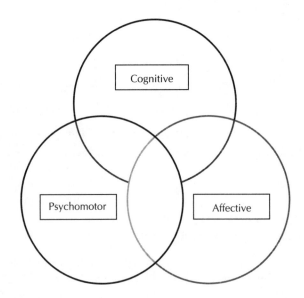

FIGURE 2.1 Integrated Learning

An architectural student needs to demonstrate more than the ability to draw: the ability to draw does not by itself define an architect. Knowledge and understanding about the properties of building materials, environmental and climatic conditions, and building codes, for example, as well as a predisposition to research limitations of a particular building site, contribute to an architect's final design. Faculty who teach drawing courses assess architectural students' ability to design a structure; faculty who teach environmental courses assess architectural students' knowledge about how environments limit designs. Program-level assessment focuses on how students integrate their learning across these and other courses to become architects. Identifying appropriate times to assess for integrated learning, then, defines the role of institution- and program-level assessment.

COORDINATING COMMITTEES

Reaching consensus about collective expectations for student learning at both the institution and program levels marks the first stage of the actual assessment process. Initiating this first stage is, typically, the role of a coordinating body—an assessment committee—that seeks community consensus about expectations for student learning based on an institution's mission, purpose, and values. Generally, there are two levels of assessment committees within a college or university:

- A campus-wide assessment committee
- Program-level assessment committees (also established in schools, divisions, departments, or services)

A Campus-Wide Assessment Committee

A campus-wide assessment committee develops an institutional student learning assessment plan (see pages 4–5 in Chapter 1). This plan, often developed in concert with other constituencies of an institution and in collaboration with a college or university institutional research and planning office, develops a timetable that triggers annual cycles of inquiry into student learning at both the institution and program levels. A campus-wide committee becomes the structure that sustains assessment of student learning across an institution.

Generally, members on this committee serve term appointments, two to three years, after which a new representative from each constituency joins the committee for a term period. There may well be permanent members such as a representative from institutional research or the institution's vice president of academic affairs. Rotational membership broadens institutional understanding of assessment over time. Diverse membership on this standing committee also assures that there are sustained conversations about student learning and achievement throughout the institution and among the various contributors to students' learning. The following list includes those who might serve on a campus-wide assessment committee or in an advisory capacity:

- Institution's chief academic leader
- Representative from an institution's faculty and staff governance
- Representative from each academic program, department, division, or school within an institution
- Representative from academic support services
- Representative from student affairs
- Representative from library and information resources
- Full- and part-time graduate and undergraduate student representative
- Teaching assistant representative
- Student tutor representative who experiences firsthand the levels of difficulties students confront in learning
- Representative from the local community who educates students in internships, cooperative education programs, or community service
- Representative from alumni
- Representative employer who contributes knowledge about what students bring to their employment, as well as identifies new abilities students will need to bring into the workplace or into civic life
- Member of an institution's business or advisory board
- Representative from institutional research and planning who provides guidance and support along the life of the assessment process

As you will read in this and the remaining chapters, over time, campus-wide assessment committees

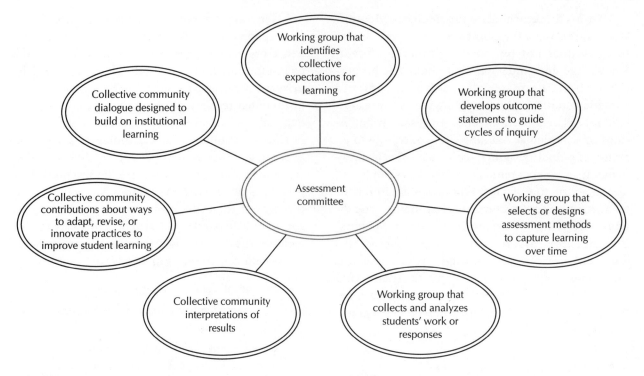

FIGURE 2.2   Assessment Committee Core Working Groups and Tasks

form or appoint core working groups, task forces, or cluster groups, consisting of faculty, staff, administrators, students, and others who contribute to students' education, to carry out specific assessment tasks, as represented in Figure 2.2. An assessment committee and its working groups sustain an institutional commitment to assessment through the following tasks:

- Reaching consensus about what the educational community expects students to represent or demonstrate along the continuum of their learning

- Designing or selecting methods to capture students' learning

- Collecting and analyzing assessment results

- Collectively interpreting assessment results and engaging in community dialogue about ways to redesign, adapt, or innovate educational practices to improve patterns of student weakness revealed in assessment results

- Establishing new cycles of inquiry to ascertain how well implemented changes improve student learning

- In collaboration with teaching and learning centers, organizing occasions to build

institutional learning based on assessment results or on innovations in educational practices designed to improve student learning

Program-Level Assessment Committees

Working in much the same way as the campus-wide assessment committee, program-level assessment committees may act as a committee of the whole program or distribute tasks through core working groups. In large programs, schools, or divisions, a central committee that focuses on core learning for students studying in that school may establish satellite committees that focus more specifically on assessing learning in areas of specialization, such as in a school of natural sciences. Program-level committees also consist of broad representation from their educational constituencies and contributors, including students and representatives from advisory boards, professions, or organizations in the local community. In addition to considering representation from the pool of constituencies listed on page 33, program-level committees might draw membership from the following:

- Administrative heads of individual departments in a program, school, or division

- Full- and part-time faculty who teach in programs
- Faculty from graduate schools who bring perspectives on accepted students
- Laboratory assistants
- Graduate assistants
- Graduates from the program
- Employers who directly hire graduates of a program

Similar to the responsibilities of a campus-wide committee, described on page 34, the tasks of program-level committees follow the same inquiry process as that of a campus-wide committee. In both campus-wide and program-level committees, dialogue about teaching and learning and students' achievement based on those processes ensures that assessment reflects educators' values.

DIALOGUE FOCUSED ON EXPECTATIONS FOR STUDENT LEARNING

Marking the first phase of a campus-wide or program-level assessment plan is dialogue focused on identifying shared expectations for student learning:

- What do members of a college or university and members of specific programs expect their students to be able to demonstrate or represent based on pedagogy, the design of the curriculum, co-curriculum, instruction, other educational opportunities and practices, and the use of educational tools?
- What should students be able to demonstrate or represent at points along their studies based on these educational practices?
- What do the curricula and other educational experiences "add up to"?

These kinds of questions initiate institution- and program-level dialogue that eventually leads to consensus about what members of an academic community wish to explore along students' chronology of learning, such as their ability to perform the following tasks:

- Reason quantitatively in different kinds of contexts outside of quantitatively based courses
- Solve complex global problems through interdisciplinary perspectives

- Integrate general education learning into their major fields of study
- Apply disciplinary habits of mind and ways of behaving in solving a problem

A core working group within an institution-level or program-level assessment committee might be appointed to respond or gather responses to these kinds of questions. There are a couple of ways this core working group might progress through this consensus-building phase:

1. A core working group of a campus-wide or program-level committee might draft responses to these kinds of questions. To focus on institution-level or program-level core curricula, a committee might appoint, select, or elect a more specialized group consisting of individuals who specifically teach courses in an institution's or a program's core curriculum or who contribute to it through programs and services such as representatives from academic support services.

2. A core working group (or the committee as a whole) might schedule several occasions for community dialogue to address these kinds of questions, creating cross-disciplinary and cross-functional groups (such as academic affairs and student affairs groups). These occasions for dialogue also contribute to and foster collaboration, a key ingredient in an institutional commitment to assessing for learning that values collective and diverse contributions to student learning as students construct meaning over time.

Positioning assessment as a collaborative process begins in this initial phase of information gathering. The following strategies also engage the wider community:

1. Posting results of core working groups' responses or the results of community dialogue on a campus Web site
2. Inviting larger response—even from other constituencies outside of a campus or program who contribute to students' learning or have a vested interest in their learning
3. Redrafting and posting a final list of expectations for student learning on a campus Web site

Building institutional knowledge across the assessment process promotes dialogue about teaching and learning and the practices that contribute to students' learning.

Program-level assessment committees also contribute to institution-wide dialogue about shared expectations for student learning. Program-level curricula and educational opportunities contribute to institution-level expectations for student learning. For example, a university comprised of schools or divisions may structure occasions for interrelated dialogue about how schools or divisions and the separate programs or departments within them contribute to university-wide expectations for student learning. Specifically, if a university asserts that its students explore and are aware of the ethical dimensions of their decisions, then verifying that schools, divisions, and their programs contribute to the development of this attribute—beyond a required course—becomes a focus of dialogue. On the other hand, an institution's focus on developing leadership abilities and qualities may, in turn, contribute to a program's focus on that quality as well. As is shown in Appendix 2.1 (referenced in Box 2.1), a curriculum map is a way to visualize this interdependent relationship that fosters student learning through multiple learning opportunities.

Program-level dialogue also focuses on identifying disciplinary, cross-disciplinary, or professional expectations for fields of study. That is, program-level dialogue focuses on discipline-bound expectations. Thus, for example, members of a biology department, together with students, members of an advisory board, and local biologists, might agree that they expect students to communicate disciplinary principles and concepts to different audience levels—from expert to lay audiences. They might also agree that students should be able to demonstrate that they practice disciplinary procedures and ways of knowing and behaving that characterize the work of biologists solving representative kinds of problems.

DIALOGUE FOCUSED ON VERIFYING EXPECTATIONS

- How intentionally do members of an academic community provide opportunities for students to learn what an institution and its programs assert they teach or inculcate?
- How do faculty, staff, and other contributors to student learning build on each others' work?

- Do students have multiple and diverse opportunities to build on previous learning, receive feedback, and reflect on their progress toward achieving what an institution and its programs expect?
- How do academic programs, services, and educational opportunities promote institution- and program-level understanding, abilities, habits of mind, ways of thinking, and behaving?
- What educational processes and experiences contribute to and reinforce collective educational expectations?

Bringing to the surface and agreeing upon shared expectations for student learning at both the institution and program levels pave the way for a second level of community dialogue. This level focuses on exploring where, when, and even how the design of curriculum, co-curriculum, instruction, pedagogy, and educational opportunities intentionally promotes these shared expectations. Specifically, it examines *coherence*—how well collective expectations translate into intentional educational practices, providing multiple and varied opportunities for students to learn. These kinds of conversations extend across academic programs and services, across the co-curriculum, and even into the surrounding local community that educates our students in internships, residencies, cooperative learning experiences, field experiences, community service, and work-study opportunities.

This kind of dialogue also may reveal gaps in students' opportunities to learn. For example, within a department or program, colleagues may believe they have adequately sequenced courses in a major program of study based on a developmental model of how students learn. However, a collective look at course content, curricular design, and pedagogy might reveal there are insufficient opportunities for students to build upon or use previous learning. Courses may exist as separate entities, disconnected from students' previous learning. Students may be responsible for memorizing formulas, principles, or concepts in one course in a major program of study with little opportunity to practice, apply, and extend this learning until later in their studies. Without threaded opportunities in the curriculum or related educational experiences to apply this memorized information, students will most likely be unable to recall, much less apply, what they once memorized. As a result, learning for students in this case remains course-bound; opportunities to use and build on initial learning simply do not exist between this course and a final course.

MAPS AND INVENTORIES

Maps and *inventories* may be used to verify collective expectations within actual educational practices; that is, they reveal the distribution of opportunities to learn across an institution and its programs and services. More important, these representations provide a rich context for writing *learning outcome statements,* sentences that describe what students should be able to demonstrate or represent based on how and what they have learned, the subject of Chapter 3. Dialogue and work focusing on what students' learning continuum looks like lead to collectively agreed-upon and clear outcome statements. Without this preparatory work leading to the development of outcome statements, there may well exist disjunctures between shared expectations for student learning and actual opportunities for students to achieve these expectations along their chronologies of learning. Developing a broad view of students' progression enables us to see how frequently students have had opportunities to hone a particular ability, for example, or to build up a repertoire of strategies to solve discipline-specific problems.

Maps

Maps provide information about what and even how students learn over time: they profile intentionality over the continuum of students' learning. Representing the underlying logic of curricular and co-curricular design, they provide a shared context for authoring outcome statements, methods to assess outcome statements, and criteria and standards by which to judge student work, topics addressed in Chapter 3 through Chapter 5.

A curriculum map, or a map of the curriculum and co-curriculum, charts where faculty and others who contribute to student learning integrate educational opportunities that address institution- and program-level expectations for student learning. These maps also identify gaps in student learning opportunities or identify concentrations of learning experiences without further opportunity for students to transfer, build upon, or apply learning. Most important, in the early dialogue that grounds assessment, maps help us see if the learning priorities we collectively articulate translate into underlying coherence among our efforts. If not, we have the opportunity during these early discussions to reprioritize learning outcomes, identify other outcomes that have taken precedence because of societal or workplace changes, or reassert their significance as core outcomes by discussing ways to deepen and broaden attention to them in the curriculum and co-curriculum and other sets of experiences.

Maps of the curriculum and co-curriculum serve three main purposes in building a collective institutional commitment to assessment:

1. They stimulate discussion about and critical reflection on collective learning priorities.
2. They illustrate how well collective expectations match with educational practices that foster those priorities.
3. They provide a visual representation of students' contexts for learning that may assist later on in interpreting assessment results.

Because students learn in different ways, under different pedagogies and educational practices, holding a couple of courses solely responsible for developing students' ability to write, for example, assumes that students continue to retain from year to year what they learned in those courses. In fact, they need to continue to apply and build on that learning over the remainder of their undergraduate and graduate studies, including learning about and using disciplinary conventions, formats, rhetorical styles, and ways of presenting information or evidence to solve problems for different audiences and purposes. Valuing multiple educational opportunities that contribute to students' writing abilities broadens institutional responsibility and students' opportunities to learn.

For example, besides responding to assignments in their coursework, students have multiple opportunities to extend their writing abilities outside of the classroom through

- contributions to a college's or university's newspaper or other publications;
- proposals for independent studies;
- proposals for honors projects;
- documentation of meeting discussions and results;
- summaries and analyses of campus surveys.

The institutional value placed on writing actually translates into the life of the institution in multiple

---

BOX 2.1   INSTITUTIONAL EXAMPLE: *New Jersey City University*

At New Jersey City University, the Business Administration Program's curriculum map locates where both program-level and institution-level learning outcomes are addressed and distributed across the program (see Appendix 2.1 at the end of this chapter). Using a labeling system of *I* (introduced), *R* (reinforced), and *E* (emphasized), members of the program indicate how courses build on desired learning over time, providing a sense of relationships among and between courses and a chronology of how students learn. Listed in the left-hand column are both institution- and program-level learning outcomes. The map and the labeling system provide a visual representation of students' curricular progression as it relates to shared expectations among faculty in the Business Administration Program and as it relates to institution-level expectations. An important collaborative strategy, mapping provides a picture of the whole that may prompt further dialogue about ways to distribute or redistribute learning opportunities.

BOX 2.2   INSTITUTIONAL EXAMPLE: *Rose-Hulman Institute of Technology*

Another approach to curriculum mapping is illustrated in Figure 2.3. At Rose-Hulman Institute of Technology, faculty map where and how they address institution-level learning outcomes, referred to as learning objectives, such as students' awareness of the ethical dimensions of engineering problems for engineers. Faculty receive an electronic form that lists institutional learning objectives, along with criteria that further identify those objectives. This form asks faculty to respond to four questions about how intentionally they address these objectives in their courses, including whether or not students are asked to demonstrate objectives and whether or not faculty provide feedback to students on these objectives, an indicator of intentionality.

A composite curriculum map of these practices, similar to Figure 2.3, provides evidence about program- and institution-level intentionality. This evidence may demonstrate sustained attention over programs and across the institution, or it may demonstrate declining or sporadic attention. Declining or sporadic attention raises the following questions for faculty and staff to answer:

- Is this outcome still one of our priorities?
- If so, how do we redirect attention to it?
- If not, why do we state it is a priority?

Source: Contributed by Gloria M. Rogers, Rose-Hulman Institute of Technology. Reproduced with permission.

learning contexts or opportunities and thereby expands and deepens students' learning about the various forms, strategies, and conventions of writing. A map of the curriculum and co-curriculum, then, would chart not only courses that focus on or integrate writing, but also complementary learning experiences outside of formal coursework that expand students' opportunities to write. (See Box 2.1 and Box 2.2.)

Inventories

Maps provide an overview of students' learning journey—a place to locate where educational opportunities are specifically designed to address institution-

and program-level expectations. *Inventories* drill down into actual educational practices to develop shared understanding of and discussion about how students learn over time and how educators value that learning through assessment methods. These kinds of inventories build institution- and program-level knowledge and provide the foundation upon which to design and develop the "bigger picture" assessment methods described in Chapter 4. Agreeing on shared expectations initiates the process of assessment. Exploring questions about the efficacy and relevance of collective educational practices, however, sustains collective curiosity. The following inventory is useful at either the institution or pro-

Objective Explicit. This objective is explicitly stated as being a learning objective for this course.
Demonstrate Competence. Students are asked to demonstrate their competence on this objective through homework, projects, tests, etc.
Formal Feedback. Students are given formal feedback on their performance on this objective.

Not covered. This objective is not addressed in these ways in this course.

Note: Clicking on the link "view criteria" will bring up the list of criteria for that particular institutional objective in a floating window.

Objective	Objective Explicit	Demonstrate Competence	Formal Feedback		Not Covered
1. Recognition of ethical and professional responsibilities. view criteria or make a comment (optional)	☐ Yes	☐ Yes	☐ Yes		☐
2. An understanding of how contemporary issues shape and are shaped by mathematics, science, and engineering. view criteria or make a comment (optional)	☐ Yes	☐ Yes	☐ Yes		☐
3. An ability to recognize the role of professionals view criteria or make a comment (optional)		Yes	☐ Yes		☐
4. An ability to understand diverse cultural and the view criteria or make a comment (optional)		Yes	☐ Yes		☐
5. An ability to work effectively in teams. view criteria or make a comment (optional)		Yes	☐ Yes		☐
6. An ability to communicate effectively in oral, w forms. view criteria or make a comment (optional)	☐ Yes	☐ Yes	☐ Yes		☐
7. An ability to apply the skills and knowledge necessary for mathematical, scientific, and engineering practices. view criteria or make a comment (optional)	☐ Yes	☐ Yes	☐ Yes		☐
8. An ability to interpret graphical, numerical, and textual data. view criteria or make a comment (optional)	☐ Yes	☐ Yes	☐ Yes		☐
9. An ability to design and conduct experiments. view criteria or make a comment (optional)	☐ Yes	☐ Yes	☐ Yes		☐
10. An ability to design a product or process to satisfy a client's needs subject to constraints. view criteria or make a comment (optional)	☐ Yes	☐ Yes	☐ Yes		☐

When given the opportunity, students will;
1. **Demonstrate knowledge of professional codes of ethics.**
2. **Evaluate the ethical dimensions of a problem in their discipline.**

Submit/Reconfirm

Rose-Hulman Institute of Technology
2002–2003 Curriculum Map
www.rose-hulman.edu

FIGURE 2.3 Rose-Hulman Institute of Technology Curriculum Map. *Source:* Contributed by Gloria M. Rogers, Rose-Hulman Institute of Technology. Reproduced with permission.

gram level to examine how students learn what an institution and its programs expect them to learn:

- What educational philosophy, principles, theories, models of teaching, research on learning, or shared assumptions underlie curricular or co-curricular design, instructional design, pedagogy, or use of educational tools?

- What pedagogies or educational experiences develop the knowledge, understanding, habits of mind, ways of knowing, and problem solving that the institution or its programs value?

- How do students become acculturated to the ways of thinking, knowing, and problem solving in their field of study?

- How do faculty and staff intentionally build upon each others' courses and educational experiences to achieve programmatic as well as institutional learning priorities?

- Which students benefit from which teaching strategies, educational processes, or educational experiences?

Pooling assessment methods used in individual courses or at the end of educational opportunities or experiences is a second type of inventory. This inventory provides longitudinal documentation of the range and frequency of assessment methods students experience along the progression of their education. Identifying patterns of course-based assessment methods over a program of study shapes and informs program- and institution-level assessment methods that build on students' previous assessment experiences, the subject of Chapter 4. Asking students to make inferences based on multiple sources of data is one way to determine their critical thinking abilities. If, however, an inventory of course-based assessment practices reveals that students have had limited experience making inferences and, instead, have been asked primarily to recall or recognize information, then a program-level inference-drawing assessment method would not fairly and appropriately match their learning history. Knowing when to assess chemistry students' ability to formulate a hypothesis or when to assess computer science students' ability to apply rules of formal logic rests on understanding the chronology of their learning and the chronological value faculty place on these abilities demonstrated through their assessment methods. The following inventory invites conversation about how individuals design assessment tasks in response to institution- and program-level expectations:

- Describe how you design a course or experience to contribute to students' demonstration or representation of an institution- or program-level expectation.

- Identify ways in which students actually learn what you intend, for example, in collaboratively based projects, through simulations, through memorization, through the use of equipment, or through self-reflection in response to a task.

- Describe your assessment method and the context within which students respond to it, for example, at the end of an internship, in a multiple-choice test, or as part of a laboratory assignment.

- Describe the content that you expect students to know in order to respond to a particular method, for example, content learned in the course or content you assume they learned in previous courses or educational experiences.

The accumulated results of individual inventories profile the frequency and range of assessment methods that occur along students' studies. This profile illustrates how intentionally institution- or program-level learning priorities become valued in the kinds of assessment methods distributed across students' studies.

THE DESIGN OF OUR WORK

Given that learning is a complex process, that students learn as a result of different pedagogies, and that they face different obstacles based on misunderstanding or long-held beliefs, exploring the design of our collective work enables us to identify underlying connections and avenues for learning or to identify how we might strengthen connections or build additional avenues for learning. Routine discussions about teaching and learning with representatives from across a campus or from across a program, department, school, or division provide an essential platform for verifying the coherence that underlies collective intentions for student learning. Department or program chairs and directors of services and programs can integrate these discussions within the fabric of their units' work—a rhythm of professional life.

In a collective commitment to assessment, our complex intentions for students, such as their ability to solve disciplinary problems or their ability to evaluate and choose among compelling and competing solutions to a problem, are achieved across our programs and services. Focus is not on what "I" do; focus is on what "we" do. Ownership of teaching stretches across courses, services, and educational practices. It holds us collectively responsible for contributing to learning over students' studies, providing multiple and varied opportunities for them to learn and practice what we value. Conversations about how we translate our teaching philosophies, sets of assumptions about learning, or theories of learning into pedagogy and curricular and co-curricular design establish a common ground for how we choose to assess our students based on their learning chronologies.

Representation of multiple voices in assessment dialogue contributes to achieving consensus about what an institution values and how those values are integrated into institutional culture. This representation also begins to establish institutional channels of communication among all who educate to enhance understanding of the myriad ways in which students learn within and outside of a college or university. Without this context, assessment becomes divorced from our professional work.

WORKS CITED

Anderson, L. W., & Krathwohl, D. R. (Eds.). (2001). *A taxonomy for learning, teaching, and assessment: A revision of Bloom's taxonomy of educational objectives.* New York: Longman.

Bloom, B. S., & Collaborators. (1956). *The taxonomy of educational objectives: Cognitive domain.* New York: David McKay.

Krathwohl, D. R., Bloom, B. S., & Masia, B. B. (1964). *Taxonomy of educational objectives: Affective domain.* New York: David McKay.

Lynton, E. A. (1998, March). Reversing the telescope: Fitting individual tasks to common organizational ends. AAHE *Bulletin,* 50, 8–10.

ADDITIONAL RESOURCES

Teaching Practices, Theories, and Research on Learning that Guide Dialogue about Curricular and Co-Curricular Coherence

Anderson, J. A., Reder, L. M., & Simon, H. A. (1996). Situated learning and education. *Educational Researcher, 25*(4), 5–11.

Angelo, T. A. (1993, April). A teacher's dozen: Fourteen research-based principles for improving higher learning in our classrooms. *AAHE Bulletin*, 13, 3–7.

Association of American Colleges & Universities. (1991). *The challenge of connecting learning.* Washington, DC: Author.

Association of American Colleges & Universities. (1998). *Statement on liberal learning:* *www.aacu.org/about/liberal_learning.cfm.*

Balsom, P. D., & Tomie, A. (Eds.). (1985). *Context and learning.* Hillsdale, NJ: Lawrence Erlbaum.

Bean, J. C. (1996). *Engaging ideas: The professor's guide to integrating writing, critical thinking, and active learning in the classroom.* San Francisco: Jossey-Bass.

Biggs, J. (1999). *Teaching for quality learning at university: What the student does.* Birmingham, Great Britain: Society for Research into Higher Education & Open University Press.

Brookfield, S. D. (1987). *Developing critical thinkers.* San Francisco: Jossey-Bass.

Brown, D. G. (Ed.). (2000). *Teaching with technology.* Bolton, MA: Anker Press.

Brown, J. S. (2000). Growing up digital: How the Web changes work, education, and ways people learn. *Change, 32*(2), 11–20.

Brown, J. S., Collins, A., & Duguid, P. (1989). Situated cognition and the culture of learning. *Educational Researcher,* 18, 32–42.

Clark, R. C., & Mayer, R. E. (2002). *E-learning and the science of instruction.* San Francisco: Jossey-Bass.

Colby, A., Ehrlich, T., Beaumont, E., & Stephens, J. (2003). *Educating citizens: Preparing America's undergraduates for lives of moral and civic responsibility.* San Francisco: Jossey-Bass.

Diamond, R. M. (1997). *Designing & assessing courses & curricula: A practical guide.* San Francisco: Jossey-Bass.

Donald, J. D. (2002). *Learning to think: Disciplinary perspectives.* San Francisco: Jossey-Bass.

Edgerton, R., Hutchings, P., & Quinlan, K. (1995). *The teaching portfolio: Capturing the scholarship of teaching* (3rd reprinting). A Publication of the AAHE Teaching Initiative. Washington, DC: AAHE.

Entwhistle, N. (1983). *Understanding student learning.* New York: Nichols.

Fink, D. L. (2003). *Creating significant learning experiences: An integrated approach to designing college courses.* San Francisco: Jossey-Bass.

Gabelnick, F., MacGregor, J., Matthews, R. S., & Smith, B. L. (1990). *Learning communities: Creating connections among students, faculty, and disciplines.* New Directions for Teaching and Learning, 41. San Francisco: Jossey-Bass.

Gardner, H. (1993). *Multiple intelligences: The theory into practice.* New York: Basic Books.

Hutchings, P. (Ed.). (1998). *The course portfolio: How faculty can examine their teaching to advance practice and improve student learning.* A Publication of the AAHE Teaching Initiative. Washington, DC: American Association for Higher Education.

Hutchings, P., Bjork, C., & Babb, M. (2002). *An annotated bibliography of the scholarship of teaching and learning in higher education* (Revised and updated Fall, 2002). The Carnegie Foundation for the Advancement of Teaching: *www.carnegiefoundation .org/elibrary/docs/bibliography.htm.*

Kuh, G. D. (2001). Assessing what really matters to student learning: Inside the national survey of student engagement. *Change, 33*(3), 10–17, 66.

Light, R. J. (2001). *Making the most of college: Students speak their minds.* Cambridge, MA: Harvard University Press.

Light, R. J., Singer, J. D., & Willett, J. B. (1990). *By design: Planning research on higher education.* Cambridge, MA: Harvard University Press.

McLaughlin, T., & MacGregor, J. (1996). *Curricular learning communities directory.* Olympia, WA: Washington Center for Improving the Quality of Undergraduate Education.

Mezirow, J., & Associates. (2000). *Learning as transformation: Critical perspectives on theory in progress.* San Francisco: Jossey-Bass.

Miller, J. E., Groccia, J., & Miller, M. (Eds.). (2001). *Student-assisted teaching: A guide to faculty-student teamwork.* Bolton, MA: Anker Press.

Oblinger, D. G., & Rush, S. C. (1997). *The learning revolution: The challenge of information technology in the academy.* Bolton, MA: Anker Press.

Oblinger, D. G., & Rush, S. C. (Eds.). (1998). *The future compatible campus: Planning, designing, and implementing information technology in the academy.* Bolton, MA: Anker Press.

Palloff, R. M., & Pratt, K. (2003). *The virtual student: A profile and guide to working with online students.* San Francisco: Jossey-Bass.

Palmer, P. J. (1999). *Building learning communities in cyberspace.* San Francisco: Jossey-Bass.

Palmer, P. J. (2000). *The courage to teach: Exploring the inner landscape of a teacher's life.* San Francisco: Jossey-Bass.

Palmer, P. J. (2001). *Lessons from the cyberspace classroom: The realities of online teaching.* San Francisco: Jossey-Bass.

Pascarella, E. T., & Terenzini, P. T. (1991). *How college affects students: Findings and insights from twenty years of research.* San Francisco: Jossey-Bass.

Perry, W. G. (1999). *Forms of intellectual and ethical development in the college years: A scheme.* San Francisco: Jossey-Bass. (Originally published in 1970).

Poindexter, S. (2003, January/February). Holistic learning. *Change, 35*(1), 25–30.

Prosser, M., & Trigwell, K. (1999). *Understanding learning and teaching: The experience in higher education.* Buckingham, UK: Open University Press.

Schon, D. A. (1990). *Educating the reflective practitioner.* San Francisco: Jossey-Bass.

Seldin, P., & Associates. (2000). *Improving college teaching.* Bolton, MA: Anker Press.

Sheckley, B. G., & Keeton, M. T. (1997). *A review of the research on learning: Implications for the instruction of adult learners.* College Park, MD: Institute for Research on Adults in Higher Education, University of Maryland.

Shulman, L. S. (1999, July/August). Taking learning seriously. *Change, 31*(4), 10–17.

Shulman, L. S. (2002, November/December). Making differences: A table of learning. *Change, 34*(6), 36–44.

Smith, B. L., & McCann, J. (2001). *Reinventing ourselves: Interdisciplinary education, collaborative learning, and experimentation in higher education.* Bolton, MA: Anker Press.

Stark, J. S., Shaw, K. M., & Lowther, M. A. (1989). *Student goals for college and courses.* Report No. 6. Washington, DC: School of Education and Human Development, The George Washington University.

Stirnberg, R. J. (1997, March). What does it mean to be smarter? *Educational Leadership,* 20–24.

Strassburger, J. (1995). Embracing undergraduate research. *AAHE Bulletin, 47*(9), 3–5.

Tinto, V., et al. (1997). *Building learning communities for new college students: A summary of findings from the collaborative learning project.* Syracuse, NY: National Center on Postsecondary Teaching, Learning, and Assessment, Syracuse University.

21st Century Learning Initiative. (1997). *A transnational program to synthesize the best of research and development into the nature of human learning, and to examine its implications for education, work, and the development of communities worldwide: A work in progress.* Washington, DC: Author.

Wehlburg, C. M., & Chadwick-Blossey, S. (Eds.). (2003). *To improve the academy: Resources for faculty, instructional, and organizational development.* Bolton, MA: Anker Press.

Weimer, M. (2002). *Learner-centered teaching: Five key changes to practice.* San Francisco: Jossey-Bass.

Wiggins, G., & McTighe, J. (1998). *Understanding by design.* Alexandria, VA: Association for Supervision and Curriculum Development.

Wiske, M. S. (Ed.). (1998). *Teaching for understanding: Linking research with practice.* San Francisco: Jossey-Bass.

Zahornik, J. A. (1997, March). Encouraging—and challenging—students' understandings. *Educational Leadership,* 30–33.

Resources That Focus on Diverse Learners, Diverse Learning Styles, and Diverse Teaching Styles

Anderson, J. (2001). Developing a learning/teaching style assessment model for diverse populations. In L. Suskie (Ed.), *Assessment to promote deep learning* (pp. 21–30). Washington, DC: American Association for Higher Education.

Bash, L. (2003). *Adult learners in the academy.* Bolton, MA: Anker Press.

Brookfield, S. D. (1987). *Developing critical thinkers: Challenging adults to explore alternative ways of thinking and acting.* San Francisco: Jossey-Bass.

Brookfield, S. D. (1991). *Understanding and facilitating adult learning.* San Francisco: Jossey-Bass.

Caffarella, R. S. (2002). *Planning programs for adult learners: A practical guide for educators, trainers, and staff developers.* San Francisco: Jossey-Bass.

Farmer, J. A., Jr., Buckmaster, A., & LeGrand, B. (1992, Fall). Cognitive apprenticeship: Implications for continuing professional education. In V. J.

Marsick & H. K. Baskett (Eds.), Professionals' ways of knowing: New findings on how to improve professional education. *New Directions for Adult and Continuing Education, 55,* 41–49.

Nilson, L. B. (2003). *Teaching at its best: A research-based resource for college instructors* (2nd ed.). Bolton, MA: Anker Press. See, especially, chapter on teaching to different learning styles.

Morgan, C., & O'Reilly, M. (1999). *Assessing open and distance learners.* London: Kogan Page.

Ross-Gordon, J. M. (Ed.). (2002). *Contemporary viewpoints on teaching adults effectively.* San Francisco: Jossey-Bass.

Stein, D. S., & Imel, S. (Eds.). (2002, Fall). Adult learning in community. *New Directions for Adult and Continuing Education.*

Taylor, K., Marienau, C., & Fiddler, M. (2000). *Developing adult learners.* San Francisco: Jossey-Bass.

Tennant, M., & Pogson, P. (2002). *Learning and change in the adult years: A developmental perspective.* San Francisco: Jossey-Bass.

Wilson, A. L., & Hayes, E. R. (2000). *Handbook of adult and continuing education.* San Francisco: Jossey-Bass.

Wlodkowski, R. J., & Ginsberg, M. B. (2003). *Diversity & motivation: Culturally responsive teaching.* San Francisco: Jossey-Bass.

Meta-sites on Active Learning and Teaching and Learning Inventories

The Active Learning Site. The Active Learning Site supports the scholarship of teaching by providing research-based resources designed to help educators use active learning. Its resources include learning bibliographies in business, humanities, sciences and applied science, and social sciences, including general research on active learning; learning research summaries; Internet links on active learning; and a starter kit for the VARK learning styles inventory: *www.active-learning-site.com.*

The Learning Styles Resource Center. Sponsored by the University of Maryland University College and Towson University, the Learning Styles Resource Center provides teaching and learning inventories that may contribute to dialogue about the ways in which students learn and the ways in which faculty teach: *polaris.umuc.edu/~rouellet/learning/about.htm.* Learning inventories help educators understand how students perceive, organize, and process information. Teaching inventories stimulate and promote discussion about the range or lack of range of ways in

which educators teach, thus occasioning dialogue about the multiple, varied, and ample opportunities students experience to learn and develop over time.

Learning Styles Resources at Questia. For more information about publications and research on learning styles, go to Learning Styles Resources at Questia, an online library of books, journals, magazines, and newspapers: *www.questia.com/ Index.jsp?CRID = learning_styles&OFFID5se1.*

The Kolb Learning Styles Inventory. Among the most well-recognized learning inventories is the Kolb Learning Styles Inventory, designed to determine students' preferences in learning and the ways in which they process ideas and experiences. For information about this inventory, go to the following Web site: *pss.uvm.edu/pss162/learning_styles.html.*

Solomon and Felder. Solomon and Felder have integrated several learning inventories, including perceptual ways of learning, into one inventory available at: *www2.ncsu.edu/unity/lockers/users/ f/felder/public/ILSdir/ilsweb.html.*

Student Affairs

The American College Personnel Association (ACPA). This association provides principles, resources, and publications that guide effective assessment of student learning: *www.myacpa.org/pub/pub_ar.cfm.*

The National Association of Student Personnel Administrators (NASPA). NASPA continually provides readings and resources on assessment through its online journal, NetResults: *www.naspa.org/netresults.*

Upcraft, M. L., & Schuh, J. H. (1996). *Assessment in student affairs: A guide for practitioners.* San Francisco: Jossey-Bass.

Meta-site Leading to Articles on Assessment in Student Affairs

The California State University www.calstate.edu/acadaff/sloa/links/student_affairs.shtml.

Resource for Collaboration between Academic Affairs and Student Affairs

Marcia B. Baxter Magolda (Executive Eds.). *About Campus.* A bi-monthly journal sponsored by the American College Personnel Association, *About Campus* is dedicated to the idea that student learning is the responsibility of all educators on campus. It is, therefore, designed to foster work between student affairs and academic affairs. *About Campus* is abstracted/indexed in *Current Index to Journals in Education* (ERIC); *Higher Education Abstracts: www.interscience.wiley.com.*

WORKSHEETS, GUIDES, AND EXERCISES

1. *A Coordinating Body.* Campus leaders oversee the formation of a campus assessment committee to initiate, coordinate, and orchestrate cycles of inquiry into student learning. Provosts, vice presidents, faculty, staff, and students work together to design a campus assessment committee purposefully composed of representatives from across an institution who bring different sets of lenses to explore student learning. As a campus leader, in conjunction with key members of your college or university, identify the range of members who will either serve on or contribute to a campus committee. If you already have a committee, discuss how you might expand its membership or its relationship to other members of the campus. Membership in either case might include those in the local business community, advisory board members, parents, and representatives of the wider public, for example. As a division head or department chair, follow a similar process to design a program-level committee that invites representation from other internal or external constituencies. Use the following list to help identify these constituencies as representatives on your committee or as ad hoc members:

- ❏ Institution's chief academic leader
- ❏ Representatives from faculty and staff governance
- ❏ Full- and part-time faculty
- ❏ Representative from each academic program, department, division, or each school within an institution
- ❏ Representative from academic support services
- ❏ Representative from library and information resources
- ❏ Representative from student support services
- ❏ Full- and part-time graduate and undergraduate students
- ❏ Teaching assistants
- ❏ Tutors
- ❏ Local community members who educate students in internships, cooperative education programs, and community service
- ❏ Members of community and business advisory groups
- ❏ Department, division, school, or program leaders
- ❏ Laboratory assistants who are familiar with how well students have learned or are learning
- ❏ Graduate assistants
- ❏ Alumni who provide a perspective on what they learned in a program and the currency of that learning
- ❏ Employers who identify what students bring to their employment as well as identify new abilities students will need to bring into the workforce
- ❏ Parents
- ❏ Representatives from institutional research and planning who provide expertise and support for assessment

2. *Expectations for Student Learning.* Use Figure 2.1 in this chapter as a way to generate discussion and consensus about institution-level and program-level expectations for student learning. Initially, discussion may begin by identifying discrete abilities, such as critical thinking. However, because program- and institution-level assessment focuses on how students integrate over time, work toward articulating what you expect them to be able to accomplish mid-point and end-point in their studies, such as evaluating alternative solutions to disciplinary problems, identifying behavioral patterns that lead to a specific diagnosis, or integrating disciplinary or interdisciplinary perspectives into solutions to problems.

   An institution-wide committee or core working group might use this figure as a way to focus on articulating what it believes all students who graduate from an institution should be able to demonstrate, represent, or produce. A program-level committee might use this figure to promote dialogue about what it believes all students who graduate from that program should be able to demonstrate, represent, or produce. Programs and services that contribute to and support student learning, such as in the areas of library and information resources or student affairs and support services, might use this figure to promote similar discussions. Representatives from these areas should also participate in academic institution- and program-level discussions to assure there is coherence underlying curricular and co-curricular intentions.

3. *Integration.* You may wish to select one or more of the readings listed under "Additional Resources" in this chapter as a way to deepen dialogue about how students learn over time in a department, school, program, or service at the institution.

For example, your department might read Donald's book, *Learning to Think: Disciplinary Perspectives,* to stimulate discussion about how learning develops in a discipline over time.

Perry's book, *Forms of Intellectual and Ethical Development in the College Years: A Scheme,* might guide institution-level dialogue about how a theory of development translates itself into the design of the curriculum and co-curriculum to develop students' attitudes and dispositions.

Brown's article, "Growing Up Digital: How the Web Changes Work, Education, and Ways People Learn," might focus dialogue on the design of delivery systems as they contribute to program- and institution-level learning outcomes.

The Association of American Colleges & Universities' writings, www.aacu.org/integrative_learning/index.cfm or www.carnegiefoundation.org/LiberalEducation/ Mapping_Terrain.pdf, could generate discussion about the learning relationships between students' majors and their liberal education.

Mentkowski & Associates' seven principles of learning, in *Learning that Lasts: Integrating Learning, Development and Performance in College and Beyond* (pp. 227–246), may focus dialogue on ways to deepen student learning at the program and institution levels.

4. *Coherence.* Once your institution- or program-level committee has agreed upon expectations for student learning, discuss the range of ways in which people teach or create learning environments that contribute to students' learning. Dialogue might involve discussing philosophies of teaching, principles of or assumptions about teaching and learning, theories of learning, research on learning and development, or research on learning in a discipline, topics that lead to collective understanding of the ways in which students learn over time. Use the following set of questions to guide institution-level discussions focused on how students learn what an institution and its programs and services value:

- What educational philosophy, principles, theories, models of teaching, research on learning, or shared assumptions underlie curricular or co-curricular design, instructional design, pedagogy, or use of educational tools to promote institution- or program-level expectations for student learning?

- What pedagogies or educational experiences develop the knowledge, understanding, habits of mind, ways of knowing, and problem solving that the institution or its programs value?

- How do students become acculturated to the ways of thinking, knowing, and problem solving that the institution or its programs value?

- How do faculty and staff intentionally build upon each others' courses and educational experiences to achieve institution- as well as program-level learning priorities?

- Which students benefit from specific teaching strategies, educational processes, or educational experiences?

5. *Mapping.* The following format developed by the New Jersey City University Business Administration Program is useful after working groups have achieved consensus about shared expectations for student learning. At either the institution or program level, this map documents the distribution of learning opportunities that contribute to shared expectations for student learning. Representatives from institutional constituencies and even constituencies who contribute to student learning outside of the institution fill out these maps as a way to verify curricular and co-curricular coherence. Expectations for student learning, or outcomes, are listed on the left-hand side of the map, and courses or experiences are listed across the top of the map. Using the labels, *I* (introduced), *R* (reinforced), and *E* (emphasized), individuals indicate the focus of students' learning in the courses they teach or the educational experiences or opportunities they provide.

6. *Inventories.* The following two inventories can be used at either the program or institution level to develop a rich understanding of how educational practices promote shared expectations for student learning. They are particularly useful after groups have developed a map. That is, they provide a deeper look at educational practices and individual assessment methods that promote expected learning. Collective discussion of these worksheets identifies gaps in the continuum of students' learning, directing focus on how educators can integrate or redistribute opportunities for students to build on and demonstrate their learning over time.

Program- or Institution-Level Map

I = Introduced R = Reinforced E = Emphasized	Course or Educational Experience	Course or Educational Experience	Course or Educational Experience	Course or Educational Experience	Course or Educational Experience	Course or Educational Experience	Course or Educational Experience
Learning Outcomes:							
1.							
2.							
3.							
4.							
5.							
6.							
7.							
8.							

Source: Adapted from the New Jersey City University Business Administration Program. Reproduced with permission.

Inventory 1: Analysis of Assessment Method Used in a Course or Educational Experience to Assess Students' Achievement of an Institution- or Program-Level Expectation Course or Educational Experience: _____

Design	Pedagogy and Use of Educational Tools	Assessment Method: Context	Assessment Method: Content
Describe how you design a course or educational experience to contribute to students' demonstration or representation of an institution- or a program-level expectation:	Identify ways in which students actually learn what you intend, for example, in collaboratively-based projects, through simulations, through memorization, through the use of equipment, or through self-reflection in response to a task:	Describe your assessment method and the context within which students respond to it, for example, at the end of an internship, in a multiple choice test, or as part of a laboratory assignment:	Describe the content that you expect students to know in order to respond to a particular method, for example, content learned in the course or content you assume they learned in previous courses or educational experiences:

Inventory 2: Documentation of Focus on and Assessment of An Institution- or Program-Level Expectation for Learning Course or Educational Experience: _____

Program- or Institution-Level Learning Expectation	Course or Educational Experience Explicitly States This Expectation	Students Demonstrate or Represent Their Learning of This Expectation	Students Receive Formal Feedback About Their Demonstration or Representation of Learning	This Expectation Is Not Addressed in this Course or Educational Experience
	Yes/No If yes, describe how.	Yes/No If yes, describe how.	Yes/No If yes, describe how.	Addressed/ Not Addressed
1.				
2.				
3.				
4.				
5.				
6.				
7.				

APPENDIX 2.1   BUSINESS ADMINISTRATION PROGRAM'S CURRICULUM MAP

Business Administration Competencies/Expected Outcomes for the Common Professional Component

Business Administration Map I=Introduce; R=Reinforce; E=Emphasize	Econ 207 Macro-Economics	Econ 208 Micro-Economics	CS 214 Microcomp App for Bus	Eng 200 Writing for Bus	Math 1165 Pre-Calc (Bus)	Busi 201 Intro to Bus	Busi 203 Bus Statistics	Busi 211 Prin Mgmt	Busi 231 Prin Mktg	Busi 241 International Bus	Busi 251 Prin Acctg I	Busi 252 Prin Acctg II	Busi 281 Bus Law I	Busi 371 Mgl Finance	Busi 411 Bus Policy
Writing Competencies															
Identify a subject and formulate a thesis statement.						I			R						E
Organize ideas to support a position.				I		R			R				R		E
Write in a unified and coherent manner appropriate to the subject matter.				I		R			R				R		E
Use appropriate sentence structure and vocabulary.				I		R			R				R		E
Document references and citations according to an accepted style manual.						I			R				R		E
Critical Thinking Competencies															
Identify business problems and apply creative solutions.								I	R	R	R	R	R	R	E
Identify and apply leadership techniques.								I			R	R		R	E
Translate concepts into current business environments.								I	R	R	R	R		R	E
Analyze complex problems by identifying and evaluating the components of the problem.								I			R	R	E	E	E

Competency													
Quantitative Reasoning Competencies													
Apply quantitative methods to solving real-world problems.			I		R	R			E				
Perform necessary arithmetic computations to solve quantitative problems.			I		R	R			E				
Evaluate information presented in tabular, numerical, and graphical form.			I		R	R			E		E		
Recognize the reasonableness of numeric answers.			I		R	R			E		E		
Oral Communications Competencies													
Organize an oral argument in logical sequence that will be understood by the audience.			I	R	R	R			E				
Use visual aids effectively to support an oral presentation.			I	R	R	R			E				
Demonstrate professional demeanor, speak clearly in well-modulated tone, and engage the audience.			I	R	R				E				
Exhibit good listening skills when others are speaking.			I	R	R				E				
Technology and Information Literacy													
Identify problem/topic.			I	R						R			
Demonstrate familiarity with information resources and technologies.			I	R						R			
Conduct search query.			I	R						R			
Evaluate sources of information.			I	R						R			

Continued

Business Administration Competencies/Expected Outcomes for the Common Professional Component

Business Administration Map I=Introduce; R=Reinforce; E=Emphasize	Econ 207 Macro-Economics	Econ 208 Micro-Economics	CS 214 Microcomp App for Bus	Eng 200 Writing for Bus	Math 1165 Pre-Calc (Bus)	Busi 201 Intro to Bus	Busi 203 Bus Statistics	Busi 211 Prin Mgmt	Busi 231 Prin Mktg	Busi 241 International Bus	Busi 251 Prin Acctg I	Busi 252 Prin Acctg II	Busi 281 Bus Law I	Busi 371 Mgl Finance	Busi 411 Bus Policy
Computer Literacy															
Demonstrate computer literacy in preparation of reports and presentations.			I												
Demonstrate ability to use software application to solve business problems.								R						E	E
Conduct search queries through the use of the Internet.							I	R			R			R	R
Values Awareness															
Recognize ethical issues.						I		R	R	R			E	E	E
Identify ethical issues.						I		R	R	R			E	E	E
Identify theoretical frameworks that apply to corporate social responsibility.						I		R	R	R		R		E	E
Translate ethical concepts into responsible behavior in a business environment.						I		R	R			R	R	R	
Develop values awareness.						I		R		R					E

CONTENT-SPECIFIC COMPETENCIES
Global Business Competencies

Competency													
Demonstrate knowledge of contemporary social, economic, and political forces; their interrelationship; and their impact on the global business environment.	I			I	R	R	RE				R		R
Identify the integration of global markets from both financial and product/service perspectives.				I		R	RE				R		R
Incorporate diverse cultural perspectives into business decisions.				I	R	R	RE				R		R

Accounting Competencies

Competency													
Understand the role of the accounting information system within an organization's overall information system.								I	R		R		
Demonstrate knowledge of the accounting cycle and the ability to perform necessary procedures at each step of the cycle for both corporate and noncorporate entities.								I	R				
Describe, prepare, and interpret comparative financial statements using analytical techniques such as ratios and common-size statements.								I	R		E		
Understand the differences between financial and managerial accounting.													
Understand the role of managerial accounting analysis, control, and planning of costs within the corporation.								I	R				

Continued

APPENDIX 2.1   (CONTINUED)

Business Administration Competencies/Expected Outcomes for the Common Professional Component

Business Administration Map

I = Introduce; R = Reinforce; E = Emphasize

Finance Competencies

Competency	Macro-Economics Econ 207	Micro-Economics Econ 208	Microcomp App for Bus CS 214	Writing for Bus Eng 200	Pre-Calc (Bus) Math 1165	Intro to Bus Busi 201	Bus Statistics Busi 203	Prin Mgmt Busi 211	Prin Mktg Busi 231	International Bus Busi 241	Prin Acctg I Busi 251	Prin Acctg II Busi 252	Bus Law I Busi 281	Mgl Finance Busi 371	Bus Policy Busi 411
Integrate knowledge of economics, accounting, and quantitative analysis in the process of making fiancial decisions.	I	I												IRE	
Access and interpret financial market data using both Internet and print sources.						I		R	R	R				RE	
Apply basic computational techniques and/or spreadsheet software to solve financial problems.							I				R			E	
Compute return and risk measures for basic financial assets (stocks and bonds).														I	
Analyze corporate financial statements to pinpoint strengths and weaknesses.											I	R		E	R
Identify the impact of investment, financing, and dividend policy decisions on the value of an enterprise.														I	

APPENDIX 2.1   (CONTINUED)

Competency							
Use financial tools for life decisions about items such as housing, credit, retirements, and investments.					I		
Management Competencies							
Define basic terms used in management.		I		E			R
Develop a basic strategic planning process for an organizational unit.		I		E			R
Derive policies and practices that meet the cultural and global challenges of a changing workforce.		I		E			R
Translate productivity, quality and efficiency concepts to current business environments.		I		E			R
Marketing Competencies							
Identify, evaluate, and translate basic marketing problems into powerful business solutions.				IRE			
Analyze buyer behavior.				IRE			
Utilize a marketing information system to achieve a competitive advantage.				IRE			
Improve ability to develop new products and evaluate pricing, promotional, and distribution strategies.				IRE			

Source: Contributed by the Business Administration faculty (William Craven, John Egan, Marilyn Ettinger, Richard Fabris, Shimshon Kinory, Patricia McGuire, Robert Matthews, Leonard Nass, Barbara O'Neal, Jeanette Ramos-Alexander, Afaf Shalaby, Joseph Stern, Susan Williams, and Rosalyn Young), New Jersey City University, for the rubric on information literacy. Reproduced with permission.

Chapter 3

MAKING CLAIMS ABOUT STUDENT LEARNING WITHIN CONTEXTS FOR LEARNING

If the students are dealing with a narrow range of problems in their studies, the likelihood of their being able to deal with other kinds of problems in relation to which their studies are potentially relevant would be much less than if they had encountered more variation. In order to be able to make use of what one has learned in a course of studies, a new situation has to be seen by the individual in such a way that certain knowledge and certain skills appear relevant, and what we can make use of and apply depends on how we see, interpret, and define the situation. This also makes the most fundamental form of learning into learning to see, learning to experience, and learning to understand certain things in certain ways, as for instance when a scientist develops a scientific way of seeing scientific phenomena, a lawyer develops a juridical way of seeing legal problems, or a physician develops a medical way of listening to heartbeats, seeing x-ray pictures, and so on.

—Ference Marton, 1998

OVERVIEW: The dialogue and tasks described in Chapter 2 provide the foundation for making claims about student learning, the focus of Chapter 3. These claims reflect the kinds of learning that the institution and its programs value and that emerge more specifically from the dialogue, maps, and inventories described in the previous chapter. This chapter takes the work of the previous chapter to a greater level of specificity to develop learning outcome statements that describe what students should be able to represent, demonstrate, or produce based on how and what they have learned. Building on the verification strategies described in the previous chapter, it presents strategies for developing and reviewing learning outcome statements to ascertain how well they align with institution- and program-level expectations and practices. The Worksheets, Guides, and Exercises at the end of this chapter are designed to (1) foster collective authorship of and agreement on learning outcome statements; (2) foster collective review and approval of these statements; and (3) orient students to institution- and program-level learning outcome statements. The work of this chapter also connects with the work of the following chapter that focuses on deciding when and how you will take stock of students' progress along the continuum of their learning.

LEARNING OUTCOME STATEMENTS

The dialogue, mapping, and inventorying in Chapter 2 function to establish generally agreed-upon outcomes. The work of this chapter aims to achieve consensus about the public claims institutions make about student learning, *learning outcome statements*. These statements build on the consensus achieved in Chapter 2 but are at a greater level of specificity based on further dialogue about the design of curriculum, co-curriculum, instruction, educational experiences and opportunities, and students' learning histories that were the ending focus of the previous chapter. They describe what students should demonstrate, represent, or produce in relation to how and what they have learned.

Characteristics of Institution- and Program-Level Learning Outcome Statements

Collectively developed across an institution or a program, a learning outcome statement is a sentence that

* describes what students should be able to demonstrate, represent, or produce based on their learning histories;

* relies on active verbs that identify what students should be able to demonstrate, represent, or produce over time—verbs such as *create, apply, construct, translate, identify, formulate,* and *hypothesize*;

* aligns with collective program- and institution-level educational intentions for student learning translated into the curriculum and co-curriculum;

* maps to the curriculum, co-curriculum, and educational practices that offer multiple and varied opportunities for students to learn;

* is collaboratively authored and collectively accepted;

* incorporates or adapts professional organizations' outcome statements when they exist;

* can be quantitatively and/or qualitatively assessed during students' undergraduate or graduate studies.

The institutional example in Box 3.1 illustrates the specificity of learning outcome statements.

BOX 3.1   INSTITUTIONAL EXAMPLE: *California State University Monterey Bay*

Ethics, one of the foci in California State University Monterey Bay's general education curriculum, seeks to develop students who "recognize the complexity and importance of choices available to humans in their personal, professional and social lives"; are aware of deeply held beliefs about how humans relate to each other in specific contexts; are able to recognize and understand others' approaches to ethical decision making; and are able to "participate meaningfully and successfully in dialogue across these differences" (csumb.edu/academic/ulr/index.html). What capacities identify students' achievement of this requirement? That is the focus of a learning outcome statement. The following five learning outcome statements identify those capacities in graduates of the university:

Outcome 1: Graduates are able to identify and analyze real-world ethical problems or dilemmas, and identify those affected by the dilemma.

Outcome 2: Graduates are able to describe and analyze the complexity and importance of choices that are available to the decision makers concerned with this dilemma.

Outcome 3: Graduates are able to articulate and acknowledge their own deeply held beliefs and assumptions as part of a conscious value system.

Outcome 4: Graduates are able to describe and analyze their own and others' perceptions and ethical frameworks for decision making.

Outcome 5: Graduates are able to consider and use multiple choices, beliefs, and diverse ethical frameworks when making decisions to respond to ethical dilemmas or problems.

   Drawn from multiple and varied opportunities to learn at the university, these outcomes identify the ways of thinking and knowing that students should demonstrate within societal and personal frameworks. In addition, these outcomes reflect the university's focus on developing learners who are predisposed to self-reflection about their own value system and ethical decision-making process.

Source: Contributed by California State University Monterey Bay: University Learning Requirements, 2002. Reproduced with permission.

The Difference between Program or Institutional Objectives and Learning Outcomes or Learning Objectives

As the example in Box 3.1 illustrates, learning outcome statements are anchored in verbs that identify the actions, behaviors, dispositions, and ways of thinking or knowing that students should be able to demonstrate. Confusion sometimes exists between the terms *program* or *institutional objectives* and *learning outcome statements*, sometimes also referred to as *learning objectives* or *educational objectives*. Program or institutional objectives identify content or learning parameters—what students should *learn, understand,* or *appreciate* as a result of

their studies. Mission statements often contain the language of program or institutional objectives, providing an overall description of what an institution and its programs intend students to learn. Learning outcome statements, learning objectives, or educational objectives identify what students should be able *to demonstrate* or *represent* or *produce* as a result of what and how they have learned at the institution or in a program. That is, they translate learning into actions, behaviors, and other texts from which observers can draw inferences about the depth and breadth of student learning. Another institutional example is provided in Box 3.2.

BOX 3.2   INSTITUTIONAL EXAMPLE: *University of Washington*

Figure 3.1 illustrates how faculty in the Development and Regional Studies Concentration at the University of Washington have translated two of their program objectives into outcome statements. These outcome statements describe what students should be able to do based on the concentration's content and curricular sequence, students' learning experiences, and the ways in which they learn in that program. Notice how the descriptors of what students should understand in the two program objective statements translate into a complex intellectual process: *analysis*. As the figure also illustrates, program-level outcome statements are more specific statements than institution-level statements. That is, these statements reflect the purposes and intentions of a specific field or focus of study or work.

Program Objective: Understand the processes of urbanization and modernization in the developing world.

⇩

Student Learning Outcome: Analyze cities as products of modernization, as expressions of various processes, such as investment and employment.

Program Objective: Understand ways political and economic relationships are shaped by history and geography.

⇩

Student Learning Outcome: Differentially analyze colonialism according to geographical and scalar variation: how different colonial regimes and technologies have affected development in different places—how structural tools look and are used differently in various places.

FIGURE 3.1   Development and Regional Studies Concentration in Geography at the University of Washington: Sample Program Objectives Translated into Student Learning Outcome Statements. *Source:* Contributed by Richard Roth and members of the Geography Department, University of Washington. Reproduced with permission.

LEVELS OF LEARNING OUTCOME STATEMENTS

Across an institution there exist levels of outcome statements. At an institutional level, outcome statements are more general statements reflecting students' entire educational experiences. For example, an institution might state that its students "write a range of texts to address different audiences and achieve different purposes." Collectively, then, programs and individual courses and services, such as those offered through writing centers, intentionally contribute to this larger institutional outcome. That is, they provide students with a plethora of writing experiences that develop students' ability to write different kinds of discourse. Outcome statements become more specific at the program level, reflecting the kinds of writing within a discipline, profession, or field of study. An outcome statement at a program level might state that students "write a range of representative documents in chemistry that solve problems for different audiences and purposes."

Taken altogether, then, students' collective writing experiences during their undergraduate and graduate studies contribute to their flexibility as writers. That is, they become individuals who learn how to use the conventions and modes of discourse that represent how humans communicate generally and how they communicate in specific fields of work.

Figure 3.2 represents the relationship among levels of outcome statements. Individual courses and services, such as learning support services, contribute to academic programs that contribute to institution-level outcomes. Not every course or service or program addresses all program- or institution-level outcomes. However, mapping how and where outcomes are addressed at each level assures that there are multiple and layered opportunities for students to develop the understanding, behaviors, habits of mind, ways of knowing, and dispositions valued at both the institution and program levels. That is, there is an underlying coherence that contributes to students' learning.

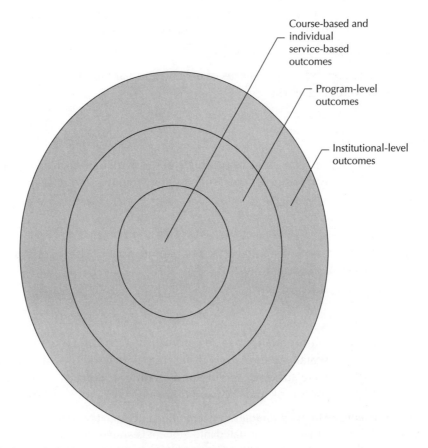

FIGURE 3.2   Underlying Coherence among Levels of Outcomes.

TAXONOMIES

Helpful in developing outcome statements are *taxonomies* that classify the cognitive, behavioral, and affective domains of learning and identify levels of learning through verbs that capture that learning (Bloom, Engelhart, Furst, Hill, & Krathwohl, 1956; Gronlund, 1970; Anderson et al., 2001). Bloom's cognitive domain taxonomy, for example, classifies cognitive learning along a developmental continuum that extends from knowledge to comprehension, application, analysis, synthesis, and evaluation. Verbs such as *define, describe, enumerate,* or *reproduce* identify acts of knowing, for example. Verbs such as *criticize, defend,* or *interpret* identify acts of evaluation. An updated version of Bloom's taxonomy extends that taxonomy to cover learning, teaching, and assessing (Anderson et al.).

Although these and other inventories are helpful in developing outcome statements, selecting from them is not an arbitrary process. The focus of outcome statements is related to the design and sequence of the curriculum, co-curriculum, and complementary educational experiences. Some programs may structure curricula based on Bloom's cognitive domain—from lower-order to higher-order cognitive complexity, for example. Other programs may build on a different philosophy, set of assumptions, or model of learning. Dialogue about the philosophy of teaching and learning and about how philosophies or sets of assumptions are translated into educational practices should guide choice within the context of these taxonomies. For example, course progressions in a major might be based on a developmental model of cognition because faculty believe that this best correlates to how students build their learning. Course progressions in another major might be based on a different model, such as a problem-based curricular model that asks students to generate hypotheses earlier rather than later in their sequence of studies. The verbs that anchor an outcome statement need to take into account students' chronology of learning, as well as their ways of learning, so that outcome statements *align* with educational practices.

COLLABORATION TO DEVELOP AND REVIEW OUTCOME STATEMENTS

Collaboration across a program or service, as well as across an institution, is key to creating learning outcome statements. They should be developed by the sorts of core working groups described in Chapter 2 that consist of representatives from across an institution or across a program. A core working group within a history program, consisting of faculty, staff, students, alumni, and local community members, for example, may work together to create an outcome statement or statements that describe how students demonstrate program-level quantitative reasoning. Similarly, an interdisciplinary core working group consisting of mathematicians, faculty from other disciplines, and representatives from academic support services might work together to develop an outcome statement or statements that describe how students should demonstrate institution-level quantitative reasoning. Other interdisciplinary core working groups may develop outcome statements for additional institution-level expectations focused on information literacy, lifelong learning, interdisciplinary perspectives, or spiritual development, depending upon an institution's mission and purposes.

To build and achieve consensus across a department or program and across an institution, members of these larger communities need to agree on these outcomes. Whether that consensus building occurs informally in department or program meetings or formally as part of a campus-wide meeting or forum—often through discussion and debate translated into drafts—consensus is essential in building a sustainable institutional commitment. Without that consensus, faculty, staff, and administrators may easily become disconnected from the larger institutional priorities and from department-, program-, division-, or service-level priorities. Achieving consensus maintains institution- and program-level focus on educational priorities. These may, in fact, change over time depending on societal changes or new institutional commitments that emerge as an institution engages in strategic planning or undertakes a change in leadership or mission revision.

For that reason, both institution- and program-level assessment plans must undertake, over time, to review outcome statements as part of a cycle of inquiry into student learning to assure that these statements remain current, relevant, and intentionally addressed through a coherent design of experiences and opportunities. To build in this important process, institutions and programs often limit the number of outcomes they assess at one time. Similar to the process at Rose-Hulman Institute of Technology, described in Box 2.2 in Chapter 2, a cyclical review of outcome statements must begin by examining curricular integrity and coherence in relation to what institutions and their programs claim students are able to demonstrate.

STRATEGIES FOR DEVELOPING OUTCOME STATEMENTS

The following five strategies, often used interdependently, represent ways in which institution- and program-level core working groups or task forces develop agreed-upon outcome statements.

Strategy 1: Mission Statements

Existing institution- and program-level mission statements provide one way to develop outcome statements. Representatives from across an institution and across a program develop outcome statements drawn from institution- or program-level mission statements. What, specifically, do an institution and its programs and services believe students should be able to demonstrate based on these mission statements? If a mission statement asserts that students learn to "write effectively," "reason quantitatively," or become "responsible citizens," how do those descriptors translate into claims about what students should be able to do or demonstrate? The California State University example in Box 3.1 earlier in this chapter illustrates how that institution has translated general statements about ethics into specific outcomes it wishes its graduates to demonstrate.

Reaching consensus about what students should be able to demonstrate or represent rests on verifying the relevance and accuracy of these statements within the context of the curriculum and co-curriculum. Mapping those statements to the institution and its programs or mapping program-level outcomes to courses and educational experiences that contribute to program learning develops that consensus. Mapping, discussed in Chapter 2, is a way to verify the relevance and accuracy of these statements, as well as the degree of curricular coherence that supports desired student learning. An institutional example using mapping of outcomes to assure educational coherence is provided in Box 3.3.

Strategy 2: Professional Organizations

Another way to jump-start efforts to develop outcome statements is to use or adapt statements that disciplinary and professional organizations have developed. Institutions and programs may revise these statements to reflect their more specific intentions. Increasingly, professional organizations are developing statements that describe what graduates should be able to demonstrate. The three disciplinary organizations discussed in the following paragraphs are doing work that represents this trend.

Responding to the question about what quantitative literacy requirements colleges and universities should establish for students who receive a bachelor's degree, the Commission on Undergraduate Programs in Mathematics of the Mathematics Association of America, in *Quantitative Reasoning for College Graduates: A Complement to the Standards* (1996), states that a quantitatively literate college graduate should be able to exhibit the following skills (www.maa.org/pubs/books/qrs.html):

1. Interpret mathematical models such as formulas, graphs, tables, and schematics; and draw inferences from them.

BOX 3.3   INSTITUTIONAL EXAMPLE: *Stonehill College*

As a part of its long-range institutional plan, Stonehill College is currently deriving and mapping its outcomes within its current and emerging institutional context to assure educational coherence. Specifically, the institution is deriving its institution-level outcomes from the following sources:

- College mission
- Long-range planning effort—college vision
- General education philosophy
- Major and minor requirements
- Co-curricular goals

Source: Contributed by Dr. Karen Talentino, Dr. Susan Mooney, Elizabeth Newman, and Kathryne Drezek, Stonehill College. Reproduced with permission.

2. Represent mathematical information symbolically, visually, numerically, and verbally.

3. Use arithmetical, algebraic, geometric, and statistical methods to solve problems.

4. Estimate and check answers to mathematical problems in order to determine reasonableness, identify alternatives, and select optimal results.

5. Recognize that mathematical and statistical methods have limits.

Information literacy outcomes and statements of abilities for college and university graduates are comprehensively articulated in the work of the Association of College and Research Libraries (ACRL), a Division of the American Library Association, in *Information Literacy Competency Standards for Higher Education: Standards, Performance Indicators, and Outcomes* (2000) under five standards (www.ala.org/ala/acrl/acrlstandards/informationliteracycompetency.htm).

The American Psychological Association has articulated "Undergraduate Psychology Major Learning Goals and Outcomes: A Report" that provides a guide for setting undergraduate goals and outcomes in the areas of science and application, liberal arts, and career and personal development (www.lawrence.edu/fac/revieg/acminfolit/apa.html).

Even when professional organizations establish outcome statements, periodically verifying where and how those statements are addressed across an institution or across a program is an essential collaborative process to assure the coherence of our work. Faculty in each program within the College of Engineering at North Carolina State University map their program outcomes against the eleven standards and criteria of the Accrediting Board of Engineering and Technology (ABET) to determine curricular coherence. An example of that work is provided in Figure 3.3: faculty in Textile Engineering list their program outcomes, document where those outcomes are addressed and how those outcomes are assessed, and align that work with the standards and criteria of ABET. Documentation of methods to assess learning outcomes also helps groups identify appropriate formative and summative methods to assess students' learning, the focus of Chapter 4.

Strategy 3: Student Work

Deriving outcome statements based on collective examination of student work over time is a third strategy. That is, reviewing the kinds of work that students submit informs and even challenges consensus

Program Learning Outcomes for Engineering at North Carolina State University	Strategies for Implementing Program Outcomes	Assessment Methods	Relation to ABET Standards and Criteria
2b. Design new systems, components, and products to address needs.	Course 201 laboratory includes a design component where the students go through a design process to fill an established need.	• Lab reports in TE 205 • Report in TE 402 • Graduating Senior Survey, Question 3	3c: An ability to design a system, component, or process to meet desired needs
2c. Use modern engineering tools for desired solution.	Introduction to tools and skills begins in TE 105, including Microsoft® Excel and Lab programs.	• Exam in TE 205 • Report in TE 424 • Employer Survey, Question 3 and Question 4	3k: An ability to use the techniques, skills, and modern engineering tools necessary for engineering practice

FIGURE 3.3   Map of Outcomes against ABET Standards. *Source:* Contributed by Marian McCord, Joni Spurlin, and engineering faculty at NCSU. Reproduced with permission.

about what we expect them to be able to do over time. Selecting sample work that students produce midpoint in their studies and at the end of their studies provides direct evidence of their achievement. Examining this evidence becomes a reality-based strategy for achieving consensus about our students' learning. At the same time, this strategy may also unearth differences in opinion about what students should be able to demonstrate, thus promoting further dialogue about curricular and co-curricular coherence.

For example, sampling students' mid-level work in a major; sampling representative work at a midpoint in students' general education; and sampling senior theses, research papers, collaborative projects, and performances become strategies for deriving outcomes. Faculty, librarians, and information resource professionals might, for example, examine a range of senior research papers to develop consensus about what seniors in a particular program should be able to demonstrate by their senior year. This strategy develops a realistic context for developing outcomes based on reading actual work and the ways in which students represent their learning. This strategy also readies groups for the work described in Chapter 5 that focuses on establishing standards for judging student work.

Strategy 4: An Epistemological and Ethnographic Process

Developing a "thick description" based on interviews and dialogue among colleagues in a program represents another strategy that yields outcome statements grounded in an epistemological approach to learning and curricular design (Ryle, 1971). Faculty in the Geography Department at the University of Washington engaged in a fourpart ethnographic process to identify and negotiate learning outcomes in relationship to the courses they teach. A member of that program transcribed the results of this process. The thick description that recorded the collaborative work of program faculty became the means by which faculty achieved consensus about shared outcome statements within the context of different pedagogical strategies and intellectual foci. From this text, faculty gained a rich understanding of what and how students learn over time through the department's collective practices. The four-part process identified and then verified outcome statements

embedded in the program curriculum. (See Appendix 3.1 at the end of this chapter.)

In describing this process in correspondence to Peggy Maki in April and October 2003, Richard Roth, member of the advising staff in the Geography Department, concludes that this strategy is an effective way to achieve the following results:

- Generate substantive, engaged discussions of curricular restructuring because it exposes not only continuities but also overlaps, duplications, and gaps in the curriculum. It makes the curriculum a source of collective public ownership rather than a collection of private, individual curricular islands. The whole is truly greater than the sum of its parts.

- Engage faculty in talking about the logic and rationale of their courses: what material they have selected; why they have selected that material rather than other material; why they have sequenced this material in a particular way; and what the cumulative effects of the course are meant to be.

- Help faculty better appreciate the epistemological position of their students. In fact, the faculty themselves tend to recapitulate the epistemological progress of the students, going from general to specific (and back to general); from simple to complex; from being awash in disconnected bits of fact, information, data, etc., to learning how to make many different kinds of arguments; from merely becoming "knowledgeable" about a topic to learning the conditions and criteria for establishing and judging that knowing. The constructivist dimension of learning (category construction, canons of the validity of evidence, doctrine of cause and origin, versions of same and different, etc.) is thus revealed.

- Help students appreciate the ways that the various aspects of a course are contingent upon one another.

- Develop ownership of the process of articulating outcome statements.

- Provide students with a way to articulate and situate their own intellectual and professional development.

- Link assessment (formative and summative), accountability, and epistemology.

For the final learning outcome statements that resulted from this epistemological and ethnographic process, go to depts.washington.edu/geog/courses.

Strategy 5: Deep and Surface Approaches to Learning

Exploring how courses and educational experiences position students as learners across their continuum of learning is yet another strategy for developing outcome statements. Of particular assistance in this strategy is the work of Marton and Saljo (1976a, 1976b). Curious to know why certain students developed a comprehensive understanding of academic texts, while others did not, in the late 1970s Marton and Saljo interviewed students after reading academic texts. They concluded that students who took a *deep approach* to reading a text were internally motivated to make meaning during their reading. Students who took a *surface approach* to reading a text were externally motivated to recall bits of the text in response to questions they anticipated being asked. Those students who took a surface approach to reading texts stored information about the reading but failed to connect that information to other contexts. They were motivated to store information in anticipation of questions they believed they would be asked. In contrast, those students who took a deep approach to reading connected new information to previous learning to make meaning for themselves as they read. They were motivated to interpret information as they read; that is, they were internally motivated to learn through the process of reading.

Focusing on the relationship between deep and surface approaches to learning is helpful in identifying outcomes for student learning as well, raising questions about the kinds of learning we value. To what degree do we promote and value surface approaches to learning? To what degree do we promote and value deep approaches to learning? Certainly, memorization and recognition become a part of students' ability to solve and analyze problems and construct responses. Yet, how and when do curricular and other educational experiences position students to take a deep approach to their learning, promoting problem solving and self-reflection as ways of understanding? These broad brushstroke distinctions may assist program- and institution-level groups to collectively identify learning outcomes. Identifying transitional points in students' learning during which they shift from surface to deep learning may also contribute to achieving consensus about outcome statements. At what points in their continuum of learning do students construct and analyze solutions to problems? That is, when do we expect them to think divergently?

Appendix 3.2 and Appendix 3.3 illustrate how two programs aim to foster students' deep approach to their learning by engaging students in thinking across multiple intellectual and personal dimensions. That is, they are designed to stimulate students to process and self-reflect on their learning, not solely to take in information. North Carolina State University's outcome statements for its service learning programs (Appendix 3.2) focus on students' abilities to address both the academic and personal dimensions of their learning. These outcome statements reflect the multidimensionality of learning and development. That is, learners construct meaning within the context of their academic learning. They also reflect on the significance of their learning on a personal level: how their learning is shaping their commitments, behaviors, actions, and dispositions.

At Azusa Pacific University (Appendix 3.3), the nursing program developed its outcome statements within the context of the institution's mission. Taking a developmental approach to learning, the program states levels of outcomes that document nursing students' expected professional progression under multiple dimensions.

COMMUNITY CONSENSUS ABOUT LEARNING OUTCOME STATEMENTS

Although the previously mentioned core working groups of institution- and program-level committees develop learning outcome statements on behalf of their larger communities, achieving consensus within those larger communities is essential in building an institutional commitment to assessing for learning. Subjecting the final drafts of learning outcome statements to the representative or collective institution- and program-level approval processes is essential to build a shared commitment to assessing for student learning. The collaborative tasks and dialogue described in Chapter 1 and Chapter 2 lead to learning outcome statement drafts that represent collective intentions translated into the life of the institution and its programs. Assuring that members of an educational community have the final say in approving such statements through institution- or program-level governance and decision-making processes acknowledges and values the collective contribution of all stakeholders in students' learning. More important, achieving acceptance of learning outcome statements contributes to the early positioning of assessment as a core institutional process.

SITUATING STUDENTS TO TAKE RESPONSIBILITY

Situating students to take responsibility for their learning can occur once programs and institutions have developed and published outcome statements. Students may contribute to the dialogue that leads to outcome statements, and their work may help us to verify the accuracy of our statements. However, how we position them within our assessment efforts is critical to their own learning over time. We can either view them as recipients of our commitment to learn about their learning, or we can directly engage them in active reflection on and ownership of their learning. On the one hand, assessment is an institution's means of learning about the efficacy and relevancy of its educational practices to improve student learning; and that is one tier of assessment. On the other hand, assessment is a means for students to learn about their own progression over time; and that is the second tier of assessment—a tier that holds students accountable for their own learning.

Engaging students in their learning begins by providing them with outcome statements at the time they matriculate into the institution and into their programs of study. That is, students need to know what we expect them to be able to demonstrate along their continuum of learning. Without that knowledge, they may remain uncertain about our expectations; in fact, they may view much of what we expect as shrouded in mystery. Furthermore, students need to become acculturated to what outcome statements require them to demonstrate. For example:

- What does it mean to analyze a piece of discourse in a discipline?

- What does it mean to critique a performance?

- What does it mean to take an interdisciplinary approach to solving a problem?

Clarity about our expected learning outcomes grounds and guides students. Specifically, students

- become initiated into our educational cultures;

- develop an understanding of what institutions expect of them;

- learn to view themselves as responsible for their learning through multiple educational opportunities the institution offers;

- learn how to accomplish their individual learning goals by becoming familiar with institution- and program-level public outcome statements that inform their educational choices or needs

Clarity about our intentions underlies the dialogue and work described in Chapter 4. It also anchors the decisions members of a community make about how they will assess students' achievement along the continuum of their studies, as well as at the end of their formal education.

WORKS CITED

American Psychological Association: *www.apa.org/ed/pcue/taskforcereport.pdfReport.*

Association of College and Research Libraries: *www.ala.org/ala/acrl/acrlstandards/ informationliteracycompetency.htm.*

Anderson, L., et al. (2001). A *taxonomy for learning, teaching, and assessing: A revision of Bloom's taxonomy of educational objectives.* New York: Addison Wesley Longman.

Bloom, B. S., Engelhart, M. D., Furst, E. J., Hill, W. H., & Krathwohl, D. R. (1956). *The taxonomy of educational objectives, the classification of educational goals, Handbook I: Cognitive domain.* New York: David McKay.

Gronlund, N. E. (1970). *Stating behavioral objectives for classroom instruction.* New York: Macmillan.

Krathwohl, D. R., Bloom, B. J., & Masia, B. B. (1964). *The taxonomy of educational objectives: The classification of educational goals. Handbook II: Affective domain.* New York: David McKay.

Mathematics Association of America: *www.maa.org/ pubs/books/qrs.html.*

Marton, F. (1998). Towards a theory of quality in higher education. In B. C. Dart & G. Boulton-Lewis (Eds.), *Teaching and learning in higher education* (p. 84). Melbourne, Australia: Melbourne, Victoria. Australian Council for Educational Research, Ltd.

Marton, F., & Saljo, R. (1976a). On qualitative differences in learning: I—Outcome and process. *British Journal of Educational Psychology, 46,* 4–11.

Marton, F., & Saljo, R. (1976b). On qualitative differences in learning: II—Outcome and process. *British Journal of Educational Psychology*, 46, 115–127.

Ryle, G. (1971). *The thinking of thoughts. Collected papers*. II. London: Hutchinson of London.

ADDITIONAL RESOURCES

Developing Outcome Statements

Adelman, C. (Ed.). (1987). *Performance and judgment: Essays on principles and practice in the assessment of college student learning*. Washington, DC: U.S. Department of Education, Office of Research.

Astin, A. W. (1991). *Assessment for excellence: The philosophy and practice of assessment and evaluation in higher education*. New York: American Council on Education/ Macmillan.

Banta, T. W., et al. (1996). *Assessment in practice: Putting principles to work on college campuses*. San Francisco: Jossey-Bass.

Case, J., & Gunstone, R. (2002, October). Shift in approach to learning: An in-depth study. *Studies in Higher Education*, 27(4), 459–470.

Chaffee, E. E., et al. (1997). *Assessing impact: Evidence and action*. Washington, DC: American Association for Higher Education.

Diamond, R. (1998). *Designing and assessing courses and curricula*. San Francisco: Jossey-Bass.

Dressel, P. L. (1976). *Handbook of academic evaluation*. San Francisco: Jossey-Bass.

Erwin, T. D. (1991). *Assessing student learning and development: A guide to the principles, goals, and methods of determining college outcomes*. San Francisco: Jossey-Bass.

Gronlund, N. E. (1998). *Assessment of student achievement*. Needham Heights, MA: Allyn & Bacon.

Harrow, A. (1972). *A taxonomy of the psychomotor domain: A guide for developing behavioral objectives*. New York: Macmillan.

Huba, M., & Freed, J. (2001). *Learner-centered assessment on college campuses: Shifting the focus from teaching to learning*. Needham Hights, MA: Allyn & Bacon.

Mentkowski, M., & Loacker, G. (1985). Assessing and validating the outcomes of college. In P. T. Ewell (Ed.), *Assessing educational outcomes*. New Directions for Institutional Research, 47, 47–64. San Francisco: Jossey-Bass.

Mentkowski, M., Moeser, M., & Straight, M. J. (1981). *Using the Perry scheme of intellectual and ethical development as a college outcome measure: A process and criteria for assessing student performance*. Milwaukee, WI: Office of Research and Evaluation, Alverno College.

Mentkowski, M., & Rogers, G. P. (1988). *Establishing the validity of measures of college student outcomes*. Milwaukee, WI: Office of Research and Evaluation, Alverno College.

Palomba, C. A., & Banta, T. W. (1999). *Assessment essentials*. San Francisco: Jossey-Bass.

Rogers, G. P. (1988). *Validating college outcomes with institutionally developed instruments: Issues in maximizing contextual validity*. Milwaukee, WI: Office of Research and Evaluation, Alverno College.

Stark, J. S., & Lowther, M. (1986). *Designing the learning plan: A review of research and theory related to college curricula*. Ann Arbor, MI: The National Center on Postsecondary Teaching and Learning (NCRPTAL), University of Michigan.

Stark, J. S., Shaw, K. M., & Lowther, M. A. (1989). *Student goals for college and courses* (Report No. 6). Washington, DC: School of Education and Human Development, The George Washington University.

Walvoord, B. E., & Anderson, V. J. (1998). *Effective grading: A tool for learning and assessment*. San Francisco: Jossey-Bass.

Deep and Surface Approaches to Learning

Entwhistle, N. (1998). Approaches to learning and forms of understanding. In B.C. Dart & G. Boulton-Lewis (Eds.). *Teaching and learning in higher education* (pp. 72–101). Melbourne: Australia: Melbourne, Victoria. Australian Council for Educational Research, Ltd.

Entwistle, N. J., & Ramsden, P. (1983). *Understanding student learning*. New York: Nichols.

Marton, F. (1975). *On non verbatim learning—II: The erosion of a task-induced learning algorithm* (Reports from the Institute of Education, University of Gothenburg, No. 40).

Marton, F. (1976). What does it take to learn? Some implications of an alternative view of learning. In N. J. Entwistle (Ed.). *Strategies for research and development in higher education*. Amsterdam: Swets and Zeitlinger.

Meta-site on Student Affairs Outcomes and Outcomes Assessment

The California State University:
www.calstate.edu/acadaff/sloa/links/student_affairs.shtml.

Meta-site on Taxonomies

The following sites list further references and Internet resources on taxonomies:
faculty.washington.edu/krumme/guides/bloom.html.

George Mason University:
assessment.gmu.edu/AcadProgEval/guide.shtml. Provides Internet resources for Bloom's taxonomy.

Bill Huitt's Homepage at Valdosta State University:
chiron.valdosta.edu/whuitt/col/cogsys/bloom.html. Provides a chart of Bloom's taxonomy for the cognitive domain.

WORKSHEETS, GUIDES, AND EXERCISES

1. *Developing Outcome Statements.* As an initial exercise with colleagues in a core working group established to develop learning outcome statements, focus discussion on students' continuum of learning at the program- or institution-level by exploring the value placed on surface and deep approaches to an expectation that the core group identified in Chapter 2. Translate that discussion into outcome statements that reflect what students should be able to represent, demonstrate, or produce as a result of their learning chronology.

2. *Developing Outcome Statements.* As an initial exercise with colleagues in a core working group established to develop learning outcome statements at either the institution- or program-level, prepare drafts of outcome statements that build on the more general expectations agreed upon in Chapter 2. As you draft institution- and program-level outcome statements, you may find some of the taxonomies in the following list helpful:

Taxonomies to Guide Authorship of Learning Outcome Statements

www.kent.k12.wa.us/KSD/MA/resources/blooms/student_blooms.html

www.kcmetro.cc.mo.us/longview/ctac/blooms.htm

edtech.clas.pdx.edu/presentations/frr99/blooms.htm

home.att.net/~jaohlma/writings/taxonomy/taxonomies.html

www.acu.edu/academics/adamscenter/resources/coursedev/taxonomies.html

Focusing on verbs that center your outcome statements will also promote dialogue about how the design of the curriculum and co-curriculum and other educational experiences contributes to the learning identified in your outcome statements. These discussions may cause members of your group to want to establish levels of outcome statements such as appear in Appendix 3.3 in this chapter. Or, members may decide to develop two sets of outcome statements:

1. One set that defines what students should be able to demonstrate or represent by midpoint in their studies

2. A second set that defines what students should be able to demonstrate or represent at the end of their studies

3. *Developing Outcome Statements.* If you are beginning to develop outcome statements at the institution level, well before your initial meeting ask members of your core working group to use one or more of the five strategies described in this chapter to prepare a list of five or six outcome statements and discuss those outcomes. Pass each member's outcome statements to others in the group, and ask each member to indicate if each statement fulfills criteria for an effective outcome statement and include comments about the effectiveness of each statement. Use the following chart to evaluate each outcome statement. After everyone has had a chance to evaluate each outcome, determine if there is consensus about these statements. That consensus may take more than one meeting. When you have reached consensus, circulate a draft of those statements in a faculty-staff forum that provides opportunity for further feedback before the statements are officially adopted through governance structures and processes; or, post these learning outcome statements on your institution's Web site, seeking further institution-wide responses before the statements move toward a final approval process at the institution level. The development of program-level learning outcome statements may also follow this same process to build consensus.

Checklist to Review an Institution- or Program-Level Draft of Learning Outcome Statements

	Describes what students should represent, demonstrate, or produce?	Relies on active verbs?	Aligns with collective intentions translated into the curriculum and co-curriculum?	Maps to curriculum, co-curriculum, and educational practices?	Is collaboratively authored and collectively accepted?	Incorporates or adapts professional organizations' outcome statements when they exist?	Can be assessed quantitatively and/or qualitatively?
Outcome:							
Outcome:							
Outcome:							
Outcome:							

4. *Developing Learning Outcome Statements and Orienting Students.* To develop departmental learning outcome statements, the Geography Department at the University of Washington (described in Appendix 3.1 in this chapter) established the following time line to develop its outcomes, as well as make them public to students on the program's Careers Web site. This project focuses on assisting students in taking ownership of their learning as they develop a professional portfolio; that is, developing outcome statements educates them about program-level expectations and becomes the means for them to determine how they will build that portfolio. Use or adapt this timetable to develop learning outcome statements based on the epistemological and ethnographic process described on page 66 in this chapter. Determine how you will publish and orient students to these statements as a way for them to chart their educational journey.

TIME LINE FOR THE DEVELOPMENT OF THE DEPARTMENT OF GEOGRAPHY'S OUTCOME STATEMENTS

Project Schedule

September 16, 1997–January 15, 2001

Task 1. Objectives and outcomes narrative synthesis

- Establish protocol for interviews.
- Conduct interviews.
- Create drafts of 35 individual course profiles.
- Negotiate and revise overviews of learning outcomes within concentrations.
- Coordinate with faculty to finalize learning goals and objectives for concentrations and entire curriculum.

January 16, 2001–September 15, 2001

Task 2. Objectives and outcomes analytical synthesis

- Create objectives and outcome matrices for each course.
- Synthesize matrices to concentration level.
- Synthesize matrices to department curriculum level.

September 16, 2000–August 15, 2002

Task 3. Objectives and outcomes career articulation

- Develop UW Geography Department Careers WWW site.
- Develop alumni e-network.
- Develop alumni contact directory.
- Develop a searchable database designed to match current job qualifications and learning outcomes that helps students translate between learning outcomes and professional development. (Geography My Action Portfolio: G-MAP)

September 16, 2001–August 15, 2002

Task 4. Objectives and outcomes assessment

- Link instructor-graded assessments to anticipated outcomes and, hence, back to course objectives.
- Enable faculty to interview one another in a second, more iterative round of conversations.
- Assess a cross-section of portfolios of geography majors by faculty and outside professional panels.

September 16, 2000–August 15, 2002

Task 5. Geography My Action Portfolio (G-MAP)

- Agree on purposes and final architecture of the G-MAP site.
- Design user interface and navigation strategies for site.
- Link existing documents conceptually and as hypertext documents.
- Test functionality of site.
- Integrate site into major requirements (required portfolio, etc.).

Source: Contributed by Richard Roth and members of the faculty, Department of Geography, University of Washington. Reproduced with permission.

5. *Reviewing and Distributing Outcomes.* Building a sustainable institutional commitment occurs over time. Periodically, institution- and program-level committees and institutional leaders take stock of how this commitment is taking shape. The following checklist can be used in assessment committees, by leadership, during program- or department- or division-level meetings, or during more public forums bringing together members of the academic community to periodically track progress. Asking members in these meetings to respond to each question by responding to a level of progress— "Some Progress," "Making Progress," or "Achieved," as well as asking members to provide evidence for each response and summarizing those responses, builds collective commitment over time. Collective responses identify progress that has been made as well as areas that need attention.

Using this checklist, assessment committees can monitor progress toward achieving this first phase of an institutional commitment to assessment. Developing learning outcome statements, making them public and accessible, orientating students to them, informing students of the institution's commitment to assessing their work, and informing students of their responsibility for tracking their own learning characterize this initial phase.

Tracking Progress toward Developing and Disseminating Learning Outcome Statements

	Some Progress	Making Progress	Achieved	Evidence
Has your institution developed outcome statements that describe what all graduates should be able to represent, demonstrate, or produce?				
Has each program, division, school, department, and major educational service developed outcome statements that describe what students should represent, demonstrate, or produce?				
Are these statements published in the institution's catalog, on its Web site, and in other relevant publications?				
Are there ways in which students are oriented to institution-level outcomes upon matriculation, such as during first-year orientation or first-year programs?				
Are there ways in which students are oriented to program-level outcomes when they enter a program of study?				
Can students map or design their own learning history, based on institution- and program-level outcomes and related curricular and co-curricular information?				
Are students aware that the institution will assess their learning over time?				
Are students aware that they are responsible for assessing their learning over time?				

APPENDIX 3.1   INSTITUTIONAL EXAMPLE: *University of Washington, Department of Geography's Learning Outcome Project*

TOWARD "THICK DESCRIPTION": THE ITERATIVE INTERVIEWING PROCESS

To develop its learning outcome statements, the Department of Geography at the University of Washington, has, so far, gone through four distinct, cumulative phases, the first three of which were ethnographic, the final one collaborative and collective:

Phase I: An Initial Ten-Minute Exercise.
In a department meeting, faculty were asked to "state a specific learning objective for one course they teach in the Geography Program and to explain what indicators they use to assess students' achievement of this objective (content, topics, or methods, not just performance on an exam or paper)."

One respondent's "course-specific learning objectives" were "critical thinking skills" and "writing skills." Her outcome indicators of the attainment of these skills included

1. application of theoretical approaches to empirical material in a clear, cogent, well-organized research or service learning project;

2. accurate and precise definition of concepts and approaches used and introduced in readings and lectures;

3. application of knowledge gained in the course to answer questions or solve problems.

Phase II: Follow-up Faculty-to-Faculty
Interviews. In each of the five concentrations within the major, faculty interviewed one another and asked for further elaboration of learning objectives leading to learning outcomes. The faculty member mentioned translated two of her objectives into outcome statements:

LEARNING OBJECTIVES: GEOG 371 (WORLD HUNGER AND RESOURCE DEVELOPMENT)

To understand the dimensions and causes of world poverty

To understand the dimensions and causes of world hunger

LEARNING OUTCOMES: GEOG 371 (WORLD HUNGER AND RESOURCE DEVELOPMENT)

Diagnose and offer solutions for global food problems.

Critique arguments related to food and hunger.

Phase III: Second Interview: Supplying the Missing Links and Narrative Stitchery.
The second follow-up interview, with the transcriber, produced a more complex description of learning objectives and outcomes. The transcriber "played dumb" by asking "What do you mean by hunger? What do you mean by development? How are those two concepts linked?" etc. Basically, this iteration produced:

1. more complex causal thinking, including consideration of linkages and hierarchies ("understanding of how poverty and hunger are linked across geographic scales");

2. more of a sense of the narrative flow of a course ("having defined poverty as x, and hunger as y, and having seen how they are linked across various geographic scales, faculty could better frame their discussion of the world food system, agricultural modernization," etc.);

3. a better-defined sense of what kinds of arguments students should be able to make at the end of a course. For example, instead of just saying students should be able to "critique arguments related to food and hunger," the faculty member who teaches World Hunger and Resource Development now states students should be able to "critique concepts of agrarian development and reform";

4. a generated supplemental list of targeted "acquired skills" students would come away with from each course—an inventory.

Phase IV: Negotiation of Learning Outcome Statements. The final phase entailed a round-robin, consisting of a collaborative process of writing the learning objectives and outcomes for the entire development concentration within the major. This meant integrating six faculty members and about eighteen courses. The developer of the thick text made a first stab at consolidating and then circulated a draft to members of the program. Learning outcomes were negotiated over an intense three-week period until consensus about learning outcomes was achieved. Results of this process are available at the University of Washington's Web site: depts.washington.edu/geog/courses.

Source: Contributed by Richard Roth and members of the faculty, Department of Geography, University of Washington. Reproduced with permission.

APPENDIX 3.2   INSTITUTIONAL EXAMPLE: *North Carolina State University's* Service Learning Program-Wide Learning Outcomes

ACADEMIC DIMENSION

1. **Identify and describe course-related concepts in the context of your service-learning-related activities.**

   - Describe the course concept that relates to your service learning experience.—AND—

   - Describe what happened in the service learning experience that relates to that course concept.

2. **Apply course-related concepts in the context of your service-learning-related activities.**

   - How does the course-related concept help you to better understand, or deal with, issues related to your service-learning experience? —AND/OR—

   - How does the service-learning-related experience help you to better understand the course-related concept?

3. **Analyze course-related concepts in light of what you have experienced in the context of your service-learning-related activities.**

   - In what specific ways are a course-related concept (or your prior understanding of it) and the experience the same and/or different? —AND—

   - What complexities do you see now in the course-related concept that you had not been aware of before?—AND/OR—

   - What additional questions need to be answered or evidence gathered in order to judge the adequacy/accuracy/appropriateness of the course-related concept when applied to the experience?

4. **Synthesize and evaluate course-related concepts in light of what you have experienced in the context of your service-learning-related activities.**

   - Based on the preceding analysis, does the course-related concept (or your prior understanding of it) need to be revised and, if so, in what specific ways? Provide evidence for your conclusion.—AND—

   - If revision is necessary, what factors do you think have contributed to the inadequacy in the concept as presented or in your prior understanding of it (e.g., bias/assumptions/agendas/lack of information on the part of the author/scientist or on your part)?—AND—

   - Based on the preceding analysis, what will/might you do differently in your service learning or other academic-related activities in the future and what are the challenges you might face as you do so?—OR—

   - Based on the analysis above, what should/might your service organization do differently in the future and what are the challenges it might face as it does so?

PERSONAL DIMENSION

1. **Identify and describe an awareness about a *personal* characteristic that has been enhanced by reflection on your service-learning-related activities.**

   - What personal strength, weakness, assumption, belief, conviction, trait, etc., have you become aware of as a result of reflection on your service-learning-related activities?

2. **Apply this awareness in the context of your service-learning-related activities and to other areas of your life now or in the future.**

   - How does/might this characteristic affect your interactions with others associated with your service activities and in other areas of your life?—OR—

   - How does/might this characteristic affect your decisions/actions taken in your service activities and in other areas of your life?

3. **Analyze the sources of this characteristic and the steps necessary to use or improve on it in your service-learning-related activities or other areas of your life.**

   - What are the possible sources of/reasons for this personal characteristic?—AND—

- In what specific way(s) can you use this strength, improve upon this weakness, etc., in your service-learning-related activities and other areas of your life?—AND—

- What are the potential personal benefits *and* risks or challenges you might face as you do so?

4. **Develop and evaluate your strategies for personal growth.**

- Based on the preceding analysis, what is an appropriate and significant way to use this new awareness in your service-learning-related activities or other areas of your life?—AND—

- How will you deal with any challenges or setbacks you might face?—AND—

- How will you assess or monitor your progress or success?

Source: Contributed by Sarah Ash and Patti Clayton, North Carolina State University. Reproduced with permission.

APPENDIX 3.3   EXAMPLE OF LEVELED OUTCOME STATEMENTS: Undergraduate Program Outcomes for the School of Nursing, the University Mission to Level Competencies, Azusa Pacific University

UNIVERSITY MISSION STATEMENT

Azusa Pacific University is an evangelical Christian community of disciples and scholars who seek to advance the work of God in the world through academic excellence in liberal arts and professional programs of higher education that encourage students to develop a Christian perspective of truth and life.

SCHOOL OF NURSING MISSION STATEMENT

Consistent with the mission and purpose of the University, the School of Nursing is a Christian community of discipleship, scholarship, and practice. Its purpose is to advance the work of God in the world through nursing education, collaborative projects, and church and community service that encourage those affiliated with the School of Nursing (whether faculty, staff, student, graduate, or colleague) to grow in faith and in the exercise of their gifts for service to God and humanity.

SCHOOL OF NURSING PROGRAM LEARNER OUTCOME

The graduate of Azusa Pacific University's baccalaureate nursing program integrates faith and ethics as a skilled and knowledgeable practitioner, accountable professional, health care educator and advocate, and coordinator of care.

Program Competencies

I. Utilizes Christian worldview to integrate beliefs, values, ethics, and service in personal and professional life.

II. Provides nursing care utilizing professional knowledge and core competencies (critical thinking, communication, assessment, and technical skills) derived from a foundation of nursing science, general education, and religious studies.

III. Demonstrates initiative for continual personal and professional growth and development.

IV. Acts as a patient and family educator and advocate to promote optimal health and well-being.

V. Functions independently and collaboratively, as both a leader and/or member of a health care team, to manage and coordinate care.

Level Competencies

Outcome I. Utilizes Christian worldview to integrate beliefs, values, ethics, and service in personal and professional life

Level I

- Describes the beliefs, values, and ethics that influence personal behaviors and potentially impact professional behaviors.

- Describes the spiritual subsystem of self and patient.

- Defines what a worldview is and how it affects one's behavior.

Level II

- Integrates selected values and ethical principles in personal and professional interactions with patients, peers, faculty, and other health care professionals.

- Utilizes data from the assessment of the spiritual subsystem to develop a nursing plan of care.

- Continues to develop a structure and framework for a Christian worldview for selected nursing topics.

Level III

- Differentiates Christian worldview from other worldviews as applied to professional nursing practice.

- Integrates selected values and *Nursing Code of Ethics* in personal and professional interactions.

- Implements spiritual care with the patient and the family based on identified strengths, challenges, and resources.

- Articulates areas of personal spiritual growth.

Level IV

- Applies the *Nursing Code of Ethics* in professional nursing practice.

- Identifies how one's own Christian beliefs and spirituality are impacted when caring for vulnerable populations and patients/families facing acute health crises.

- Articulates a personal reflection on the concept of ministry as a Christian nurse.
- Evaluates the effectiveness of spiritual care interventions in professional nursing practice.

Outcome II. Provides nursing care utilizing professional knowledge and core competencies (critical thinking, communication, assessment, and technical skills) derived from a foundation of nursing science, general education, and religious studies

Level I

- Begins to utilize the elements of professional knowledge and core competencies (critical thinking, communication, assessment, and technical skills) to provide nursing care to well and selected ill adults.
- Identifies the relationship among general education, nursing science, and religious studies.

Level II

- Utilizes professional knowledge and core competencies (critical thinking, communication, assessment, and technical skills) to provide nursing care to individuals across the life span, including neonates and elderly.
- Applies selected concepts from general education and religious studies to nursing practice.

Level III

- Utilizes professional knowledge and core competencies (critical thinking, communication, assessment, and technical skills) to provide nursing care to individuals within a family context.
- Integrates concepts from general education and religious studies in provision of care to individuals and families.

Level IV

- Utilizes professional knowledge and core competencies (critical thinking, communication, assessment, and technical skills) to provide nursing care in a diversity of settings with individuals, families, and community aggregates.
- Applies core knowledge of health promotion, risk reduction, and disease prevention in managing the care of vulnerable populations.
- Applies core knowledge of illness and disease management and health care technologies in

managing the care of individuals and families facing acute health crises.

- Applies professional and clinical standards including evidence-based practice to guide professional decision making.
- Synthesizes concepts from general education and religious studies in the provision of individual comprehensive care to families and aggregates.

Outcome III. Demonstrates initiative for continual personal and professional growth and development

Level I

- Identifies and reflects on experiences for personal and professional learning and growth.

Level II

- Identifies and chooses a variety of opportunities that will contribute to personal and professional growth.

Level III

- Demonstrates initiative for continual personal and professional growth and development.
- Selects personal and professional experiences for learning and growth.
- Participates in nursing opportunities that contribute to personal and professional growth based upon identified needs.
- Examines the value of personal and professional experiences on growth and development.

Level IV

- Creates personal and professional experiences for continued learning and professional development.
- Analyzes own nursing practice, compares to professional practice standards, and determines areas for improvement.

Outcome IV. Acts as a patient and family educator and advocate to promote optimal health and well-being

Level I

- Recognizes the basic role of patient educator and advocate based upon the identification of selected patient needs and rights within the health care system.

Level II

- Serves as a patient educator and advocate at a beginning level based on the identification of patient needs and rights.

Level III

- Assumes the role of health care educator and advocate for patients and their families.

Level IV

- Assumes the role of health care educator and advocate for patients, families, communities, and aggregates.

Outcome V. Functions independently and collaboratively, as both a leader and/or member of a health care team, to manage and coordinate care

Level I

- Identifies professional guidelines that define nursing roles and responsibilities.
- Makes beginning contributions to the health care team under supervision of the nursing clinical instructor.

Level II

- Defines independent and collaborative role of the nurse as a member of the health care team.
- Provides nursing care under the supervision of the RN team leader and the nursing clinical instructor.

- Utilizes professional guidelines to provide safe patient care.

Level III

- Implements independent and collaborative aspects of the nursing role.
- Provides nursing care and team leadership in collaboration and consultation with preceptor and nursing clinical instructor.
- Independently follows professional guidelines in all aspects of professional practice.

Level IV

- Functions in a leadership role in collaboration with preceptors and members of the health care team in coordinating services to patients, families, and aggregates.
- Demonstrates independence in clinical decision making based on comprehensive assessment and prioritization.
- Demonstrates professional accountability and clinical responsibility for outcomes of nursing care.

Source: Developed by the undergraduate nursing department at Azusa Pacific University under the leadership of Shila Wiebe, Program Director; D. Vicky Bowden, Curriculum Committee Chair; Professor Connie Austin, eportfolio Program Director; and Dr. Julia Jantzi, Director of Institutional Assessment Planning. Reproduced with permission.

Chapter 4

IDENTIFYING OR DESIGNING TASKS TO ASSESS THE DIMENSIONS OF LEARNING

Assessments do not function in isolation; an assessment's effectiveness in improving learning depends on its relationships to curriculum and instruction. Ideally, instruction is faithful and effective in relation to curriculum, and assessment reflects curriculum in such a way that it reinforces the best practices in instruction. In actuality, however, the relationships among assessment, curriculum, and instruction are not always ideal. Often assessment taps only a subset of curriculum and without regard to instruction, and can narrow and distort instruction in unintended ways.

—National Research Council, 2001

OVERVIEW: Dialogue about teaching, philosophies of teaching, and models of learning, as well as collaborative articulation of outcomes, necessarily lead to dialogue about the assessment methods or tasks that prompt students to represent the dimensions of their institution- and program-level learning. Focused on engaging core working groups in identifying or designing formative and summative assessment methods, this chapter identifies the considerations that surround the choices we make, including how well a method aligns with what and how students learn and receive feedback on that learning and how well a method "fits" its purpose. The Worksheets, Guides, and Exercises at the end of this chapter, together with the Inventory of Direct and Indirect Assessment Methods (Appendix 4.2), are designed to deepen discussions leading to decisions about methods by focusing on the (1) parameters of decision making that lead to choices; (2) properties of methods that make them fit for use; and (3) the range of direct and indirect methods that capture the dimensions of learning.

THE RANGE OF TEXTS THAT DEMONSTRATE OR REPRESENT LEARNING

"Will this be on the test?" "What will the test cover?" and "Do we have to know this for the test?" are frequent questions students raise as they gear up for an examination. These queries represent students' surface approach to learning—an approach that focuses on memorizing or rehearsing in response to an *external motivator*—passing the test itself and "getting it out of the way"—as opposed to an *internal motivator*—constructing meaning over time. That is, the test becomes a container, a receptacle, into which students deposit what they have rehearsed or hope that they have rehearsed well enough. Often what students store in their short-term memories and then deposit on a test vaporizes after they have completed the test—unless, of course, they have future opportunities to build on that learning. If historically conditioned to learn this way, students become facile in recall and recognition, banking their short-term memories in response to what "the test," viewed as an end point, will require them to know.

This chapter identifies the parameters of decision making that lead to selecting or designing assessment methods that extend or build upon recall and recognition and reveal the multidimensions of institution- and program-level learning. A range of written, spoken, and visual texts can become the basis for drawing inferences about the depth and breadth of the learning described in outcome statements. Consider the kinds of situations that prompt students to generate texts that demonstrate how well they

- integrate and transfer their learning over time;
- apply knowledge and understanding into new contexts;
- analyze and explore representative professional, disciplinary, and interdisciplinary problems;
- interpret, construct, express, and create meaning;
- represent or express thinking and problem solving in different forms of discourse, within different kinds of contexts, for different audiences.

At the institution and program levels, assessment committees establish core working groups to select or design assessment methods to assess the learning described in the collectively agreed-upon learning outcome statements described in the previous chapter. A collaborative process based on multiple perspectives, this decision-making process should draw on the experience and expertise of a range of individuals. For example, in a graduate-level program, faculty, representative graduate students, members of a professional advisory board, a librarian, and a representative from the institution's office of research and planning might work together to identify assessment methods. Their collective expertise and experience bring multiple perspectives

to the underlying dialogue that eventually narrows the pool of appropriate possibilities:

- Faculty contribute information about how pedagogy, curricular design, and the design of course-based assessment methods develop intended learning outcomes.
- A representative graduate student or students contribute learner-centered information about their sets of learning experiences and the ways in which they have represented their learning over time.
- A member of a professional advisory board contributes information about current external needs or demands.
- A librarian contributes knowledge about the demands or dimensions of a method in relationship to expectations for graduate-level research.
- A representative from institutional research and planning deepens understanding about the logistics of using, collecting, analyzing, and interpreting results of methods (see also Chapter 6, pages 154 and 161).

MULTIPLE METHODS OF ASSESSMENT

Capturing the complexity of our students' learning requires identifying or designing multiple methods of assessment. A method that prompts students to define disciplinary terms supports inferences about what students know; it does not support inferences about how well they use that knowledge to solve representative disciplinary problems. The limitations of one method stimulate the design or selection of other methods that altogether capture the dimensions of learning. Relying on one method to assess the learning described in outcome statements restricts interpretations of student achievement within the parameters of that method. Using multiple methods to assess the learning expressed in an outcome statement is advantageous in several ways:

- Reduces straightjacket interpretations of student achievement based on the limitations inherent in one method
- Provides students with opportunities to demonstrate learning that they may not have been able to demonstrate within the context of another method, such as timed tests

- Contributes to comprehensive interpretations of student achievement at both institution and program levels
- Values the dimensionality of learning
- Values the diverse ways in which humans learn and represent their learning

Combinations of quantitative and qualitative assessment methods add depth and breadth to interpretations of student learning. *Quantitative methods* place interpretative value on numbers—the number of right versus wrong answers, for example. *Qualitative methods* place interpretative value on the observer—observations of group interaction or an individual's performance in a simulation. Qualitative methods also enable an observer concurrently to assess broader dimensions of learning, such as how individuals translate understanding into behaviors, dispositions, reactions, and interactions. Behaviors, attitudes, and beliefs resist easy quantification and lend themselves to narrative interpretation as, for example, in assessing group interactions through videotaping. In their research on learning, Entwhistle and Ramsden argue that

> . . . in our experience, neither qualitative nor quantitative methods of research taken separately can provide a full and a convincing explanation of student learning . . . it seems essential that an understanding of student learning should be built up from an appropriate alternation of evidence and insights derived from both qualitative and quantitative approaches to research. In our view the strength of our evidence on student learning is the direct result of this interplay of contrasting methodologies, and has led to a realistic and useful description of approaches and contexts of learning in higher education.

Source: Noel J. Entwhistle and Paul Ramsden. (1983). *Understanding student learning* (p. 219).

The institutional example in Box 4.1 illustrates how a qualitative method, enhanced through technology, provides a means to capture robust learning.

The recent National Board of Medical Examiners' decision to observe medical students' clinical skills with standardized patients acknowledges the value of relying on more than one method to assess student learning. Historically, medical students have represented their professional knowledge and understanding in standardized medical examinations. This method, however, limits drawing inferences about students' actual behaviors with and dispositions toward different patients, including their communicative styles. Written responses restrict drawing such inferences. Now, observers will assess medical students with a range of standardized patients to draw inferences about how medical students translate knowledge and understanding into professional practices across a range of representative patients (www.amednews.com/2002/prse0902).

Educators may well decide to design or develop their own assessment methods as alternatives or complements to commercially developed standardized instruments. Locally developed methods enable us to translate educational practices into tasks that specifically capture our intentions. As designers, we gain because such methods fit with what and how students learn over time within our institution- and program-level contexts. More important, these methods provide the opportunity to track students' complex ways of understanding, thinking, and behaving. Further, as designers we can explore how our students understand and integrate learning from various experiences, as well as apply and build on previous learning. Designing our own methods provides us with high-powered lenses to observe the multidimensionality of our students' progress in relation to our intentions.

The institutional examples in Box 4.2 and Box 4.3 illustrate how locally designed methods capture the dimensions of learning.

BOX 4.1 INSTITUTIONAL EXAMPLE: *Stanford University, California*

Stanford University's Virtual Labs Project uses Web technology, media-rich images, and interactive multimedia to track physiology students' understanding and behaviors in simulations during which they examine, diagnose, and treat virtual patients. Associated with these patients is information about their medical history and current complaints (summit.stanford.edu/hhmi). Importantly, the simulation aligns with the simulation-based curriculum modules delivered through the Web. These modules promote learning through visual and conceptual understanding of temporal and causal relationships. (To view current projects, viewers need to install Shockwave™ and Quicktime™.)

BOX 4.2   INSTITUTIONAL EXAMPLE: *University of Michigan*

At the University of Michigan, to assess students' emerging definitions of spirituality among individuals representing different worldviews, Mayhew relies on three methods: students' visual representations, written texts, and semistructured interviews. He provides students with digital/disposable cameras to take pictures or images that reflect their working meanings of "spirituality." Students write full-sentence captions for each of the final ten pictures they select and then enter them into an album, along with a rationale for including each of the ten photographs. These mini-albums become the basis of a 30- to 45-minute semistructured interview. During these interviews, Mayhew questions students about their images and choice of words, thus providing him with a rich data set from which to make inferences about students' definitions of spirituality.

Source: Contributed by Matthew Mayhew, Center for the Study of Higher and Postsecondary Education, University of Michigan. Reproduced with permission.

BOX 4.3   INSTITUTIONAL EXAMPLE: *North Carolina State University*

Students in North Carolina State University's Service Learning Program produce written products multiple times throughout a semester. Through these documents, called Articulated Learnings, students describe what and how they have learned in their service-related experiences, as well as how these experiences have shaped their subsequent thinking, actions, or commitments. The writings capture the dimensions of their knowing, thinking, and reflection. Four questions prompt these final documents:

1. What did I learn?
2. How, specifically, did I learn it?
3. Why does this learning matter, or why is it important?
4. In what ways will I use this learning, or what goals shall I set in accordance with what I have learned in order to improve myself and/or the quality of my learning and/or the quality of my future experiences/service?

Source: Contributed by Sarah Ash and Patti Clayton, North Carolina State University. Based on the Integrative Processing Model developed by Pamela Kiser at Elon University. Kiser, P. M. (1998). The Integrative Processing Model: A framework for learning in the field experience. *Human Service Education, 18,* 3–13. Reproduced with permission.

DIRECT AND INDIRECT METHODS OF ASSESSMENT

Developing a comprehensive understanding of the dimensions of student learning involves the selection or design of direct and indirect methods. *Direct methods* prompt students to represent or demonstrate their learning or produce work so that observers can assess how well students' texts or responses fit institution- or program-level expectations. Performances, creations, results of research or exploration, interactions within group problem solving, or responses to questions or prompts represent examples of direct methods. Observers draw inferences based on what students produce, how they perform, or what they select in response to a universe of questions or stimuli designed to assess dimensions of their learning.

Indirect methods capture students' perceptions of their learning and the educational environment that supports that learning, such as access to and the quality of services, programs, or educational offerings that support their learning. Student satisfaction, alumni, and employer surveys are examples of indirect methods that document perceptions, reactions, or responses. Results of indirect methods may well complement the results of direct methods. A student satisfaction survey that reveals patterns of dissatisfaction with an academic support service, for example, may help to explain why certain cohorts of students are less able to achieve specific institution-level expectations. By themselves, results of indirect methods cannot substitute for the evidence of learning that direct methods provide. They can, however, contribute to interpreting the results of direct methods, as is discussed in Chapter 6.

METHODS ALONG THE CONTINUUM OF LEARNING: FORMATIVE AND SUMMATIVE

Seeking evidence of learning along the progression of students' studies—*formative assessment*—as well as at the end of their studies—*summative assessment*—records students' progress toward and achievement of institution- and program-level learning. After a certain number of courses and educational experiences, after a certain number of credits and educational experiences, or at points that index when students should be able to master certain abilities or ways of behaving, assessment methods provide evidence of how well students are learning.

Results of formative assessment provide useful information about program- and institution-level learning that can stimulate immediate change in pedagogy, design of instruction, curriculum, co-curriculum, and services that support learning. Although all students do not have to be assessed for

us to learn about the efficacy of educational practices, if all students are assessed and they receive results of their performance, this information can also dramatically change the advising process, allowing students and advisors to talk about and reflect on how students can improve their performance. Typically, formative assessment methods are built into the performing and visual arts curricula: faculty provide continuous feedback to students as emerging professionals. That is, formative assessment becomes a way for students to learn; it also becomes a way for faculty to learn about the efficacy of their practices.

The institutional example in Box 4.4 illustrates how formative assessment methods capture students' integrated learning. Student work and patterns of feedback provide programs with evidence of student learning in relation to expected learning outcomes.

Patterns of students' performance identify their strengths as well as their weaknesses. Collectively, faculty and others who contribute to student learning determine how to address patterns of weakness in students' remaining coursework and sets of learning experiences. They might, for example, wish to improve one or more of the following practices as ways to improve students' learning:

- Increase opportunities for students to transfer learning or rehearse or practice learning.

BOX 4.4 INSTITUTIONAL EXAMPLE: *Alverno College*

Alverno College's practice of using multiple methods of assessment both formatively and summatively is illustrated in chemistry students' third-year assessment. Multiple methods capture these majors' learning as they collaboratively and individually solve a problem. For example, a group of three to four students might be asked to provide input to an advisory committee for the Milwaukee Estuary Remediation Action Plan regarding contamination in the Milwaukee Harbor. Each student is given approximately two weeks to research the situation in advance of the actual assessment. For the assessment, each student prepares a position paper on an issue specifically assigned to her related to contaminated sediment. She also prepares a procedural document for monitoring a contaminant in the harbor. At the time of each student's individual assessment, each member of the group defends her own position and recommended procedures for treating, preventing, or disposing of contamination in the harbor.

Working collaboratively, using the information provided by each student, the group then drafts a long-term plan for the management of contaminated sediment in Milwaukee Harbor. The meeting is videotaped for two audiences: (1) the chemistry faculty who assess the students' performance; and (2) the students who will assess their own performance.

Source: Contributed by Georgine Loacker, Senior Assessment Scholar and Professor of English, Alverno College. Reproduced with permission.

- Diversify teaching and learning practices to expand opportunities for students to deepen their learning.

- Examine the efficacy of prerequisites or curricular sequencing, including students' ability to navigate the curricular sequence to avoid enrolling in certain kinds of courses that would contribute to their learning.

- Provide more focused practice with technological tools.

- Review advising practices.

Summative assessment methods provide evidence of students' final mastery levels. They prompt students to represent the cumulative learning of their education and answer the question: How well do our students actually achieve our institution- and program-level expectations? Again, results of summative methods are useful to improve the curriculum; co-curriculum; pedagogy; and the design of instruction, programs, and services. If they are used along with formative assessment methods, they provide students with a final perspective on their work as it has emerged over time. If the institution and its programs use only summative assessment methods as points of learning, there is no opportunity to revise, adapt, or innovate practices that will improve the achievement of a current graduating class. Results are useful to improve educational practices for future classes but not for a class about to graduate. Thus, an institutional commitment to assessing for learning builds in formative as well as summative assessment to respond to patterns of weakness along students' learning progression. In this commitment, educators become flexible designers who adapt, revise, or develop new practices in response to what they learn along students' educational journey.

POSITIONS OF INQUIRY

Where and how we choose to position ourselves as observers of our students' work and where and how we position our students in relation to institution- and program-level assessment also contribute to the selection or design of assessment methods. We can dip down and take snapshots of our students' learning by embedding these methods into required courses or by asking students to respond to these methods during scheduled times out of class. Based on inferences from these snapshots, we derive a composite picture of learning and can generalize about students' achievement against our collective expectations. Rising junior examinations, for example, represent this approach. These examinations also sometimes serve a gatekeeping function to identify students who are unable to achieve expected levels of achievement and, consequently, need to demonstrate that learning before they graduate.

A collaborative approach to assessment involving faculty and students may take other forms, such as ongoing review of student work from course to course in a major so that students receive feedback about their abilities to build on, apply, and integrate learning. Practiced in the arts, ongoing review of student work based on public and shared criteria promotes integration of learning and students' self-reflection about their achievement. This review also enables faculty to identify patterns of student weaknesses along the continuum of students' learning. These findings then become the focus of routine program-level dialogue during which colleagues determine ways to implement changes to address those patterns in sequences of courses, pedagogy, or other educational practices. In this approach, students' ongoing work or culminating projects represent chronological evidence of their achievement. This embedded approach to assessment values student-generated texts that emerge from specific educational contexts, as opposed to externally created contexts.

In the institutional examples in Box 4.5 and Box 4.6, students are positioned to generate work within their contexts for learning. Assessment practices are integrated into these internally created contexts for learning.

ISSUES OF ALIGNMENT: OUTCOMES, INFERENCES, AND STUDENTS' LEARNING HISTORIES

The learning described in outcome statements guides the selection or design of assessment methods. *Alignment* refers to the degree to which a method captures that learning. Just as exploring students' learning histories and educational practices leads to collective articulation of learning outcome statements, exploring the relationship between learning outcome statements and proposed assessment methods leads to consensus about relevant and effective ways to prompt students to represent the dimensions of that learning. Asking members of core working groups to

---

BOX 4.5   INSTITUTIONAL EXAMPLE: *Marian College*

As a culminating project in the curriculum and assessment class of the graduate educational leadership program at Marian College, students build a shared online faculty development program for creating effective methods to assess student learning based on the texts and documents they have read and discussed over time. A paperless project, each student creates two Microsoft Power Point™ assessment workshops with follow-up materials and URLs for classroom teachers to use. The completed workshops are placed in a common folder in an online platform for the culminating course in the program. All class members assess their peers' work electronically based on professional criteria. As part of their practicum, students select a workshop from this common folder that best fits the needs of their particular school and field test that workshop as a staff development training opportunity. Practitioners, in turn, assess students' workshops against agreed-upon criteria. Students are positioned in this culminating project as contributors to the wider educational community that draws upon their work to enhance professional practices. In turn, they receive feedback from professionals in their field.

Source: Contributed by Carleen VandeZande, Marian College. Reproduced with permission.

BOX 4.6   INSTITUTIONAL EXAMPLE: *Keystone College*

In the Fine Arts Department at Keystone College, one of the department's formative assessment methods involves (1) visual recording of students as they work on key projects and (2) digital photographing of students' "before" and "after" works of art. Assessment of students' behaviors provides program-level evidence of students' progress toward professional practices in relation to the design of curriculum and educational practices. Pictures of "before" and "after" creations provide the comparative basis for faculty, peer, and self-assessment along the continuum of students' evolution as artists.

Source: Digital Images: David Porter, Judith L. Keats, and William Tersteeg, Keystone College. Reproduced with permission.

address the following alignment questions identifies a pool of methods for assessing students at points along the continuum of their learning, some of which have proven value based on their historical use within a program or across the campus:

- What kinds of methods or tasks prompt students to represent the learning described in outcome statements?

- Do students' learning histories include ample and multiple opportunities to demonstrate, receive feedback about, and reflect on the learning described in outcome statements? That is, how frequently have students represented the dimensions of that learning in similar kinds of tasks?

- What dimension or dimensions of learning is a method or task designed to capture? What dimension is it unable to capture?

- What inferences will observers or raters be able to draw from students' responses to each method? What will they not be able to draw?

Beyond identifying methods that assess students' abilities to select "right" answers, dialogue facilitates focusing on identifying methods that represent institution- and program-level expectations across the progression of students' learning. Different methods provide students with opportunities to construct responses; solve problems; and create, interpret, design, perform, and translate learning over time into various kinds of products.

Maps of the curriculum and co-curriculum described in Chapter 2 provide a visual representation of students' opportunities to practice the learning described in outcome statements. Recall that the curriculum map at Rose-Hulman Institute of Technology, presented in Box 2.2 in Chapter 2, documents (1) where students have opportunities to learn what a program or institution values; and (2) where students receive feedback about their achievement. Categorizing the kinds of feedback students receive contributes to determining how well assessment methods align with students' learning histories.

For example, suppose students' predominant form of feedback in a major program of study consists of receiving scores on objective tests that value selecting correct answers. Yet, if one of that program's outcome statements values students' ability to identify and then evaluate the feasibility of several solutions to a problem, there will be a disconnect between students' dominant ways of performing and receiving feedback and the ways of performing necessary to fulfill that program-level outcome. That is, there is lack of alignment between values—between those practiced in a program and those expected. The design or selection of an assessment method needs to take into consideration collective intentions translated into educational practices. According to the Mathematics Association of America, selecting a method to assess quantitative literacy is based on clarity about the type of learning a program or an institution values:

> Assessment should fit the nature of a quantitative literacy program using methods which reflect the type of learning to be measured, rather than methods which are most easily constructed or scored. For example, if students are to learn how to respond to open-ended problem settings, they must be asked to do so in the assessment procedure. Facing them with a multiple-choice test for the measurement of such a goal would be inappropriate.
>
> Source: *Quantitative Reasoning for College Graduates: A Complement to the Standards* (www.maa.org/past/ql/ql_part4.html)

Typically, it is unlikely that students accustomed to receiving feedback on objective tests will perform well on open-ended methods or tasks, tasks designed to assess students' generative abilities, such as interpreting evidence from multiple perspectives. Case and Gunstone's (2002) research on the difficulties students experience in developing a conceptual approach to solving quantitatively based chemistry problems is illustrative of this point. Their study of chemistry students' approaches to learning reveals that students who initially take a recall and recognition approach to quantitative reasoning in chemistry—that is, they memorize algorithms or take a solely information approach to learning—have difficulty shifting later on in their studies to a conceptual approach to quantitative problem solving. That is, students' conditioned ways of knowing impede their ability to move toward conceptual understanding (pp. 459–470).

Ascertaining if students' educational chronology includes opportunities for them to self-reflect and receive feedback on the learning described in outcome statements deepens discussions about alignment. *Self-reflection* reinforces learning by engaging learners in focused thinking about their understanding and misunderstanding. In addition, feedback from multiple individuals—faculty, staff, peers, internship advisors, outside reviewers, or representatives from a profession—provides students with realistic responses to their work, causing them to reflect on their achievement. Limited feedback, coupled with little opportunity for students to self-reflect on their development or understanding, may well contribute to some students' inability or low ability to represent the learning described in outcome statements, especially given that humans learn differently over time.

PROPERTIES OF A METHOD: VALIDITY AND RELIABILITY

Collecting and reporting assessment results can be translated into charts and graphs that provide a summary of student achievement. However, assessing for learning dives beneath reporting percentages to interpret the relationship between students' achievement and the practices that contribute to that achievement. Those who teach and educate students, members of the programs and services that contribute to students' learning, become the interpreters of assessment results. The relevance of those interpretations depends on the usefulness of collected results. If results do not lead to interpretations about student learning—interpretations that are based on patterns of strength and weakness in relation to expectations for learning—then the methods have minimal usefulness in an organization committed to learning about the efficacy of its practices. (Chapter 5 focuses on developing scoring rubrics: criteria and standards that provide useful institution- and program-level results upon which to identify patterns of student performance.)

The process of selecting or designing assessment methods, then, involves analyzing properties of each proposed assessment method to determine (1) how well a method prompts students to represent the learning described in outcome statements and (2) how consistently raters score students' responses or work and can discern patterns of students' strengths and weaknesses that are, in turn, useful in stimulating dialogue about the efficacy of educational practices. With the support and expertise of representatives from institutional research or other individuals knowledgeable about statistical measures and processes, core working groups can narrow down the pool of possible summative and formative methods by testing the *validity* and *reliability* of a proposed method.

Validity

The property of *validity* refers to the extent to which a method prompts students to represent the dimensions of learning desired. A valid method enables direct and accurate assessment of the learning described in outcome statements. If a program is based on a problem-based model of learning that values students' abilities to articulate and justify solutions to problems, resorting to a multiple-choice method to assess students' learning will not prompt students to represent the valued learning they have practiced. This method will provide evidence of students' ability to select answers without evidence of the thinking that justifies a selection. It will not provide evidence of their ability to construct or create responses, including unanticipated ones. The discussions that surround learning outcome statements, curricular and co-curricular design, pedagogy, models of teaching and learning, and philosophies of teaching provide the necessary institution- and program-level context within which to analyze the validity of methods. Given the complex institution- and program-level outcomes of higher education, these discussions are increasingly leading working groups to design methods that emerge from institution- and program-level teaching and learning processes to assure a method's validity.

Reliability

The property of *reliability* refers to the extent to which trial tests of a method with representative student populations fairly and consistently assess the expected traits or dimensions of student learning within the construct of that method. In addition, it measures how consistently scorers or scoring systems grade student responses. Inquiry into the reliability of a method is prompted by the following kinds of questions:

* How well do trial tests yield the same results after multiple administrations?
* More specifically, how well do representative populations respond to levels or types of questions or stimuli?
* Does the language of questions or instructions or the sequence or format of questions or tasks disadvantage certain populations?
* How consistent are scores across observers, graders, or an automated grading system?

Interrater reliability—that is, the degree to which different individual observers or graders agree in their scoring—develops through multiple trials of scoring sample student work or responses to achieve common calibrations among graders. Calibrating graders or observers so that they respond similarly to what students produce is a component of pilot testing a designed method. An example of how an institution weaves tests of validity and reliability into its commitment to assessment is illustrated in the institutional example in this chapter, Box 4.7.

Standardized Tests

Historically, standardized instruments have served as the primary method to assess student learning. Often required for placing students in appropriate level courses in colleges and universities, for certifying achievement in a major or profession, or for gatekeeping purposes to identify students who are unable to perform according to institution- or program-level expectations, standardized instruments are accompanied with large-scale validity and reliability studies conducted over years of administration with representative populations. T. Dary Erwin's definitions and comparison of validity and reliability properties and their subcomponents across frequently used standardized tests provide valuable information about these properties (U.S. Department of Education, 2000). In addition, his analysis of what each test specifically aims to assess contributes to campus discussions about how well standardized tests align with program and institution-level outcome statements or provide results that complement alternative assessment methods developed within an institution. A similar sourcebook focusing on definitions and assessment methods for communication, leadership, information literacy, quantitative reasoning and quantitative skills is currently under review. (Appendix 4.1 at the end of this chapter lists strategies for reviewing and selecting standardized instruments.)

Though backed by validity and reliability studies, traditional standardized instruments have been historically designed to report on students' discrete abilities as a "measure" of their understanding, often through multiple-choice or closed-ended questions. In writing about traditional methods to assess students' writing, in *Assessment of Writing: Politics, Policies, Practices,* Murphy and Grant (1996) describe the paradigm that has anchored traditional testing:

> Most traditional assessment measures are anchored in a positivist paradigm, a paradigm that is dominant in education in general and to some degree in the field of writing assessment. Positivism treats knowledge as skills, as information that can be divided into testable bits, or as formulaic routines. With positivism there is a truth, a correct interpretation, a right answer that exists independently of the learner. . . . Within a positivist framework, there is no room for the idea that several equally valid interpretations might be possible. (p. 285)

Stating institution- and program-level outcomes and exploring how well methods align with those statements and students' learning histories and how well standardized tests capture the multidimensions of learning drive dialogue focused on designing local methods. These locally designed methods serve as alternatives or complements to standardized tests. They value students' abilities to perform authentic tasks that parallel or replicate real-world tasks and prompt students to represent the dimensions of their learning (Wiggins, 1998). In addition, these methods provide opportunity for feedback from faculty, staff, administrators, peers, and others who contribute to student learning; they also provide opportunity for students' self-reflection on their achievement. If not to replace standardized tests, alternative methods complement evidence of learning assessed through standardized tests. Indeed, they provide rich evidence of institution- and program-level outcomes, thereby representing higher education's complex expectations for student learning.

Designed Methods

Representing student learning through commercially and nationally normed methods, such as standardized tests, satisfies external audiences focused on making budgetary decisions or decisions aimed at comparing institutions' performance. How well externally validated methods align with institution- and program-level outcomes, the pedagogy, curricular and instructional design, and educational practices is another question. Many institutions and programs resort to narrowing the curriculum and students' approaches to learning to more greatly assure that students will achieve passing scores on these standardized methods. In such cases, standardized methods lack internal institution- and program-level validity. Pressures of external mandates or efficient reporting of results conditions pedagogy and curriculum to prepare students to perform on these standardized instruments.

Increasingly, however, as institutions internally validate alternatives to standardized methods, the results of these methods should complement nationally normed results because they more closely align with institution- and program-level values. In addition, internally validated methods represent a complementary interpretation of student achievement that may, in fact, refute or challenge externally validated results. To demonstrate the complexity of our intentions and the dimensions of student learning, the results of internally developed and validated methods need to be presented alongside externally validated methods. Furthermore, the results of internally designed assessment methods provide us with the richest information about the efficacy of our own educational practices.

Maps and inventories provide an early opportunity to validate formative and summative assessment methods because they illustrate how well methods align with what and how students learn. Because educators assess students' learning in courses and after educational experiences—that is, they develop methods that align with their teaching—establishing a pool of these practices is helpful in identifying program- or institution-level formative and assessment methods. Indeed, there may already be locally designed methods that can be used to track student learning over time, such as a case study or problem that community members agree would best stimulate students to represent their learning. The following questions underlie approaches to validating locally designed methods:

- Does the method align with what and how students have learned?

- Have students practiced and received feedback on what the method will assess?

- Have students had multiple and varied opportunities to learn?

- Are students aware that they are responsible for demonstrating this learning?

- Have there been opportunities to pilot test the method across student populations to assure the method does not bias certain populations?

Aligning, pilot testing, and administering designed methods over semesters has been the hallmark of Alverno College's pioneering efforts to develop and model practices that assure the validity and reliability of its designed methods. The work of Mentkowksi, Rogers, Doherty, and Loacker provides direction and models for institutional processes that assure the validity and reliability of designed methods (Mentkowski & Associates, 2000; Mentkowski & Rogers, 1988; Mentkowski & Loacker, 1985; Mentkowski & Doherty, 1984, 1980). The institutional example in Box 4.7 summarizes the processes that underlie the College's internally developed validation process.

As the institutional example in Box 4.7 illustrates, the process of designing assessment methods is yet another example of the collaboration that underlies an institutional commitment. This collaboration leads to consensus about the appropriateness of a method in relationship to learning outcome statements; the intentional design of educational experiences; and the degree to which methods are valid, reliable, and useful in providing results that identify patterns of student performance.

The inventory presented in Appendix 4.2 at the end of this chapter contributes to collective dialogue and decision making focused on the selection or design of assessment methods. Deriving evidence of student learning from direct and indirect methods provides rich information about how and when and under what kinds of opportunities students learn or face obstacles to learning. Identifying assessment methods prepares core working groups to reach consensus about standards and criteria for judging student responses, the subject of Chapter 5.

BOX 4.7   INSTITUTIONAL EXAMPLE: *Alverno College*

At Alverno College validation of methods includes a set of questions closely aligned with the values of the institution. These questions are specifically designed to foster faculty inquiry into the validity of the assessments that they use to foster and credential each student's learning outcomes (Alverno College Faculty, 1979/1994, p. 121). Because the questions are about the validity of the college's curriculum-embedded assessments, which are a regular part of how students learn, they reflect not only what and how students have learned but also the expectation that these student learning outcomes transfer to post-college settings. In this context, the alignment of assessment methods with outcome expectations is doubly important. Some of the alignment questions include

- "Is the mode of assessment appropriate to the outcome(s)?"

- "Does the instrument assess both content and ability?"

- "Do the criteria taken collectively sufficiently measure the outcomes?"

Other questions call attention to additional validity concerns.

- "Can the instrument elicit performance with sufficient data to provide for diagnostic, structured feedback to the student on her strengths and weaknesses?" The validity of an educational assessment includes its learning consequences, which is why the presence and nature of feedback are fundamental to the validity of assessment as learning at Alverno. When assessments have

(Continued)

BOX 4.7 (Continued)

embedded learning and credentialing consequences, they, in addition, motivate students to do their best and so avoid the kind of low motivation that often threatens the validity of judgments drawn from add-on assessments.

- "Does the instrument integrate previous levels of the competence?" Increased curricular coherence heightens the role that local context plays in assessment validity. This question assumes that assessments need to developmentally build upon a particular kind of integration of prior learning because Alverno educators require that students demonstrate higher levels of the curriculum's abilities in more advanced coursework.

- "Can the instrument elicit the fullest expression of the student ability at a level appropriate to context?" Performance-based assessments are often updated with new stimuli or are intentionally revised in other ways, and so, faculty observation of change in student performance becomes a key source of validity evidence. For assessments that occur outside of the classroom, Alverno faculty design teams have an ongoing responsibility for reviewing performance to determine implications for improvement of the assessment and curriculum.

For purposes such as accreditation, more formal processes for aggregating and documenting evidence from curriculum-embedded assessments are increasingly necessary. An assessment that senior education majors and minors complete as part of their student teaching requirements provides an example of how curriculum-embedded assessments can serve both accountability and improvement needs. Research staff from Educational Research and Evaluation thematically analyzed 40 performance assessments, which included the student teachers' lesson plans, the assessments they used, and how well they analyzed their pupils' learning. The researchers also coded the student teachers' self-assessments against curriculum-based and research-validated criteria. The report included estimates of interrater reliability and examples of the thematic categories, representing typical performance as well as the range observed. A visiting site team from the U.S. Department of Education was able to use the report as summative evidence of the quality of the education program.

But, across the college, collective review by faculty of student performance has been the strongest support to improving curriculum and the validity of assessment judgments. For example, in a follow-up study, 13 education department faculty rated and discussed the performance of 11 preservice teachers on the student teaching assessment. Because each preservice teacher provided extensive evidence of her performance, including examples of her pupils' performance on an assessment she designed, the review process was tightly scripted to make it feasible. Each individual faculty reviewed only three or four performances, one of which students had in common. Their small- and large-group discussions led to affirmations of prior faculty judgments of these student teaching assessments, which had indicated that these students were ready to teach based on criteria that integrated departmental criteria and state standards. But, these discussions also yielded concerns about the quality of the student teachers' analyses of their pupils' performance. These concerns have guided specific changes in the assessment and preparation of student teachers' analyses of their students in prior field experiences. Such collaborative inquiry by faculty into the validity of assessments is supported by broadly conceptualizing the scholarship of teaching (Mentkowski & Associates, 2000).

Source: Contributed by Glen Rogers, Senior Research Associate, Educational Research and Evaluation, and Kathy Lake, Professor of Education, Alverno College. Reproduced with permission. Citations from: Alverno College Faculty. (1979/1994). *Student assessment-as-learning at Alverno College.* Milwaukee, WI: Alverno College Institute. Original work published 1979, revised 1985 and 1994; and Mentkowski, M., & Associates. (2000). *Learning that lasts: Integrating learning, development, and performance in college and beyond.* San Francisco: Jossey-Bass.

WORKS CITED

Banta, T., & Associates. (2002). *The scholarship of assessment*. San Francisco: Jossey-Bass.

Cambridge, B. (Ed.). (2001). *Electronic portfolios: Emerging practices for students, faculty, and institutions*. Washington, D.C.: American Association for Higher Education.

Case, J., & Gunstone, R. (2002, October). Shift in approach to learning: An in-depth study. *Studies in Higher Education, 27*(4), 459–470.

Educational Testing Services: *www.ets.org*.

George, J., & Cowan, J. (1999). *A handbook of techniques for formative evaluation: Mapping the students' learning experience*. Kogan Page Ltd.

Greene, J. (January 21, 2003). NBME moves ahead with clinical exam plan. *amednews.com*: *www.amednews.com/2002/prsd0121*.

Halloun, I., & Hestenes, D. (1985, November). The initial knowledge state of college physics students. *American Journal of Physics, 53*(11), 1043–1055.

Kiser, P. M. (1998). The Integrative Processing Model: A framework for learning in the field experience. *Human Service Education, 18*, 3–13.

Mayhew, M. J. (2002, November). Exploring the essence of spirituality: A phenomenological study of eight students with eight different worldviews. Paper presented at the Spirituality as a Legitimate Concern in Higher Education Conference. SUNY Buffalo.

Measurement Research Associates: *www.measurementresearch.com/media/standardizedoral.pdf*.

Mentkowski, M., & Associates. (2000). *Learning that lasts: Integrating learning, development, and performance in college and beyond*. San Francisco: Jossey-Bass.

Mentkowski, M., & Doherty, A. (1980). *Validating assessment techniques in an outcome-centered liberal arts curriculum: Insights from the evaluation and revisions process*. Milwaukee, WI: Office of Research and Evaluation. Alverno College.

Mentkowski, M., & Doherty, A. (1984). *Careering after college: Establishing the validity of abilities learned in college for later careering and performance*. Milwaukee, WI: Alverno Publications.

Mentkowski, M., & Loacker, G. (1985). Assessing and validating the outcomes of college. In P. Ewell (Ed.), *Assessing educational outcomes*, 47, 47–64. New Directions for Institutional Research. San Francisco: Jossey-Bass.

Mentkowski, M., & Rogers, G. P. (1988). *Establishing the validity of measures of college student outcomes*. Milwaukee, WI: Office of Research and Evaluation. Alverno College.

Murphy, S., & Grant, B. (1996). Portfolio approaches to assessment: Breakthrough or more of the same? In E. White, S. Lutz, & S. Kamusikiris (Eds.). *Assessment of writing: Politics, policies, practices* (pp. 285–300). New York: Modern Language Association.

The National Center for Higher Education Management Systems: *www.nchems.org*.

National Center for Research on Evaluation, Standards, and Student Testing (1991). *Complex, performance-based assessments: Expectations and validation criteria* (CSE Technical Report 331). Los Angeles, CA: Author.

National Research Council. (2001). *Knowing what students know: The science and design of educational assessment*. Washington, D.C.: National Academy Press, 221.

National Research Council. (2001). *Knowing what students know: The science and design of educational assessment* (pp. 206–212). (Selected pages focus on criteria to validate tasks.)

Regis University. E-portfolio basics. Available: *academic.regis.edu/LAAP/eportfolio/index.html*.

U.S. Department of Education, National Center for Educational Statistics. (2000). *The NPEC sourcebook on assessment, Vol. 1: Definitions and assessment methods for critical thinking, problem solving, and writing*. (NCES 2000—172). Prepared by T. Dary Erwin for the Council of the National Postsecondary Education Cooperative Student Outcomes Pilot Working Group: Cognitive and Intellectual Development. Washington, DC: U.S. Government Printing Office. *nces.ed.gov/pubsearch/pubsinfo.asp?pubid=2000195*.

University of Arizona, Graduate College: *grad.admin.arizona.edu/degreecert/ppfoedc.htm*.

Van Aken, E. M., Watford, B., & Medina-Borja, A. (1999, July). The use of focus groups for minority engineering program assessment. *Journal of Engineering Education*, 333–343.

Wiggins, G. (1998). *Educative Assessment: Designing Assessments to Inform and Improve Student Performance*. San Francisco: Jossey-Bass.

ADDITIONAL RESOURCES

Considerations Affecting the Design and Selection of Assessment Methods

Allen, M. J. (2004). *Assessing academic programs in higher education*. Bolton, MA: Anker.

Brown, S., & Glasner, A. (1999). *Assessment matters in higher education: Choosing and using diverse approaches*. Philadelphia, PA: SRHE and Open University Press.

Clarke, M., & Gregory, K. (Eds.). (2003, Winter). The impact of high stakes testing. *Theory into Practice*, 42, 1.

Erwin, D. T., & Wise, S. E. (2002). A scholarly practitioner model for assessment. In T. W. Banta & Associates, *Building a scholarship of assessment* (pp. 67–81). San Francisco: Jossey-Bass.

Ewell, P. T. (1987, Fall). Establishing a campus-based assessment program. In D. F. Halpern (Ed.), *Student outcomes assessment: What institutions stand to gain* (pp. 9–24). New Directions for Higher Education, 59. San Francisco: Jossey-Bass.

Ewell, P. (1991). To capture the ineffable: New forms of assessment in higher education. In G. Grant (Ed.), *Review of research in education* (pp. 75–125). Washington, DC: American Educational Research Association.

Ewell, P. T., & Jones, D. P. (1985). The costs of assessment. In C. P. Adelman (Ed.), *Assessment in American higher education: Issues and contexts*. Washington, DC: Office of Educational Research and Improvement. U.S. Department of Education.

Grant, G. (Ed.) (1991). *Review of research in education*, 17. Washington, DC: American Educational Research Association.

Herman, J., Aschbacher, P., & Winters, L. (1992). *A practical guide to alternative assessment*. Alexandria, VA: Association for Supervision and Curriculum Development.

Jacobs, L. D., & Chase, C. I. (1992). *Developing and using tests effectively*. San Francisco: Jossey-Bass.

Kohn, A. (2000). *The case against standardized tests*. Portsmouth, NH: Heinemann.

Maki, P. (2001). From standardized tests to alternative methods: Some current resources on methods to assess learning in general education. *Change*, 29–31. Washington, DC: Heldref.

North Central Regional Educational Laboratory. (n.d.). What does research say about assessment? *www.ncrel.org/sdrs/areas/stw_esys/4assess.htm*.

Pike, G. R. (2002). Measurement issues in outcomes assessment. In T. W. Banta & Associates, *Building a scholarship of assessment* (pp. 131–147). San Francisco: Jossey-Bass.

Sacks, P. (1999). *Standardized minds: The high price of America's testing culture and what we can do to change it*. Cambridge, MA: Perseus Books.

Wiggins, G. (1989). Teaching to the (authentic) test. *Educational Leadership*, 46, 45.

Wiggins, G. (1990). The case for authentic assessment. *Practical Assessment, Research & Evaluation*, 2, 2.

Diverse Learners

Graduate Record Examinations. (1999). *New directions in assessment: Fairness, access, multiculturalism & equity* (The GRE, FAME Report Series. 3). Princeton, NJ: Educational Testing Service.

Haworth, J. G. (Ed.). (1996, Winter). Assessing graduate and professional education: Current realities, future prospects. *New Directions for Institutional Research*. San Francisco: Jossey-Bass.

Michelson, E. (1997, Fall). Multicultural approaches to portfolio development. In Assessing adult learning in diverse settings: Current issues and approaches (pp. 41–54). *New Directions for Adult and Continuing Education*, 75. San Francisco: Jossey-Bass.

Moran, J. J. (1997). *Assessing adult learning: A guide for practitioners*. Malabar, FL: Krieger.

Rose, A. D., & Leahy, M. A. (Eds.). (1997, Fall). Assessing adult learning in diverse settings: Current issues and approaches. *New Directions for Adult and Continuing Education*, 75. San Francisco: Jossey-Bass.

Sheckley, B. G., & Keeton, M. T. (1997). *A review of the research on learning: Implications for the instruction of adult learners*. College Park, MD: Institute for Research on Adults in Higher Education, University of Maryland.

Vella, J., Berardinelli, P., & Burrow, J. (1998). *How do they know? Evaluating adult learning*. San Francsico: Jossey-Bass.

Fairness in Assessment Methods

Assessment Guidelines and Standards: *www.aahe.org/assessment/web.htm#Communicating assessment results*.

Fair Test Examiner: *www.fairtest.org*.

Joint Committee on Testing Practices. Code of Fair Testing Practices in Education. Available online: *www.apu.org/science/finalcode.pdf*.

Jorgensen, S., Fichten, C. S., Havel, A., Lamb, D. James, C., & Barile, Maria. (2003). *Students with disabilities at Dawson College: Successes and outcomes.* The Adaptech Research Network: *www.adaptech.org.*

Sedlacek, W. E. (1993). *Issues in advancing diversity through assessment* (Research Report, 45–93). Counseling Center, University of Maryland at College Park: *www.inform.umd.edu/EdRes/Topic/diversity/General/Reading/Sedlacek/issues.html.*

Suskie, L. (2000, May). Fair Assessment Practices. AAHE *Bulletin: www.aahe.org/bulletin/may2.html.*

Validity and Reliability

National Postsecondary Educational Cooperative (NPEC) of the National Center for Educational Statistics. Defining and Assessing Learning: Exploring Competency-Based Initiatives: *nces.ed.gov/pubsearch/pubsinfo.asp?pubid=2002159.* Pages 10–12 are especially helpful in defining validity and reliability and its component measures.

Palomba, C. A., & Banta, T. W. (1999). *Assessment essentials: Planning, implementing, and improving assessment in higher education* (pp. 104–106). San Francisco: Jossey-Bass.

Pike, G. R. (2002). Measurement issues in outcomes assessment. In T. W. Banta & Associates, *Building a scholarship of assessment* (pp. 131–147). San Francisco: Jossey-Bass.

Methods of Assessment
Concept Maps and Mind Mapping

Meta-site: Generic Centre: Learning and Teaching Support Network: *dbweb.liv.ac.uk/ltsnpsc/AB/AB-html/node12.html.* Lists articles on concept maps and their usefulness in assessing learning.

Focus Groups

Krueger, R. A., & Casey, M. A. (2000). *Focus groups: A practical guide for applied research.* London: Sage.

Morgan, D. L. (1998). *Focus groups as qualitative research* (2nd ed.). London: Sage.

Steward, D., & Shamdasani, P. (1990). *Focus groups: Theory and practice* (University Paper series on quantitative applications in the social sciences). Newbury Park, CA: Sage.

Wilson, V. (1997, April). Focus groups: A useful qualitative method for educational research? *British Educational Research Journal, 23*(2), 209–225.

Interviews

Dobson, A. (1996). *Conducting effective interviews: How to find out what you need to know and achieve the right results.* Transatlantic.

Merton, R. K., Fiske, M., & Kendall, L. (1990). *The focused interview* (2nd ed.). Glencoe, IL: The Free Press.

Inventories

Sietar: *www.sietar.de/SIETARproject/Assessments&instruments.html#Topic26.* Lists instruments that assess intercultural competencies and sensitivities.

The University of Texas at Arlington. The Office of Institutional Research and Planning. Student Affairs-Related Outcomes Instruments: Summary Information. *wbarratt.indstate.edu/dragon/saroi/sa-indx.html.* Comprehensive inventory of outcomes-related instruments.

Locally Designed Methods

Banta, T. W., & Schneider, J. A. (1986, April). Using locally developed comprehensive exams for majors to assess and improve academic program quality. Paper presented at the Annual Meeting of the American Educational Research Association. San Francisco, CA.

Haladyna, T. M. (1999). *Developing and validating multiple choice test items.* Mahwah, NJ: Erlbaum.

Lopez, C. L. (1998, Summer). Assessment of student learning. *Liberal Education,* 36–43.

Sanders, W., & Horn, S. (1995, March). Educational assessment reassessed: The usefulness of standardized and alternative measures of student achievement as indicators for the assessment of educational outcomes. *Education Policy Analysis Archives, 3,* 6: *epaa.asu.edu/epaa/v3n6.html.*

Online and Computer-Assisted Assessment

Anderson, R. S., Bauer, B. W., & Speck, B. W. (Eds.). (2002, Fall). Assessment strategies for the on-line class: From theory to practice. *New Directions for Teaching and Learning,* 91. San Francisco: Jossey-Bass.

Brown, S., Race, P., & Bull, J. (Eds.). (1999). *Computer-assisted assessment in higher education.* London: Kogan Page Ltd.

Portfolios: Meta-sites

American Association for Higher Education.

Barrett, H. (2004). *Dr. Helen Barret's electronic portfolios: electronicportfolios.com.*

Barrett, H. (2004). *Dr. Helen Barret's favorite on alternative assessment & electronic portfolios.* Includes higher education and professional examples as well as bibliography on portfolios: *electronicportfolios.org/portfolios/bookmarks.html.*

Barrett, H. (2000). *The electronic portfolio development process.* Available: *electronicportfolios.com/portfolios/EPDevProcess.html.*

Barrett, H. (2001). *Helen Barrett's stages of electonic portfolio development: electronicportfolios.org/portfolios/eifeltools.pdf.*

Barrett, H. (2003a). *Annotated bibliography on portfolios, alternative assessments, and tools for developing electronic portfolios: electronicportfolios.com/portfolios/ bibliography.html.*

Barrett, H. (2003b). *Dr. Helen Barrett on electronic portfolio development: ali.apple.com/ali_sites/ali/ neccexhibits/1000156/Step_Guides.html.*

Barrett, H. (2003c, October). *Using technology to support alternative assessment and electronic portfolios: electronicportfolios.com/portfolios.html.*

Portfolio Resources

American Association for Higher Education: *webcenter1.aahe.org/electronicportfolios/index.html.*

Aurbach & Associates. (1996). *Portfolio assessment bibliography: www.aurbach.com/files/bibliography.pdf.*

Barker, K. (2000). *The electronic learning record (ePortfolio): Assessment and management of skills and knowledge: Research report.* Available: *www.FuturEd.com.*

Barker, K. (September, 2003). *Eportfolio quality standards: An international development project.* Available: *www.FuturEd.com.*

Barrett, H. (2003). *electronicportfolios.com/handbook/ index.html.* Information about electronic portfolio handbook CD-ROM.

Cambridge, B. (Ed.). (2002). *Electronic portfolios: Emerging practices for students, faculty, and institutions.* Washington, DC: American Association for Higher Education.

Glendale Community College: *www.gc.maricopa.edu/ English/assessment/resources_portfolio.html.*

Open Source Portfolio Initiative: *www.theospi.org.* The Open Source Portfolio Initiative (OSPI) consists of an evolving group of individuals and organizations interested in collaborating on the development of the best nonproprietary, open source electronic portfolio code possible.

Project Kaleidoscope: *www.pkal.org/template0.cfm?c_id=2.* Examples of portfolios in psychology, physics, biology, chemistry, and neuroscience, some of which focus on assessment of student learning.

Regis University. *E-portfolio basics.* Available: *academic.regis.edu/LAAP/eportfolio/index.html.*

Urban Universities Portfolio Project: *www.imir.iupui.edu/portfolio.*

Wolf, D. (1989, April). Portfolio assessment: Sampling student work. *Educational Leadership,* 46(7), 35–39.

Zubizarreta, J. (2003). *The learning portfolio: Reflective practice for improving student learning.* Bolton, MA: Anker.

Qualitative and Quantitative Methods

Banta, T. W., Lund, J. P., Black, K. E., & Oblander, F. W. (1996). *Assessment in practice: Putting principles to work on college campuses.* San Francisco: Jossey-Bass.

Cresswell, J. W. (1998). *Qualitative inquiry and research design: Choosing among five traditions.* Thousand Oaks, CA: Sage.

Denzin, N. K., & Lincoln, Y. S. (Eds.). (1994). *Handbook of qualitative research.* Thousand Oaks, CA: Sage.

DeVellis, R. F. (1991). *Scale development.* Thousand Oaks, CA: Sage.

Erwin, D. T., & Wise, S. E. (2002). A scholarly practitioner model for assessment (pp. 72–77).

Kvale, S. (1996). *InterViews: An introduction to qualitative research interviewing.* Thousand Oaks, CA: Sage.

LeCompte, M. D., Millroy, W. L., & Preissle, J. (Eds.). (1992). *The handbook of qualitative research in education.* San Diego, CA: Academic Press.

Lofland, J., & Lofland, L. H. (1995). *Analyzing social settings: A guide to qualitative observation and analysis.* Belmont, CA: Wadsworth.

Maxwell, J. A. A. (1996). *Qualitative research design: An interactive approach.* London: Sage.

Merriam, S. B. (Ed.). (2002). *Qualitative research in practice.* San Francisco: Jossey-Bass.

Merriam, S. B. (1997). *Qualitative research and case study applications in education.* San Francisco: Jossey-Bass.

Miles, M. B., & Huberman, A. M. (1994). *Qualitative data analysis* (2nd ed.). Newbury Park, CA: Sage.

Morse, J. M. (Ed.). (1993). *Critical issues in qualitative research methods.* Thousand Oaks, CA: Sage.

Morse, J. M., & Field, P. A. (1995). *Qualitative research methods* (2nd ed.). Thousand Oaks, CA: Sage.

Palomba, C. A., & Banta, T. W. (1999). *Assessment essentials: Planning, implementing, and improving assessment in higher education* (pp. 337–342). San Francisco: Jossey-Bass.

Patton, M. Q. (1990). *Qualitative evaluation and research methods* (2nd ed.). Newbury Park, CA: Sage.

Seidman, I. (1998). *Interviewing as qualitative research* (2nd ed.). New York: Teachers College Press.

Silverman, D. (1993). *Interpreting qualitative data: Methods for analyzing talk, text, and interaction.* Thousand Oaks, CA: Sage.

Smith, M. L. (1986). The whole is greater: Combining qualitative and quantitative approaches in evaluation studies. In D. Williams (Ed.), Naturalistic evaluation. *New Directions for Program Evaluation,* 30. San Francisco: Jossey-Bass.

Wolcott, H. F. (1994). *Transforming qualitative data: Description, analysis, and interpretation.* Thousand Oaks, CA: Sage.

Standardized Tests

Buros Institute. *The mental measurements yearbook test reviews online: buros.unl.edu/buros/jsp/search.jsp.*

Eric's Test Locator: *searchERIC.org.*

Factors Affecting Test Outcomes: Generic Centre: Learning and Teaching Support Network: *dbweb.liv.ac.uk/ltsnpsc/AB/AB-html/node6.html.* Source of articles on tests and alternatives to tests.

Surveys and Questionnaires

Ewell, P. T. (1983). *Student outcomes questionnaires: An implementation handbook* (2nd ed.). Boulder, CO: National Center for Higher Education Management Systems.

Sudman, S., & Bradburn, N. (1982). *Asking questions: A practical guide to questionnaire design.* San Francisco: Jossey-Bass.

Suskie, L. (1996). *Questionnaire survey research: What works.* (2nd ed.). Tallahassee, FL: Association for Institutional Research.

Areas of Assessment Focus
Advising

Miller, M. A., & Alberts, B. M. (2003). Assessing and evaluating the impact of your advisor training and development program. In *Advisor training: Exemplary practices in the development of advisor skills.* Manhattan, KS: National Academic Advising Association.

Disciplines in General

Meta-site: North Carolina State University: *www2.acs.ncsu.edu/UPA/assmt/resource.htm#hbooks.*

Banta, T. W., & Palomba, C. A. (2003). *Assessing student competence in accredited disciplines.* Sterling, VA: Stylus.

Distance Learning

Meyer, K. A. (2002). Quality in distance education: Focus on on-line learning. ASHE-ERIC *Higher Education Report,* 29, 4. San Francisco: Jossey-Bass.

Morgan, C., & O'Reilly, M. (1999). *Assessing open and distance learners.* London: Kogan Page Ltd.

First College Year

Cutright, M. (Ed.). (2003). *Annotated bibliography on assessment of the first college year.* University of South Carolina: Policy Center on the First Year of College.

Gardner, J. N., Barefoot, B. O., & Swing, R. L. (2001a). *Guidelines for evaluating the first-year experience at four-year colleges.* University of South Carolina: The National Resource Center.

Gardner, J. N., Barefoot, B. O., & Swing, R. L. (2001b). *Guidelines for evaluating the first-year experience at two-year colleges.* University of South Carolina: The National Resource Center.

Siegel, M. J. (2003). *Primer on assessment of the first college year.* University of South Carolina: Policy Center on the First Year of College.

Swing, R. L. (Ed.). (2001). *Proving and improving: Strategies for assessing the first college year.* (Monograph 33). University of South Carolina: National Resource Center.

General Education

Albert, A. R. (2004). Assessment methods for student learning outcomes in general education at urban and metropolitan universities. Dissertation in preparation, University of Central Florida. This dissertation identifies instruments and methods of data collection being used to assess core general education student learning outcomes at urban and metropolitan universities and explores the usefulness of these instruments and methods in producing data that can be used for improvement purposes. Contact Angela R. Albert at *aalbert@mail.ucf.edu.*

Association of American Colleges and Universities. (2002). *Greater expectations: A new vision for learning as a nation goes to college* (National Panel Report). Washington, DC: Association of American Colleges and Universities.

Bauer, K. W., & Frawley, W. J. (2002). *General education curriculum revisions and assessment at a research university.* Paper presented at the 2002 Association of Institutional Research (AIR) Conference, Toronto, Canada.

Gaff, J. G., & Ratcliff, J. L. (Eds.). (1997). *Handbook of the undergraduate curriculum: A comprehensive guide to purposes, structures, strategies, and change.* San Francisco: Jossey-Bass.

League for Innovation in the Community College. *21st century learning outcomes colleges: www.league.org/league/projects/pew.*

Lopez, C. L. (1998). How campuses are assessing general education. *Liberal Education, 84*(3), 36–43.

Lopez, C. L. (1999). General education: Regional accreditation standards and expectations. *Liberal Education, 85*(3), 46–51.

Ratcliff, J. L. (1993). *Linking assessment and general education.* University Park, PA: NCTLA.

Stone, J., & Friedman, S. (2002). A case study in the integration of assessment and general education: Lessons learned from a complex process. *Assessment & Evaluation in Higher Education, 22*(2), 199–210.

Information Literacy

Association of College and Research Libraries: *www.ala.org/ala/acrl/acrlstandards/informationliteracycompetency.htm.*

Dunn, K. (2002, January/March). Assessing information literacy skills in the California State University: A progress report. *The Journal of Academic Librarianship, 28.*

Hernon, P., & Dugan, R. E. (2002). *An action plan for outcomes assessment in your library.* Chicago: American Library Association.

Middle States Commission on Higher Education. (2003). *Developing research & communication skills: Guidelines for information literacy in the curriculum.* Philadelphia, PA: Author.

Interdisciplinary Assessment

Journal of Innovative Higher Education: www.uga.edu/ihe/IHE.html. Lists abstracts as far back as 1989, some of which relate to assessment.

Stowe, D. E. (2002, May–June). Assessing interdisciplinary programs. *Assessment Update. 14*(3), 3–4.

Vess, D. (2000). *Exploration in interdisciplinary teaching and learning: www.faculty.de.gcsu.edu/~dvess/ids/courseportfolios/front.htm.*

Learning Communities

MacGregor, J., et al. (2003). *Doing learning community assessment: Five campus stories* (National Learning Communities Project Monograph Series). Olympia, WA: The Evergreen State College, Washington Center for Improving the Quality of Undergraduate Education, in cooperation with the American Association for Higher Education.

Taylor, K., Moore, W. S., MacGregor, J., & Lindblad, J. (2003). *What we know now about learning community research and assessment* (National Learning Communities Project Monograph Series). Olympia, WA: The Evergreen State College, Washington Center for Improving the Quality of Undergraduate Education, in cooperation with the American Association for Higher Education.

Psychology

Meta-site: American Psychological Association. *Cyberguide to best practices in assessment: www.apa.org/ed/best_practices.html.*

American Psychological Association (in preparation). Dunn, D. S., Mehrotra, C. M., & Halonen, J. S. (Eds.). *Measuring up: Assessment challenges and practices for psychology.* Washington, DC: Author.

Science, Technology, Engineering, and Mathematics

Meta-site: The Field-Tested Learning Assessment Guide (FLAG): *www.flaguide.org.* A good source of assessment methods in science, technology, engineering, and mathematics.

Meta-site: Project Kaleidoscope: *www.pkal.org.* See especially sites focused on use of portfolios: *www.pkal.org/template2.cfm?c_id=496.*

Committee on Undergraduate Science Education, Center for Science, Mathematics, and Engineering, and Technology, National Research Council. (1999). *Transforming undergraduate education in science, mathematics, engineering, and technology.* Washington, DC: National Academy Press.

Gold, B., Keith, S., & Marion, W. (Eds.). (1999). *Assessment practices in undergraduate mathematics.* Washington, DC: The Mathematics Association of America.

Hake, R. R. *www.physics.indiana.edu/~hake.* Richard Hake has assembled an impressive amount of resources on teaching, learning, and assessing in the sciences.

Hake, R. R. (1998). *Research, development, and change in undergraduate biology education* (REDCUBE): A Web guide for nonbiologists at *www.physics.indiana.edu/~redcube.*

Mathieu, R. (2000). Assessment tools to drive learning: FLAG, SALG, and other proven assessments available online. In *Targeting* curricular change: *Reform in undergraduate education in science, math, engineering, and technology* (pp. 26–31). Washington, DC: American Association for Higher Education.

Mintzes, J. J., Wandersee, J. H., & Novak, J. D. (Eds.). (2000). *Assessing science understanding: A human constructivist view.* San Diego, CA: Academic Press.

Wiese, D., Seymour, E., & Hunter, A. (1999, June). *Report on a panel testing of the student assessment of their learning gains instrument by faculty using modular methods to teach undergraduate chemistry.* University of Colorado, Bureau of Sociological Research.

Wright, J. C., Millar, S. B., Kosciuk, S. A., Penberthy, D. L., Williams, P. H., & Wampold, B. E. (1998, August). A novel strategy for assessing the effects of curriculum reform on student competence. *Journal of Chemical Education, 75,* 986–992.

Senior Year

Gardner, J. N., Van der Veer, G., & Associates. (1997). *The senior year experience: Facilitating integration, reflection, closure, and transition.* San Francisco: Jossey-Bass.

Service Learning

Bringle, R. G., Phillips, M. A., & Hudson, M. (forthcoming, 2004). *The measure of service learning: Research scales to assess student experiences.* Washington, DC: American Psychological Association.

Eyler, J., & Giles, D. W., Jr. (1999). *Where's the learning in service learning?* San Francisco: Jossey-Bass.

Student Affairs

Bresciani, M. (2003). *Identifying projects that deliver outcomes and provide a means of assessment: A concept mapping checklist.* Washington, DC: NASPA.

Kuh, G. D., Gonyea, R. M., & Rodriguez, D. P. (2002). The scholarly assessment of student development. In T. W. Banta & Associates, *Building a scholarship of assessment* (pp. 100–127). San Francisco: Jossey-Bass.

Pascarella, E. T. (2001). Indentifying excellence in undergraduate education: Are we even close? *Change, 33*(3), 19–23.

Pascarella, E. T., & Terenzini, P. T. (1991). *How college affects students: Findings and insights from twenty years of research.* San Francisco: Jossey-Bass.

Schroeder, C., et al. (1994). *The student learning imperative: Implications for student affairs.* Washington, DC: American College Personnel Association.

Schuh, J. H., & Upcraft, M. L. (1996). *Assessment in student affairs: A guide for practitioners.* San Francisco: Jossey-Bass.

Schuh, J. H., Upcraft, M. L., & Associates. (2000). *Assessment practice in student affairs: An applications manual.* San Francisco: Jossey-Bass.

Stage, F. K. (Ed.). (1992). *Diverse methods for research and assessment of college students.* Washington, DC: American College Personnel Association.

Upcraft, M. L., & Shuh, J. H. (1996). *Assessment in student affairs: A guide for practitioners.* San Francisco: Jossey-Bass.

Winston, R. B., Jr., Creamer, D. G., Miller, T. K., & Associates. (2001). *The professional student affairs administrator: Educator, leader, and manager.* Philadelphia: Taylor and Francis.

Winston, R. B., Jr., & Miller, T. K. (1994). A model for assessing developmental outcomes related to student affairs programs and services. *NASPA Journal, 32,* 2–19.

Writing

Conference on College Composition and Communication: *www.ncte.org/groups/cccc.*

Haswell, R. H. (Ed.). (2001). Beyond outcomes: Assessment and instruction within a university writing program. *Perspectives on Writing: Theory, Research, Practice, 5.* Westport, CT: Ablex.

White, E. M. (1994). *Teaching and assessing writing: Recent advances in understanding, evaluating, and improving student performance* (2nd ed.). San Francisco: Jossey-Bass.

White, E. M., Lutz, W. D., & Kamusikiri, S. (1996). *Assessment of writing: Politics, policies, practices.* New York: MLA.

Writing Project Administrators: *www.writingproject.org.*

Representative Institutional Sites Featuring Assessment Methods

California State University-Monterey Bay: *csumb.edu.*

Dixie College. *General education assessment plan: Assessment instruments: www.dixie.edu/effective/ge_toc.htm.*

Ferris State University: *www.ferris.edu.*

King's College. *The comprehensive assessment program: www.kings.edu.*

Sinclair Community College: *www.sinclair.edu.*

Southwest Missouri State University: *www.smsu.edu.*

WORKSHEETS, GUIDES, AND EXERCISES

1. *From Outcome Statements to Methods of Assessment in Courses or Educational Experiences.* Developing an inventory of course-based or experience-based assessment practices (such as in service learning programs) results in a rich pool of practices upon which to build institution- and program-level assessment methods. In the process of selecting or designing formative and summative assessment methods, core working groups can develop this inventory by asking individuals to submit responses to the following worksheet. This worksheet becomes a way to determine how well proposed program or institution levels of assessment align with how and what students learn and how they represent their learning. Or, from this worksheet, members of a core working group may be able to design formative and summative methods of assessment that align with students' learning histories.

Assessment Methods in Individual Courses or Educational Experiences

Individual submitting worksheet:_____

Course or educational experience:_____

1. List agreed-upon outcome statement or statements your course or educational experience addresses:

    1.
    2.
    3.
    4.

2. What methods of teaching and learning contribute to or foster the learning described in this outcome statement or these outcome statements?

    1.
    2.
    3.
    4.

3. What assumptions about teaching and learning underlie these methods?

    1.
    2.
    3.
    4.

4. What assessment methods do you use to assess the learning described in the outcome statements listed under Number 1?

5. What assumptions underlie your methods?

6. What inferences can you draw from what students represent or demonstrate or produce?

2. *Designing or Selecting Direct and Indirect Methods.* Based on results of the inventory in Exercise 1, core working groups at the institution- and program-levels may decide to derive or design direct and indirect methods. They may also decide to use standardized instruments. Having members of a core working group, in consultation with colleagues, analyze the considerations that play a key role in the design or selection of direct and indirect methods helps narrow down the pool of options. The following worksheet helps members of a core working group to analyze and then agree upon methods that align with what and how students learn and represent their learning. It also asks members of a core working group to consider the validity and reliability of each proposed method.

Analysis of Direct and Indirect Assessment Methods under Consideration				
	Method	**Method**	**Method**	**Method**
Learning outcome(s)				
Alignment with curriculum and educational experiences, including assessment practices	_____	_____	_____	_____
Inferences that can be drawn about student learning	_____	_____	_____	_____
Inferences that cannot be drawn about student learning	_____	_____	_____	_____
Can be used for formative assessment	_____	_____	_____	_____
Can be used for summative assessment	_____	_____	_____	_____
Validity of the method	_____	_____	_____	_____
Reliability of the method	_____	_____	_____	_____

3. *A Schedule for Formative and Summative Assessment.* In collaboration with an office of institutional research and planning, core working groups that identify and select methods of assessment for institution-level outcomes also develop a timetable to assess students along the continuum of their learning. Use the following worksheet to develop a timetable to assess students' learning along the continuum of their studies. Using this chart, core working groups in program-level assessment committees can also establish a program-level assessment chronology. This timetable provides an overall chronology of assessment efforts at either the institution or program level. Cycles of inquiry into how well students make progress toward and eventually achieve institution- and program-level outcomes occur over time. Each year or every couple of years the institution and its individual programs focus on assessing one or two outcomes at a time to maintain a focus of inquiry.

List Each Agreed-upon Institution- or Program-level Outcome.	Formative Assessment Schedule (For Example, After Each Course; After Certain Number of Credits or Sequences of Courses or Educational Experiences?)	Summative Assessment Schedule
1.		
2.		
3.		
4.		

4. *Assessment within the Design of Curricula and Educational Experiences.* Re-conceptualizing or creating a new program is an opportunity to develop an organic relationship among educational philosophy, learning outcomes, curricular and co-curricular design, sequence of educational experiences, and methods of assessment. The following visual represents a way to think about this interrelationship. If your institution is in the early stages of designing a new program or a new core curriculum, consider how you might use this visual as a way to guide your design. That is, begin by (1) stating learning outcome statements for the proposed program; (2) discuss the philosophy of teaching, assumptions underlying teaching and learning, or models of teaching and learning that will promote desired learning and translate those discussions into curricular and co-curricular design or sets of educational experiences; (3) develop or select direct and indirect assessment methods that capture learning along the progression of students' studies to ascertain how well students transfer and build upon knowledge, understanding, behaviors, habits of mind, ways of knowing, dispositions.

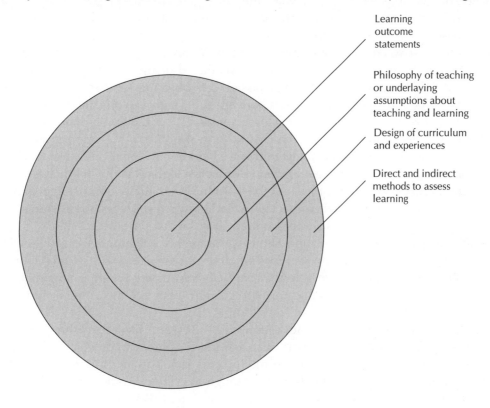

Learning outcome statements

Philosophy of teaching or underlaying assumptions about teaching and learning

Design of curriculum and experiences

Direct and indirect methods to assess learning

5. *Developing Assessment Methods.* The institutional examples in Box 4.8 and Box 4.9 represent ways in which different constituencies of an institution have worked together to develop assessment methods that provide evidence of student learning from multiple lenses. These two examples also illustrate the importance of institutional context in the collective identification of questions of curiosity that members of an educational community wish to pursue. In the design of assessment methods, consider how cross-disciplinary members of core working groups or other established groups might work together to develop complementary methods of assessment that explore students' knowledge, understanding, habits of mind, ways of knowing, attitudes, and values.

BOX 4.8   INSTITUTIONAL EXAMPLE: *Academic Librarians and Faculty: Information Literacy*

Academic libraries, like the institutions of which they are a part, are exploring the type of contribution that they can make to outcomes assessment. The broad area of library evaluation and assessment has historically focused on the "user in the life of the library" (i.e., input, output, and performance measures); but, more recently, attention has centered on the "library in the life of the user" (e.g., customer satisfaction). Now, there is even a different perspective: the "user and library in the life of the institution"—the accomplishment of the institutional mission (i.e., outcomes assessment). Each of the three perspectives has value and, to date, researchers have not sufficiently explored interconnections.

As shown in *An Action Plan for Outcomes Assessment in Your Library*,[1] professional associations (Association of College & Research Libraries, ACRL; and the Wisconsin Association of Academic Librarians), the Florida State Library (with its outcomes workbook), The Citadel (Daniel Library), and the California State Library system have viewed information literacy as the link between outcomes assessment and libraries. Outcomes focus on the ways in which library users change (know, think, and are able to do) as a result of their contact with the library's resources and programs. This is not to say that librarians cannot work with others in other areas of outcomes assessment.

The ACRL has developed Information Literacy Competency Standards for Higher Education (reprinted as Appendix H in *An Action Plan for Outcomes Assessment in Your Library*). In Chapter 6 of *An Action Plan for Outcomes Assessment in Your Library* we take the information literacy competency standards and performance indicators and convert them into measurable student learning outcomes.

The Mildred F. Sawyer Library, Suffolk University (Boston), has taken that framework and included student learning outcomes as part of an assessment plan, part of which relates to student ability to retrieve, evaluate, and use electronic information. The learning outcomes that were sought have a lifelong effect on students and, although that effect would be difficult to measure, there should be an effort to do so. While faculty involvement was essential, the staff wanted to identify and design learning modules that were in concert with carefully chosen learning objectives, known library strengths, and within the limits of available resources.

This report describes two methods of assessment related to achievement of the assessment plan. The first relies on the type of data that libraries can gather from electronic databases supplied by commercial vendors, and the second involves cooperation with teaching faculty.

Use of Boolean Search Operators

Librarians advocate the teaching of information search skills. Along with other searching skills, Boolean operators (use of AND, OR, and NOT) are used to reduce, or refine, the number of "hits" (retrievals) per search of almost every electronic database. This skill, once learned and applied, will

(Continued)

---

[1]Peter Hernon and Robert E. Dugan, *An Action Plan for Outcomes Assessment in Your Library* (Chicago: American Library Association, 2002). For other examples of the use of outcomes assessment in academic libraries, see the articles in volume 28 (2002) of *The Journal of Academic Librarianship* (January/March and November).

BOX 4.8 (Continued)

save students time by increasing the effectiveness of the search process; their retrievals will be "more on target," resulting in less information overload and less time reading through abstracts of articles or sources that do not meet their needs. Librarians at Sawyer Library gather data about the knowledge and application of Boolean searching by conducting a pretest and posttest of students receiving formal searching instruction and by retrieving the statistics from vendors supplying the databases to track the number of retrievals per search for each month of the academic term.

They retrieve the monthly statistics for "number of searches" and "number of hits" and then calculate the number of hits per search. The Boolean operator "AND" is emphasized during the instructional sessions because it is used to combine two or more keywords, thereby reducing the number of results. If the number has dropped, the library might claim that its efforts in instructing students on this specific Boolean operator have reduced the number of retrievals per search. Adding to the validity of the claim is that the library received such statistics prior to implementation of the instruction program, and there was no observable/measurable change during the school term.

The library staff compiles and reviews the pretest and posttest from the instruction sessions and the monthly vendor statistics. Analysis of the test scores is used to improve the content and methods employed during the instruction sessions; analysis of the vendor statistics verifies whether or not the instructional sessions changed student searching processes to include Boolean operators.

Technology Skills

The Accounting Department at Suffolk University recognized the importance of technology-related competencies to accountants—if they are to access and assimilate electronic information—and to solve unstructured problems found in different consulting and strategic decision-making situations. Using pretests and posttests, student ability to incorporate traditional and nontraditional sources of information into company-analysis projects was measured. There was even a multiple-choice Internet quiz.

While developing skills provides students with the competencies to access technology, improving their perceived abilities is vital to ensure the successful utilization of computers in the workplace. Combining strong skills and highly perceived abilities should allow students to access, synthesize, and analyze timely information from various information sources when working on an appropriate independent assignment, the very competencies that accounting recruiters expect.

The development of effective pedagogical tools must recognize that the benefits of technology may depend on the learning situation and the psychological and other characteristics of the students. Librarians can partner with classroom faculty to meet the learning objectives for the course, especially those related to the use of technology to navigate the Internet and to retrieve, download, and evaluate information for the completion of classroom assignments. In doing so, libraries ensure that their outcomes are ones key to the instructional programs of the college or university.

Conclusion

The same toolkit of methods that teaching faculty use to assess outcomes applies to libraries and their measurement of student learning. Both faculty and librarians can gather direct and indirect evidence of the changes that occur in student learning during a course or program of study. What are librarians trying to do in their instructional programs? Why are they doing it the way they are? How well do those approaches work—that is, accomplish the assessment plan? The assessment plan, a planning document, guides whatever course of action the library takes (see www.suffolk.edu/sawlib/plandocs/current_student_assessment_plan.htm for a sample plan). At the same time, it is critical that information literacy be related to the broader concept of critical thinking and competencies such as "formulate and state a research question, problem, or issue . . . ;" "organize information in a manner that permits analysis, evaluation, synthesis, and

(Continued)

BOX 4.8 (Continued)

understanding"; "create and communicate information effectively using various media"; and "understand the ethical, legal, and socio-political issues surrounding information."[2]

---

[2]Dunn, K. (2002, January/March). Assessing information literacy skills in the California State University: A progress report. *The Journal of Academic Librarianship*, 28.

Sources: Contributed by Peter Hernon, Professor, Simmons College, Graduate School of Library and Information Science, 300 The Fenway, Boston, Massachusetts 02115–5898: peter.hernon@simmons.edu; Robert E. Dugan, Director, Mildred F. Sawyer Library, Suffolk University, 8 Ashburton Place, Boston, Massachusetts 02108: rdugan@suffolk.edu.

BOX 4.9 INSTITUTIONAL EXAMPLE: *Student Affairs and Academic Affairs: Academic Integrity, Student Learning, and Campus Culture*

Reports of the growing numbers of cases involving academic dishonesty across the nation have stirred the faculty, student body, and administration on numerous college campuses. In 2000, members of the NC State University community began to study its Honor Code, records of infractions, and student behaviors and impressions regarding academic integrity in an attempt to understand the behaviors and drivers of those behaviors on our own campus. A committee of administrators from Academic Affairs and Student Affairs, technology staff, faculty, and students initially met to focus on whether technology makes cheating easier for students; and while that focus was retained throughout their work, it became obvious that something bigger was happening. In order to understand the larger picture, a more thorough assessment regarding attitudes toward cheating, how many people were participating in cheating behaviors, and why they were behaving in that manner was required. In short, we began to understand that we had to consider what students know about academic integrity and cheating, how they learned it, and what they might need to "re-learn" in light of inaccurate information, unfortunate perceptions (and realities), and misguided responsibility for their own behavior.

In response to national literature on cheating behaviors and their pervasiveness, we wanted to learn the specifics of our own population's behaviors and attitudes. Borrowing heavily from Rutgers' professor Donald McCabe's work on academic integrity, staff from Undergraduate Affairs and Student Affairs worked together to modify his survey to accommodate NC State's cultural and practical realities [see the survey at www.ncsu.edu/undergrad_affairs/assessment/files/projects/acadint/acad_integrity.pdf]. With the survey online, we contacted 3,000 randomly selected undergraduate students and attained a 30% response rate, which is fairly typical for this kind of survey topic. Our findings were the basis for multiple, campus-wide presentations, posted at: www.ncsu.edu/undergrad_affairs/assessment/files/projects/acadint/academic_integrity_at_ncstate.pdf.

While our findings are not atypical of such surveys, they were especially illuminating in three primary respects: (1) they demonstrated a "disconnect" between what students claim to value (integrity) and how they behave; (2) students want the definition and consequences of cheating to be clear; and (3) students want extenuating circumstances to be considered in decisions about sanctions. Most important in moving toward an institutional "remedy" is the consistent evidence that students value and need guidance from their professors regarding the complexities of cheating.

(Continued)

BOX 4.9 (Continued)

The survey's findings established the basis for the work we needed to do and, thus, are indicative of how we used the results. First, we realized the need for widespread campus conversations about academic integrity, rather than promoting the ongoing assumption that the Office of Student Conduct is solely responsible for institutional integrity. As a result, we made presentations to several groups, articulating the findings of the survey to the Provost's Staff, the Chancellor's Staff, the Faculty Senate, Staff Senate, Student Judicial Board, Deans' Steering Committee, Deans' Council, and Associate Deans. These conversations provided fuel for disseminating the results, as well as identifying some possible sources of remedy. Most significant is that every single group offered valuable recommendations for taking the discussion to larger groups and for identifying more strategies for further education of the community.

Decisions

Key to our effort of assessing academic integrity is the hope that we can reinforce the institutional culture of NC State University as one of honor, integrity, and individual choice. A number of educational initiatives were already in place when this assessment was conducted. Based on the results of the survey, some initiatives remained the same, some were altered, and others were created. Most strategies involved further partnering between Undergraduate Affairs and Student Affairs.

Decisions Implemented as a Result of the Assessment of Academic Integrity

- Prior to the implementation of the survey, students who violated the academic integrity policies were often assigned an eight-hour CD-ROM exercise that focused on academic integrity issues. This sanction was not altered as a result of the assessment. It provides students with the philosophical importance of academic integrity and ways to maintain integrity when faced with common, yet difficult, situations.

- During the development of the survey, members of a student senate committee wrote an honor statement to reflect their views on the importance of academic integrity. It was on the ballot for the spring 2001 student body elections. It passed and is currently located in the student senate constitution.

- New faculty orientation packets were created for the August orientation program. The packet included a cover letter and a number of documents with procedures for pursuing academic integrity violations and resources for helping students avoid violations. It was given to each member in hardcopy form, but it can be located on the Office of Student Conduct's Web site: www.ncsu.edu/student_conduct.

- An article titled "Academic Integrity at NC State University: Creating a Culture of Honor" was published in *Emphasis: Teaching and Learning*, the NC State Faculty Center for Teaching and Faculty Learning's newsletter. The article highlighted the survey methods, findings, and the resulting strategies and was distributed to every faculty member on campus.

- The Office of Student Conduct Web site was expanded to include more information about academic integrity. The site was expanded to include judicial statistics, academic integrity case studies to help faculty handle cases of academic dishonesty, and presentations on academic integrity. The existing information was reorganized to better assist faculty, and a quiz on academic integrity with the correct answers and explanations is in the process of being developed for students.

(Continued)

BOX 4.9   (Continued)

- Based on an informal conversation between faculty and Student Affairs staff regarding academic integrity issues, Dr. Steve Wiley, Paul Cousins, and Dr. Carrie Zelna implemented a semester-long intervention in Communications 257 in the fall 2002 semester. Academic integrity issues were infused into the course through a variety of activities and lectures. Sections of the original survey were administered, and other assessment methods were implemented to determine if the activities and lectures were effective. This assessment is still in progress.

- The Office of Student Conduct has always presented educational programs to students and faculty on the issue of academic integrity. Due to the findings of this assessment, changes to the presentations were made to include statistics when appropriate, and case studies were altered to include those that involved the violations that students incorrectly identified as "not cheating." In some situations the entire program was altered to include more philosophical information to help students better understand academic integrity as it relates to the philosophy of education.

- After presenting the survey data to the student judicial board, the members began implementing their own educational interventions. One such intervention was the creation of banners placed in various locations on campus during exam week to remind students of the importance of integrity in their academic work.

Decisions Made as a Result but Still in the Planning Phases of Implementation

- The College of Design is in the process of developing posters to reemphasize academic integrity polices in the classroom. The survey showed that 10% of the students learned the policies from posters that were last posted over five years ago. Based on this, we believe posters to be an important and effective way to disseminate information to students.

- The chancellor will send each incoming student a letter emphasizing the importance of integrity in all aspects of the university's culture.

- The Office of Student Conduct, Undergraduate Affairs, and the Student Judicial Branch of Student Government plan to partner to implement an Honor and Integrity week. Due to budget constraints, this project was put on hold until spring 2003 or fall 2003.

The Assessment Cycle

We will re-administer the survey with revisions in spring 2005 to see if any of the interventions have made a positive impact on students' behaviors, knowledge, and attitudes. In the interim, specific programs are administering portions of the survey and other assessment methods after particular interventions have been implemented.

Allen, J., & Zelna, C. L. (2002, February). Academic integrity at NC State University: Creating a culture of honor. *Emphasis: Teaching and Learning, 11,* 3.

Source: Contributed by Jo Allen, Carrie Zelna, and Marilee Bresciani, NCSU. Reproduced with permission.

APPENDIX 4.1 STRATEGIES FOR REVIEWING AND SELECTING STANDARDIZED INSTRUMENTS

- Review a sample of the instrument to determine how well it aligns with collective program- or institution-level outcome statements, the educational practices that foster the learning described in those statements, and the assessment methods students have responded to along the continuum of their learning. Particularly helpful is Buros Institute's *The Mental Measurements Yearbook Test Reviews Online* (buros.unl.edu/buros/jsp/search.jsp) that contains information on over 4,000 commercially designed tests.

- Review a sample of the instrument and its accompanying literature to determine its validity—how well it assesses what it claims to assess—and its reliability—how well scores correlate across groups tested and across test versions, how well items and parts of a test correlate, and how well different raters' scores agree based on scoring the same test.

- Identify the kinds of inferences that can be drawn from the test and the kinds of inferences that cannot be drawn in relation to your outcome statements.

- Determine how fair the test is for your representative student populations and their learning chronologies. Specifically, identify the multiple and varied ways students have had opportunities to learn and receive feedback about what the test is assessing. The following resource is especially helpful in addressing issues of fairness: National Council on Measurement in Education. Code of Fair Testing Practices in Education: www.apa.org/science/finalcode.pdf.

- Determine restrictions inherent in administering the instrument in relation to using the results to improve student learning and providing feedback to students. Are results available in a reasonable amount of time to inform educators and students about their performance and inform institution- and program-level dialogue about how to improve students' learning experiences? Or, are tests restricted primarily for summative administration and therefore cannot inform educational practices along the continuum of students' learning?

- Identify alternative direct methods that you might use to assess other dimensions of what you expect students to demonstrate based on your learning outcome statements and the design of educational practices that contribute to that valued learning.

APPENDIX 4.2 INVENTORY OF DIRECT AND INDIRECT ASSESSMENT METHODS

DIRECT METHODS

Standardized Instruments: Tests and Inventories

Description

Historically, *standardized instruments,* such as objective tests, have served as the primary direct method to assess student learning. Content or disciplinary experts identify the standard content, knowledge, and tasks that students should know and be able to perform. In addition, they determine what constitutes levels of achievement based on the construction, design, and sequencing of questions or prompts. Students' achievement is referenced against other student groups' achievement on the same instrument, referred to as *norm referencing.* Primarily designed to make decisions about students, standardized instruments perform a gatekeeping role. They certify competence in a profession or field, such as in the case of licensure examinations for nursing students, or program-level knowledge or skills, such as in the case of general education tests. Results are also used to place students in appropriate courses or to identify level of achievement at points in students' studies, such as in the case of the increasing use of junior examinations.

What Standardized Instruments Provide

- Content and tasks developed by external experts within fields or programs of study

- Psychometric approach to assessment that values quantitative methods of interpreting student achievement

- Evidence of what students know or can do within the universe and framework of questions, prompts, and tasks of an instrument

- Evidence to make gatekeeping decisions such as professional certification or end-of-study achievement or to meet state mandates that value measurement as proof of learning

- Evidence to track student learning if instrument can be used formatively and if results have utility for programs and the institution

- Quick and easy adoption and efficient objective scoring

- History of validity and reliability studies

- One possible source of evidence within an institutional commitment to assessing student learning through multiple lenses

What Standardized Instruments Do Not Provide

- Evidence of the strategies; processes; and ways of knowing, understanding, and behaving that students draw upon or apply to represent learning

- Evidence of the complex and diverse ways in which humans construct and generate meaning

- Alignment with institution- and program-level learning outcome statements and students' learning histories

- Realistic time frames or contexts that reflect how humans solve problems, seek additional information or resources, correct mistakes, or reposition their thinking (Students respond within a time frame that might well affect their decisions or actions, such as deciding to make a last-minute guess among options in a question.)

- Highly useful results that directly relate to pedagogy and educational practices (Results relate to the construct of the instrument itself and what it is designed to measure. Patterns of student performance reported in scales or scores identify discrete areas of performance, such as a skill level, that identify strengths and weaknesses in curricular or co-curricular attention. However, these patterns do not assist in learning about why students responded in the ways they did. Or did they learn successful strategies for selecting or making "good guesses"?)

Some Examples

Instruments that test general education knowledge and abilities include the following:

- Academic Profile: www.ets.org/hea/acpro
- Collegiate Assessment of Academic Proficiency (CAAP): www.act.org/caap/index.html
- ACCUPLACER: www.collegeboard.com/highered/apr/accu/accu.html

Instruments dedicated to measuring specific skills include the following:

- Watson-Glazer Critical Thinking Appraisal
- California Critical Thinking Skills Test
- Tasks in Critical Thinking
- Reflective Judgment Inventory
- Measure of Intellectual Development
- e-Write, a component of ACT's COMPASS/ESL system

Examples of achievement tests in a particular field of study or profession include the following:

- Graduate Record Examinations' Subject Tests: www.gre.org/pbstest.html
- The PRAXIS Series: Professional Assessment for Beginning Teachers: www.ets.org/praxis/index.html
- Area Concentration Achievement Tests: www.collegeoutcomes.com
- Graduate Management Admission Test: www.mba.com/mba

Examples of inventories that assess students' knowledge, behaviors, and attitudes include the following:

- Force Concept Inventory (FCI): Designed to assess the initial knowledge state of students before they begin undergraduate physics courses. Students respond to a series of force-related problems or statements that reveal their knowledge (Halloun & Hestenes, 1985).
- Intercultural Development Inventory (IDI): Forty-four-item inventory-based paper and pencil instrument designed to assess the extent of an individual's intercultural sensitivity along a continuum that ranges from ethnocentrism to ethnorelativism, identifying a person's ability to shift from denial of difference to integration of difference (www.intercultural.org).
- A list of current inventories frequently used in student services is available at The Office of Institutional Research and Planning, The

University of Texas at Arlington. Student Affairs-Related Outcomes Instruments: Summary Information: wbarratt.indstate.edu/dragon/saroi/sa-indx.html.

Locally Designed Tests and Inventories

In a collective and shared commitment to assessing student learning, core working groups may well determine that no appropriate standardized instrument exists that aligns with institution- and program-level outcomes. That decision generates the design of local tests or inventories or continuing use of existing instruments that have an institutional history of providing useful and reliable results. Technological advancements, such as WebCT (www.webct.com/transform) and Blackboard (www.blackboard.com/products/ls/index.htm) offer an online environment for constructing some locally developed instruments.

What Local Tests or Inventories Provide

- Strong alignment of content and format with learning outcome statements and course-based assessment methods students have experienced along their learning histories
- Useful results that can be interpreted within the local contexts of teaching and learning and then used to improve student learning
- Opportunity to establish local instrument criteria that reflect what an institution and its programs value in educational practices
- Opportunity for faculty, staff, administrators, students, teaching assistants, tutors, intern advisors, advisory board members, and institutional researchers, for example, to contribute their perspectives on what should be assessed and how it should be assessed

What Local Tests or Inventories Do Not Provide

- Immediate reliability and validity results that verify content, construct, format and consistency in scoring, unless instruments have been pilot tested and evaluated over several semesters (Thus, time to pilot test an instrument for an institution's representative student populations is a necessary component of an institutional commitment to assessing for learning.)

Authentic, Performance-based Methods

Authentic, performance-based methods prompt students to represent their learning in response to assignments and projects that are embedded into their educational experiences. These methods value divergent thinking and responses, as opposed to convergent thinking, most typically represented in standardized tests. How students think, problem solve, react, interpret, or express themselves becomes the focus of these kinds of direct methods. Further, these methods can easily be embedded into students' continuum of learning, providing evidence of their growth over time, which is often demonstrated in self-reflective writing and responses to feedback from those who contribute to students' education, such as peers, internship advisors, external reviewers or evaluators, faculty, and staff.

What Authentic, Performance-based Methods Provide

- Representation of integrated learning
- Direct alignment with students' learning experiences
- Opportunities for students to reflect on and receive formative feedback about their learning and development
- Student-generated opportunities to demonstrate learning, as opposed to test-generated occasions

What Authentic, Performance-based Methods Do Not Provide

- Easily quantifiable evidence given the complexity they capture
- Efficient scoring opportunities

Range of Authentic Assessments

- *Student portfolio:* A collection of multiple kinds of student-generated texts stored electronically or in paper form, a portfolio provides evidence of a learner's achievements along the continuum of learning. Developments in technology now make it possible for students to create digital portfolios. This method of storage and collection provides a longitudinal representation of learning, demonstrating how students make meaning within their contexts for learning through

assignments, projects, and narrative self-analyses and self-reflection. Portfolios provide an opportunity for students to demonstrate how they integrate learning over time from multiple learning experiences and opportunities within the curriculum, co-curriculum, and learning experiences that extend beyond their formal educational activities. They provide a valuable source of evidence for institution- and program-level learning by generating a range of texts that represent student learning. *Webfolios, digital learning records,* or *electronic learning records* are other current terms for this method. Two current resources provide a taxonomy of portfolios:

Regis University. Eportfolio basics. Available: academic.regis.edu/LAAP/eportfolio/index.html.

Cambridge, B. (Ed.). (2001). *Electronic portfolios: Emerging practices for students, faculty, and institutions.* Washington D.C.: American Association for Higher Education.

For information about Alverno College's Diagnostic Digital Portfolio, go to: www.ddp.alverno.edu.

- *Learning Record Online:* Similar to a student portfolio, the Learning Record Online (LRO) provides a running record of students' achievements. Originally developed for K–12 and now being developed for higher education, the LRO provides formative and summative evidence of students' learning within their curricula and against agreed-upon criteria and standards of judgment. Like a portfolio, the LRO provides ongoing evidence of students' emerging learning within contexts for learning, including evidence of their reflective process, their metacognition. Facilitated by online technology, educators and others interested in learning about students' development are able to aggregate or disaggregate groups to draw inferences and make decisions about students' progress and eventual levels of achievement: www.cwrl.utexas.edu/~syverson/olr/intro.html.

- *Capstone project:* A culminating independent research, collaborative, or professional project at the end of students' careers, this method provides evidence of how students solve representative higher-order disciplinary, professional, or interdisciplinary problems. This project is often represented in more than one kind of text, that is, in writing as well as in speaking or in visual texts, such as poster presentations. This method provides evidence of how well students integrate, synthesize, and transfer learning; in addition, it also can provide evidence of how well students integrate institution-level outcomes. This method can also be integrated as a formative means of assessment. The beginning of a second year of graduate study or the beginning of a third year of students' undergraduate study might index a time for students to demonstrate accumulated learning. Senior theses or senior research projects are also examples of capstone projects that provide opportunity for observers to assess students' mastery level within a field of study, discipline, or profession.

- *Performances, products, or creations:* Required over time as well as at the end of a program of study or upon the completion of undergraduate or graduate study, students' original work represents how they interpret, express, and construct meaning. Traditionally, the arts' faculty have formatively assessed students' performances to provide them with immediate feedback that shapes their future performances. This approach provides not only students with immediate feedback but also faculty and others who contribute to students' learning.

- *Visual representation:* Representing learning visually through charting, graphing, mapping, for example, provides students with alternative ways to show evidence of their learning, often a practice within disciplines such as mathematics and the sciences. Mathematicians often represent developments in their thinking in mind maps: jonathan.mueller .faculty.noctrl.edu/toolbox/examples/seaver/ mindmappingtask.htm. Visual representation offers a way to assess how well students make connections or understand a concept. In addition, visual representation extends students' repertoire of making meaning, developing a versatility in forms of representation that respond to the different needs of audiences, contexts, and the purposes of communication. The Biology Teaching Homepage provides examples of different kinds of conceptual maps,

as well as procedures for incorporating them into students' learning: www.fed.cuhk.edu .hk/~johnson/misconceptions/concept_map/ cmapguid.html. The Innovative Learning Group presents different forms of thinking maps: www.thinkingmaps.com.

- *Case studies:* Used over time, as well as at the end of students' studies, case studies, often used in business programs, provide opportunity to assess students' problem-solving abilities within a major program of study or along students' learning continuum to determine how well they are integrating the learning expressed in institutional learning outcomes—knowledge, perspectives, abilities, values, and attitudes. Parallel case studies used over time provide evidence of students' abilities to solve representative disciplinary, professional, or more generalized problems. In addition, they provide evidence of students' writing.

- *Professional or disciplinary practices:* Engaging students in practices that prepare them for the kinds of problems, activities, or situations individuals address not only in their fields of study but also as contributors to society and local communities provides evidence of how well students transfer, apply, and integrate learning. The Harrell Professional Development and Assessment Center in the University of Florida's College of Medicine has created an environment that permits observation of medical students interacting with patients. Audiovisual equipment captures, records, and displays these interactions. Replaying these interactions provides opportunities for faculty and students to assess students' knowledge, understanding, behaviors and dispositions: www.med.ufl.edu/oea/ comec/harrell.

- *Team-based or collaborative projects:* With rare exception, humans work with other humans during most of their lives in a range of workplace, social, and community environments. Team-based or collaborative projects are direct methods that enable assessment of individuals' knowledge, understanding, behaviors, and attitudes, as well as their ability to work with others to achieve a final product or solve a problem. Often videotaped, groups of faculty, staff, and students themselves have access to immediate results that inform students as well as educators. Alverno College's institutional example in Box 4.7 illustrates assessment that focuses on individual students as well as their collective achievement.

- *Internships and service projects:* How students actually apply or transfer their cumulative learning can be assessed in internship or service projects. That is, authentic experiences become a direct method of assessment, providing opportunity for students to demonstrate the dimensions of their learning within the context of a real environment. A step beyond simulations, these direct methods assess how well students translate their cumulative learning into actual practice.

- *Oral examinations:* Often used at the end of a professional program or a graduate program, as in an oral doctoral defense (University of Arizona, Graduate College: grad.admin.arizona .edu/degreecert/ppfoedc.htm), oral examinations probe the dimensions of student learning. They provide opportunities for students to represent how well they integrate learning and apply it to solving a case study or problem, responding to guided questions, or presenting a product. Measurement Research Associates provides some guidelines for conducting effective oral examinations: www.measurementresearch.com/ media/standardizedoral.pdf.

INDIRECT METHODS

Helpful in deepening interpretations of student learning are indirect methods, methods that focus on perceptions of student learning by asking students or others to respond to a set or series of questions. Indirect methods function to complement direct methods rather than to substitute for them.

What Indirect Methods Provide

- Evidence of students' attitudes, perceptions, and experiences
- Evidence that may help to explain student performance levels

What Indirect Methods Do Not Provide

- Work that represents evidence of student learning unless an instrument asks students to produce a text as evidence

Some Representative Examples

- *Focus groups* with representative students to probe a specific issue that may have been identified in a survey or identified in patterns of student performance as a result of formative or summative assessments. Van Aken, Watford, and Medina-Borja (1999) describe the successful design of a focus group to obtain perceptions of historically underrepresented students enrolled in an engineering program.

- *Interviews* with groups of students representing the institutional population. Tracking a cohort of students is one way of assessing learning for formative and summative purposes.

- Student, alumni, employer, and faculty-staff *surveys* and *questionnaires* that provide information about students' or others' perceptions of students' educational experiences and the institutions' impact on their learning. Alumni questionnaires and surveys provide a retrospective view of graduates' educational experience and create an opportunity for them to recommend improvements in education based on what is relevant to their current employment, profession, or graduate education. Faculty-staff surveys or questionnaires provide perceptions of student learning—that is, what students are able and not able to demonstrate in classroom-based assessments or observations of student behavior. Some examples follow:

  - ACT's surveys for adult learners, alumni, entering students, withdrawing students, and for institutional services: www.act.org

  - College Student Experiences Questionnaire (CSEQ), Community College Survey of Student Engagement (CCSSE): www.ccsse .org/aboutccsse/aboutccsse.html

  - Community College Student Experiences Questionnaire (CCSEQ): www.people .memphis.edu/~coe_cshe/CCSEQ_main.htm

  - The National Center for Higher Education Management Systems' Comprehensive Alumni Assessment Survey: www.nchems.org

  - National Survey of Student Engagement (NSSE): www.iub.edu/~nsse

  - Noel-Levitz Student Satisfaction Inventories: www.noellevitz.com/library/research/ satisfaction.asp#ssi

Chapter 5

REACHING CONSENSUS ABOUT CRITERIA AND STANDARDS OF JUDGMENT

If students are expected to develop a degree of independence in pursuit of learning, reach a satisfactory level of skill in communication, demonstrate sensitivity to their own values and those of their associates, become capable of collaborating with peers in defining and resolving problems, be able to recognize the relevance of their increasing knowledge to the current scene, and seek continually for insightful understanding and organization of the total educational experience, these outcomes must be specifically stated. In addition they must be made explicit in relation to learning experiences and by providing opportunities for demonstration of the developing behavior and for evaluation of it. Content, subject matter, and behavior are interrelated and must be construed by teachers, students, and evaluators. This requires an interrelated trinity of conceptual statements defining the objectives of operational statements, including how the behavior is to be evoked and appraised, and providing standards for deciding whether progress is evident and whether accomplishment is finally satisfactory.

—P. L. Dressel, 1976

OVERVIEW: How observers or raters interpret the work, projects, and creations that students generate in response to a method of assessment is the subject of this chapter. Developing criteria and standards of judgment provides a means to document and examine patterns of student achievement: the intellectual complexity, creativity, application of disciplinary logic, behaviors, and dispositions that provide evidence of integrated learning. Specifically, core working groups that design or develop methods of assessment also work together or in conjunction with representative constituencies at their institution to collaboratively develop scoring rubrics. Consisting of criteria and levels of achievement for each criterion, scoring rubrics are public grading sheets that scorers apply to the work students produce in response to an assessment method. These sheets enable scorers to assess the dimensions of student work, that is, how well a particular project or creation meets collaboratively agreed-upon criteria. The Worksheets, Guides, and Exercises at the end of this chapter are designed to guide core working groups as they (1) develop scoring rubrics that enable scorers to rate student work against criteria and standards for judgment, (2) pilot test these scoring rubrics to ascertain how well they capture the dimensions of students' learning, and (3) develop interrater reliability among scorers as they apply scoring rubrics to samples of student work.

INTERPRETATIONS OF STUDENT ACHIEVEMENT

How well do students progress toward institution- and program-level learning outcomes? How well do they achieve institution- and program-level expectations by the time they graduate? Interpreting students' achievement along the progression of their learning marks the next phase of the assessment process, that is, deciding how to interpret what students say, do, or prepare in response to an assessment method. Identifying the criteria and standards of judgment that an institution and its programs choose to apply to student work raises the following questions:

- Will criteria and standards of judgment be externally or internally established?
- What kind of results do externally and internally developed criteria and standards of judgment provide?
- How useful are results in promoting collective and targeted interpretations of student achievement within the context of educational practices?

Two approaches, norm referencing and criterion referencing, provide results that lead to different levels of community conversations.

Norm Referencing

A *norm-referenced approach* to assessing student learning primarily aims to compare a student's achievement against the achievement of other students who have performed the same task. Based on the achievement levels of a broader population, an individual student's performance is compared against the achievement of that broader population—referred to as a *norm*. A student's score, then, places that student within the context of others' performance. Unless developed within an institution based on shared criteria and standards of judgment, standardized instruments, such as tests of students' general education knowledge, are norm-referenced to certify levels of attainment against externally established criteria and standards of judgment. In this gatekeeping role, standardized tests focus on categorizing students. Interpretations of student performance, for example, serve as predictors of future achievement, such as students' attainment in graduate school, law school, or medical school. Or, they certify entry into a profession, such as

in national licensure examinations in nursing, law, or medicine. Categories of performance also enable institutions to benchmark the achievement of their students against students at comparative institutions or in comparable programs. Frequently, policy makers, legislators, and other public audiences aim to rank states or individuals based on results of standardized norm-referenced instruments, believing that a one-time "measure" of students' performance reflects an institution's or a program's effectiveness within the defined universe of a standardized instrument.

When institutions develop standardized instruments themselves, normed within an institutional context, institutions and programs may use these results to place or identify students—those who pass and those who fail; those who can write at a certain level and those who cannot—such as in rising junior year examinations. Collective interpretations of norm-referenced standardized instrument results based on students' scores may also identify areas of weakness in student learning or teaching practice, such as determining that students need more opportunities to learn how to identify assumptions that underlie an argument. Interpreting why students are and are not able to achieve within the scope of a norm-referenced method is the most important question in an institutional commitment to assessing student learning. Unless a norm-referenced method provides students with opportunities to explain their responses, or unless a method is specifically constructed to track problem-solving abilities such as in the "generalized graded unfolding models" designed to assess students' cognitive complexity, described by Erwin and Wise (2002, p.75), norm-referenced results provide limited information about students' behaviors, attitudes, habits of mind, problem-solving processes or strategies, or the interplay between understanding and action.

Criterion Referencing

Standardized norm-referenced approaches to assessment build in criteria and standards based on the collective expertise of those who develop, design, and test them. Students' results are reported in terms of numerical scores that place them in an achievement level based on these externally developed and tested criteria and standards of judgment. A *criterion-referenced approach* to assessment, on the other hand, deepens context-specific collective interpretations about student achievement based on criteria and standards of judgment developed within an institution and its programs. Criterion-referenced results report on students' performance against the multiple dimensions and possible performance levels of a task—an exhibit, a presentation, a thesis, or a collaboratively designed project. Results relate to the construct of a direct or indirect method that aligns with institution- or program-level outcomes and students' learning histories. Students learn about their achievement in relation to these criteria and achievement levels; institutions and programs learn about students' learning in the same way. Institution- and program-level value is placed on students' achievement against criteria. How well students meet specific performance criteria along a continuum of achievement, as opposed to how well they compare with other students, becomes the focus of collective interpretation. Developed to align with institution- and program-level outcome statements, assessment methods, and students' learning chronologies, criterion-referenced results lead to dialogue about the relationship among pedagogy; curricular, co-curricular, and instructional design; and educational opportunities. How well do students' work, projects, and responses fit institution- and program-level criteria and standards for learning?

Some standardized instruments, such as the Graduate Record Examination in writing, for example, provide results of student performance along criteria that identify areas of students' strengths and weaknesses (www.gre.org/descriptor.html). Again, these results may foster interpretation about what students have learned but likely do not promote interpretations about how they have learned or why they performed as they did on one particular testing day.

Further, whereas most commercially designed standardized instruments value reporting numerical results, locally designed assessment methods value both quantitatively and qualitatively stated results. These results support institution- and program-level inquiry into the efficacy of educational practices that promote integration, synthesis, and transference. The complexity of institution- and program-level outcomes cannot be solely reflected in numerical results. Observation is powerful for capturing complexity. Intellectual processes and the confluence of understanding, behaving, and responding, for example, are difficult to measure in simplistic ways. Over time, criterion-based results may lead to reporting percentages of student performance against an institution- or program-level norm, but, more important, within those percentages they offer robust evidence about the dimensions of learning that foster collective interpretation within the context of educational practices.

SCORING RUBRICS

Scoring rubrics, a set of criteria that identify the expected dimensions of a text and the levels of achievement along those dimensions, provide a means to assess the multiple dimensions of student learning represented in students' projects, work, products, and performances. Raters assess student work based on these criteria to derive inferences about students' learning represented in various kinds of texts. In effect, rubrics translate outcome statements into criteria, also referred to as *primary traits* or *performance indicators.* These criteria publicly identify the significant dimensions that raters apply to texts students generate in response to an assessment method. Results of applying these criteria provide evidence of learning patterns. At both the institution and program levels these patterns identify students' areas of strength as well as weakness. Interpreting patterns of weakness leads to adjustments or modifications in pedagogy; curricular, co-curricular, and instructional design; and educational practices and opportunities.

Scoring rubrics consist of two kinds of descriptors:

1. *Criteria descriptors:* Descriptions of the criteria or traits manifested in a project, performance, or text students produce in response to an assessment method. Criteria identify the ways of thinking, knowing, or behaving represented in what students produce, such as the following:

- Creativity
- Self-reflection
- Originality
- Integration
- Analysis
- Synthesis
- Disciplinary logic

Criteria descriptors may also identify characteristics of the text itself, such as the following:

- Coherence
- Accuracy or precision
- Clarity
- Structure

2. *Performance descriptors:* Descriptions of how well students execute each criterion or trait along an achievement continuum—score levels. This continuum, then, describes representative ways students perform or execute each criterion,

Exemplary	Commendable	Satisfactory	Unsatisfactory
Excellent	Good	Needs improvement	Unacceptable
Exceptional	Acceptable	Marginal	Unacceptable
Expert	Practitioner	Apprentice	Novice

reflecting mastery levels; national or professional levels; levels established through the collective expertise of faculty, staff, and others who contribute to students' education based on their observation of students' progression over time or the developmental process that typically occurs. Achievement along a continuum may be expressed numerically, such as through a 1–5 scale, or expressed verbally to identify levels of excellence, expertise, or proficiency as illustrated in the examples above.

The following scoring rubrics identify the criteria and standards of judgment for texts that students produce as evidence of either institution- or program-level learning. In all of the examples note that criteria are described under each level of achievement, providing students with specific feedback about their work and providing educators with specific patterns of evidence upon which to base collective interpretation:

- The institutional example in Box 5.1 presents a scoring rubric designed to assess nursing

---

BOX 5.1   INSTITUTIONAL EXAMPLE: *Azusa Pacific University*

Level II Competency Paper

Students write a one- to two-page paper reflecting on how well they meet the Level II expectations in their journey toward becoming an "Accountable Professional." It is scored by the following rubric.

Scoring Rubric

Criteria	Beginning ✔ −	On Target ✔	Exceeds Expectation ✔ +	Score
Personal and professional learning and growth	Reflection does not connect to personal needs and experiences and/or does not reflect an effort to seek out growth experiences.	Reflection identifies self-initiative in seeking experiences for personal and professional growth beyond course requirements.	Reflection analyzes areas for personal and professional learning and growth that exceed the course requirements and shows evidence of collaboration with others in at least a beginning effort to obtain additional experiences.	
Personal and Professional Accountability	Reflection demonstrates nursing actions without necessary thought for personal and professional actions.	Reflection identifies and applies personal and professional accountability.	Reflection demonstrates the foundation for consistent personal accountability and responsibility. Provides at least two examples.	

Source: Developed by the undergraduate nursing department at Azusa Pacific University under the leadership of Professor Shila Wiebe, Director; Dr. Vicky Bowden, Curriculum Committee Chair; Professor Connie Austin, ePortfolio Program Director; and Dr. Julie Jantzi, Director of Institutional Assessment Planning. Reproduced with permission.

students' abilities to integrate personal as well professional experiences into the early stages of their emerging professional lives. Scorers grade reflective writings over the course of nursing students' studies against levels of achievement they expect students to demonstrate that correlate with the design of the curriculum and related educational experiences. This particular scoring rubric also asks graders to indicate the level of achievement translated into a numerical score.

- Appendix 5.1 at the end of this chapter presents a scoring rubric designed to assess the dimensions of undergraduate students' quantitative reasoning during the duration of their undergraduate studies. Scorers use a verbal achievement scale—*developing, proficient, accomplished*—to assess samples of student work at various times in their careers.

- Appendix 5.2 presents another approach to a rubric. This one focuses on assessing students' abilities to integrate the dimensions of information literacy through periodic sampling of student writing over time. This particular rubric was developed to assess the outcomes for information literacy developed by the Association of College & Research Libraries (www.ala.org/Content/NavigationMenu/ACRL/Standards_and_Guidelines/Information_Literacy_Competency_Standards_for_Higher_ Education.htm).

- Appendix 5.3, a scoring rubric used to assess interior design majors' capstone project, focuses on assessing how well students integrate and apply principles of design into their final design projects. That is, the scoring rubric identifies the criteria upon which professionals in the field of interior design reach judgment about a final product.

- Appendix 5.4 illustrates another example of a scoring rubric for a final project in psychology, a thesis. Assessing the level at which students meet the criteria that describe the professional components of a thesis in psychology, scorers apply these criteria to each component of the document to determine how well students demonstrate professional conventions and practices, disciplinary logic, and conformity to the standards of written English. Scoring may also involve *weighting* certain criteria, that is, placing increased value on certain ones. The summary sheet that records scorers' responses to students' theses (page 151) shows that students' literature

review and the quality of their writing, for example, have increased weight assigned to them. As this summary sheet also demonstrates, it is possible to convert students' scores into grades.

Analytic and Holistic Rubrics

Scorers may grade student work using an *analytic scoring rubric* that lists each criterion scorers rate as they read or observe students' work, as illustrated in Appendix 5.4. Analytic scoring rubrics provide detailed results about patterns of student achievement. Viewing the results of analytic scoring rubrics promotes targeted interpretation and decision making. For example, results that identify students' weak abilities to solve certain kinds of problems or take multiple perspectives on an issue lead to discussions about how to modify or change pedagogy; the design of curriculum, co-curriculum, instruction; and other educational opportunities to improve these thinking processes. These analytic scoring rubric patterns become fertile evidence upon which to base focused interpretations about students' strengths or weaknesses. Washington State University's Critical Thinking Project uses an analytic scoring rubric to identify strengths and weaknesses in students' ways of thinking across the curriculum. Scorers grade sample student writing based on seven criteria:

1. Identifies and summarizes the problem/question at issue (and/or the source's position)

2. Identifies and presents the *student's own* perspective and position as it is important to the analysis of the issue

3. Identifies and considers *other* salient perspectives and positions that are important to the analysis of the issue

4. Identifies and assesses the key assumptions

5. Identifies and assesses the quality of supporting data/evidence and provides additional data/evidence related to the issue

6. Identifies and considers the influence of the context on the issue

7. Identifies and assesses conclusions, implications, and consequences (wsuctproject.wsu.edu/ctr.htm)

Or, scorers may grade student work using a *holistic scoring rubric* that lists features of a work that scorers use to make more global judgments. Figure 5.1 is an example of a holistic scoring rubric that graders use to place students' portfolios in one

1.	• Incomplete and poorly organized portfolio that does not contain artifacts that demonstrate achievement of program outcomes • No accompanying summary or self-reflective sheets that describe the significance of the artifacts to the learner • Submissions overall that do not conform with conventions of English—spelling, grammatical, punctuation, and word usage errors
2.	• Incomplete portfolio that contains some artifacts that demonstrate achievement of program outcomes • No or a few summary or self-reflective sheets that describe the significance of the artifacts to the learner • Submissions overall that do not conform to conventions of English—spelling, grammatical, punctuation, and word usage errors
3.	• Complete portfolio that includes artifacts that demonstrate achievement of program outcomes • Each artifact accompanied with summary and reflective sheets that describe the significance of the artifact to the learner • Submissions overall that conform to conventions of English—spelling, grammar, punctuation, and word usage
4.	• Complete portfolio that includes artifacts that demonstrate achievement of program outcomes • Each artifact accompanied with summary and reflective sheets that chronologically describe the significance of the artifact to the learner • Submissions that conform to conventions of English with only minor mistakes in spelling, grammar, punctuation, and word usage

FIGURE 5.1   Holistic Scoring Rubric for a Program-Level Portfolio

of four achievement levels. Each portfolio receives one numerical score based on scorers' assessment of the qualities of a portfolio. Holistic scoring rubrics are useful for categorizing student work to determine overall performance levels in response to a task, such as developing a program-level portfolio.

One of the rubrics that the service learning program asks raters to use as they read students' articulated learnings, illustrated in Chapter 3, Appendix 3.2, is a holistic critical thinking rubric that is applied to students' responses to both the academic and personal dimensions of their responses (adapted from Paul, 1993). Raters use a scale of 1–4 to assess students' critical thinking as represented in students' writing. Raters award a level four to students' writing if, overall, it meets the criteria listed in the institutional example in Box 5.2.

STRATEGIES TO DEVELOP SCORING RUBRICS

Developing internal scoring rubrics is another line of collaborative work that draws on multiple levels of expertise inside and outside of an institution and its

programs. How are they developed? Who develops them? What are the standards against which student work is applied? How do we assure they represent standards of quality? Quality in Undergraduate Education (QUE), a national project supported by the Education Trust and the National Association of System Heads (NASH) in association with Georgia State University, defines quality standards as "high, achievable, and credible to policy makers, students, families, and employers" (www.gsu.edu/~wwwque/about/advantages.html). A cluster of 10 two-year and four-year colleges and universities from four states is working to articulate expectations for undergraduate learning in six disciplines.

The core working groups that select or design direct methods may also be the same core working groups that develop scoring rubrics because these two processes are interdependent. To develop standards of quality, institutions and programs invite additional external members into this group: internship advisors, professionals within the local community, representatives from business advisory groups, representatives from professional organizations, representative from

---

BOX 5.2 INSTITUTIONAL EXAMPLE: *North Carolina State University*

- Consistently avoids typographical, spelling, and grammatical errors
- Makes clear the connection(s) between the service-related experience and the dimension being discussed
- Makes statements of fact that are accurate, supported with evidence **(Accuracy)**
  - For Academic Articulated Learning Statements: Accurately identifies, describes, and applies appropriate academic principle
- Consistently expands on, expresses ideas in another way, or provides examples/illustrations **(Clarity)**
- Describes learning that is relevant to Articulated Learning category and keeps the discussion specific to the learning being articulated **(Relevance)**
- Addresses the complexity of the problem; answers important question(s) that are raised; avoids over-simplifying when making connections **(Depth)**
- Gives meaningful consideration to alternative points of view, interpretations **(Breadth)**
- Demonstrates a line of reasoning that is logical, with conclusions or goals that follow clearly from it **(Logic)**
- Draws conclusions, sets goals that address a (the) major issue(s) raised by the experience **(Significance)**

Source: Contributed by Sarah Ash and Patti Clayton, North Carolina State University. Reproduced with permission.

organizations that employ students, colleagues from surrounding two- and four-year institutions, and colleagues from K–12 whose knowledge and expertise are useful in developing criteria that contribute to students' successful entrance and progression in learning.

In addition, this group draws on

1. emerging work in professional and disciplinary organizations focused on establishing criteria and standards for judgment;

2. available research on learning in a particular field of study focused on identifying abilities, traits, and ways of knowing and problem solving that mark progression of learning in that field of study. Understanding the progression of learning contributes to developing scoring rubrics that capture learning over time against agreed-upon criteria and standards of judgment.

Development of Scoring Rubrics

The following process is intended to guide core working groups to develop scoring rubrics. Specific strategies under each major step of the process are helpful in reaching consensus about the criteria and levels of achievement of a scoring rubric:

1. After agreement on a direct assessment method, have each member of the core working group independently list the criteria to apply to students' text and then describe each criterion.

Specific strategies that produce a pool of responses include the following:

a. Ask a member to research disciplinary or professional organizations' current work focused on student learning.

Example: The Quality in Undergraduate Education project (QUE) is designed to develop standards in six disciplines: biology, chemistry, English, history, mathematics, and physics (www.gsu.edu/~wwwque/about/index.html). Members of the project expect all of their departmental graduates to reach at least the level of proficiency against the standards they articulate. Some current work involves creating scoring rubrics for representative tasks in a discipline (www.gsu.edu/~wwwque/standards/discipline.html) similar to the scoring rubric in Appendix 5.4 designed to assess psychology majors' senior theses.

Example: In her work on making the implicit explicit, Barbara Lovitts (2002) is working with doctorate-granting institutions to develop scoring rubrics to assess dissertations. Working with different disciplines, she and those involved in the project will identify similarities and differences in the defining criteria of dissertations (www.carnegiefoundation .org/CID/ashe?lovitts.pdf).

b. Ask a member to research literature on learning in a discipline or field of study to ascertain what that current research reveals about how students learn. The National Research Council's *Knowing What Students Know: The Science and Design of Educational Assessment* provides a rich resource on this kind of research, such as criteria that distinguish novice and expert ways of thinking and behaving (2001).

c. Derive rubrics from work that students have submitted previously in response to similar tasks, such as case studies, research projects, or problems. That is, reviewing representative student work identifies the traits that distinguish exemplary from less successful work. Review representative student work graded from A to F to determine criteria and levels of achievement that identify the continuum of learning and its markers along the way.

d. Interview students to find out what they believe they have mastered over time; that is, let their experiences inform your rubric. Developing student interview protocols, similar to those developed by Marton and Saljo to learn about students' approaches to reading (see Chapter 3, page 67), may also provide valuable information about what students are able to accomplish over time that can inform development of a scoring rubric. Interviews with tutors and graduate teaching assistants also provide an opportunity to explore and identify criteria that they, themselves, directly experience in their educative roles within the institution.

e. Ask members to describe what they have observed about student learning based on students' learning continuum. That is, what are students able to achieve over time?

The scoring rubric developed at Washington State University (page 123) was developed from research on learning, as well as from local expertise about students' learning over time, and practice in using the rubric (wsuctproject.wsu.edu/ctm_1p_files/ frame.htm).

2. In a group meeting, identify overlap among the pooled criteria and descriptions to identify consensus about the criteria. Review contributions that do not overlap and discuss the necessity of including them in the scoring rubric. As a group, identify levels of achievement and write descriptions of each criterion within the context of a level of achievement. If it is not possible to achieve consensus about a criterion or its level of achievement, the following process provides the opportunity to test a draft that may have questionable criteria or unclear descriptions of achievement levels.

3. Pilot test the scoring rubric by applying it to samples of student work that have been previously handed in. Revise the rubric based on these pilot tests and continue to apply it to samples of student work until the group has reached consensus that it clearly describes each criterion along levels of achievement. If, during these pilot tests, student texts do not represent a criterion, the finding may point to gaps in students' learning opportunities.

STRATEGIES TO ASSURE INTERRATER RELIABILITY

Once a scoring rubric has been refined based on the preceding strategies and before it is applied for institution- and program-level assessment, establishing the reliability of raters as they apply a rubric is essential. This is called *interrater reliability*. This process assures that individuals' ratings are reliable across different samples and samples from representative student populations. Raters may consist of faculty and staff within the institution or external reviewers such as internship advisors, alumni, professionals within the community, or faculty from nearby institutions.

Calibration, the process of establishing interrater reliability in scoring student texts, is developed over successive applications of a scoring rubric to student work, semester after semester and sometimes over several years, to assure that rater responses are consistent across representative student populations. Specifically, do raters score students' work the same way? Do major discrepancies exist? The following steps establish interrater reliability:

1. Ask raters to independently score a set of student samples that reflects the range of texts students produce in response to a direct method.

2. Bring raters together to review their responses to identify patterns of consistent and inconsistent responses.

3. Discuss and then reconcile inconsistent responses.

4. Repeat the process of independent scoring on a new set of student samples.

5. Again, bring all scorers together to review their responses to identify patterns of consistent and inconsistent responses.

6. Discuss and then reconcile inconsistent responses.

This process is repeated until raters reach consensus about applying the scoring rubric. Ordinarily, two to three of these sessions calibrate raters' responses. In actual practice, two raters score student work; a third rater may be called upon if there is a disagreement between the two scorers' responses.

To calibrate scorers' responses to the critical thinking criteria illustrated on page 135, Ash and Clayton ask each member of a team of scorers to independently evaluate students' work. Scorers report their individual evaluations, and the team meets as a whole to compare the results, discuss discrepancies, and reconcile the differences through a process of reaching consensus on each score. This sharing of evaluative judgments supports an iterative process of revision of the educational experiences themselves that increases their ability to produce the desired student outcomes. In addition, repetition of this over time—and with an ever-widening set of scorers—assists instructors in their own use of the articulated learning process and also establishes interrater reliability to ensure consistent scoring of student texts. (Contributed by Sarah Ash and Patti Clayton, North Carolina State University.)

THREADED OPPORTUNITIES FOR INSTITUTIONAL AND STUDENT LEARNING

Internally developed, scoring rubrics become a way to align teachers and learners in tracking students' learning over time against institution- and program-level criteria and standards of judgment. Members of the institutional community learn about students' achievement and use it to focus program- and institution-level

dialogue on pedagogy and educational practices. In addition, threaded throughout students' undergraduate and graduate education, scoring rubrics provide students and educators with a running record of students' development and achievement. Scoring rubrics used in individual courses and services also promote learning as integrative, as opposed to an aggregation of experiences. Students begin to see connections between and among courses—how each of their educational experiences contributes to their learning and development.

Integration is a key element that institution- and program-level rubrics can capture. They focus on and value the whole of students' texts—their performances, interactions, creations, written and oral presentations, and research projects—through viewing the parts that contribute to a whole text. Strength in one criterion does not guarantee a final high score—a score that may be affected by weaker performance under other criteria. Scoring rubrics focus on both the content of a text as well as its execution, that is, the qualities that enable or impede others to interpret that text, such as structure, use of design principles, coherence within a text, use of disciplinary logic, precision and accuracy, and depth of analysis. Whereas individual courses or educational experiences may focus on components of learning, such as how to write or how to solve certain kinds of problems, at the institution- and program-level value is placed on how well students integrate what they have learned to solve a new problem, create a work of art, treat a patient, or address a societal issue.

Just as sharing outcomes with students upon matriculation into an institution or a major helps to orient them to their education, sharing institution- and program-level scoring rubrics with them also orients them to viewing learning as a process. Sharing outcomes and scoring rubrics encourages student responsibility for learning. Together, outcome statements and scoring rubrics create a context against which students, as well as institutions and their programs, chart progress and achievement. Along with fostering a student work ethic built on practice, chronological use of scoring rubrics in a program, a service, or across an institution develops self-reflection about the dimensions of learning and representations of learning. Scoring rubrics also foster students' commitment to improvement and an understanding that the process of learning involves synthesis—lifelong learning dispositions that higher education aspires its students to develop.

WORKS CITED

Erwin, T. D., & Wise, S. E. (2002). A scholarly-practitioner model of assessment. In T. W. Banta & Associates, *Building a scholarship of assessment* (p. 75). San Francisco: Jossey-Bass.

Dressel, P. L. (1976). *Handbook of academic evaluation* (p. 303). San Francisco: Jossey-Bass.

Lovitts, B. E. (2002, November). Making the implicit explicit: A conceptual approach for assessing the outcomes of doctoral education. Paper presented at the 2002 ASHE meeting, November 21–24, Sacramento, California. Available: *www.carnegiefoundation.org/CID/ashe?lovitts.pdf.* Additional information available from Barbara Lovitts: *Blovitts@aol.com.*

National Research Council. (2001). *Knowing what students know: The science and design of educational assessment.* Washington, DC: National Academy Press.

Paul, R. (1993). *Critical thinking: What every person needs to survive in a rapidly changing world.* Santa Rosa, CA.

Foundation for Critical Thinking. Washington State University. Critical Thinking Rubric: *wsuctproject.wsu.edu/ctr.htm.*

ADDITIONAL RESOURCES

California State University. Links to examples of scoring rubrics including disciplinary rubrics: *www.calstate.edu/acadaff/sloa/links/using-rubrics.shtml.*

Hanson, G. R. (Ed.). (2003). *Let's do assessment* (Assessment in Student Affairs; Interactive CD Rom Series 1). Washington, DC: NASPA.

Hanson, G. R. (Ed.). (2003). *Let's talk assessment* (Assessment in Student Affairs; Interactive CD Rom Series 2). Washington, DC: NASPA.

Hanson, G. R. (Ed.). (2003). *Let's use assessment* (Assessment in Student Affairs; Interactive CD Rom Series 3). Washington, DC: NASPA.

Huba, M. E., & Freed, J. E. (2000). *Learner-centered assessment on college campuses: Shifting the focus from teaching to learning* (pp. 151–200, 201–232). Boston, MA: Allyn & Bacon.

Linn, R. (2000). Assessments and accountability. ER online, 29(2), 4–14.

Murphy, P. D., & Gerst, J. (1996, May). Assessment of Student Learning in Graduate Programs. Paper presented at the Annual Forum of the Association of Institutional Research, Albuquerque, New Mexico. Abstract available: *searcheric.org/scripts/seget2 .asp?want=http://searcheric.org/ericdb/ED409765.htm.*

Sanders, W., & Horn, S. (1995, March). Educational assessment reassessed: The usefulness of standardized and alternative measures of student achievement as indicators for the assessment of educational outcomes. *Education Policy Analysis Archives,* 3(6): *epaa.asu.edu/epaa/v3n6.html.*

Walvoord, B. E., & Anderson, V. J. (1998). *Effective grading: A tool for learning and assessment.* San Francisco: Jossey-Bass.

Additional Resources for K–16

Focused primarily on K–12, the following resources may also include examples of rubrics in higher education. They serve as a useful overview of examples and strategies for creating analytic and holistic scoring rubrics, including creating them online.

Meta-sites

Relearning by Design Resource Center: *www.relearning .org/resources/PDF/rubric_sampler.pdf.*

Kathy Schrock's Guide for Educators—Assessment Rubrics: *school.discovery.com/schrockguide/ assess.html.*

Arter, J. A., & McTighe, J. (2001). *Scoring rubrics in the classroom: Using performance criteria for assessing and improving student performance.* Thousand Oaks, CA: Corwin Press.

Marzano, R. J., Pickering, D., & McTighe, J. (1993). *Assessing student outcomes: Performance assessment using the dimensions of learning model.* Alexandria, VA: Association for Supervision and Curriculum Development.

Wiggins, G. (1989, May) A true test: Toward more authentic and equitable assessment. *Phi Delta Kappan,* 703–713.

Wiggins, G. (1997). Feedback: How learning occurs. In *Assessing impact: evidence and action* (pp. 31–39). Washington, DC: American Association for Higher Education.

Wiggins, G. (1998). *Educative assessment: Designing assessments to inform and improve student performance.* San Francisco, CA: Jossey-Bass.

Examples of Some Rubrics Developed at Colleges and Universities

Meta-site: American Association for Higher education: *www.aahe.org/assessment/web.htm#Rubrics.*

Bond, L. (1996). Norm and criterion-referenced testing. *Practical Assessment, Research & Evaluation,* 5, 2.

California State University Monterey Bay: *essp.csumb .edu/capstone/criteria.html.*

Southern Illinois University Edwardsville: *www.siue.edu/ ~deder/assess/cats/rubex.html.*

WORKSHEETS, GUIDES, AND EXERCISES

1. *Development of a Scoring Rubric.* In conjunction with designing a direct method of assessment, the same or a separate core working group will develop an accompanying scoring rubric. If you are a member of that group, consider how that group might use one or more of the following strategies to develop a scoring rubric for an agreed-upon method.

Strategies for Developing a Scoring Rubric

- Research disciplinary or professional organizations' current work focused on student learning.

- Research literature on learning in a discipline or field of study to ascertain what that current research reveals about indicators of student learning.

- Derive rubrics from student work that is similar to the text the direct method will prompt students to generate.

- Interview students to find out what they believe they have mastered over time.

- Develop a protocol to track students' learning over time in order to derive criteria.

- Interview colleagues about students' learning progression based on their observations of student learning.

2. *Determination of Assessment Criteria.* Use the following format to ask members of a core working group or a wider group of individuals who contribute to students' learning to fill in descriptors for both the achievement levels and criteria that raters will use to assess a specific student assignment in response to an agreed-upon assessment method.

	Scale	Scale	Scale	Scale	Scale
Criterion 1					
Criterion 2					
Criterion 3					
Criterion 4					
Criterion 5					
Criterion 6					

3. *Development and Evaluation of a Composite Rubric.* From the individually designed rubrics, develop a composite rubric and ask members of a core working group to evaluate the composite rubric considering the following criteria and using the following sheet:

- How clearly is each criterion under each achievement scale described?
- Identify overlap in criteria and performance descriptors to assure differentiation among all criteria according to a level of achievement.
- How clearly is each criterion differentiated along the continuum of achievement?
- Is any language unclear or ambiguous?

	Particular Observation Worth Sharing with the Larger Group
Criterion 1	
Criterion 2	
Criterion 3	
Criterion 4	
Criterion 5	
Criterion 6	
Criterion 7	

4. *Interrater Reliability.* Once a core working group has reached consensus about a scoring rubric, raters go through a calibration period to ascertain how well they consistently apply that rubric to samples of student work that are also representative of the institutional population. To pilot an internally developed rubric, ask raters to apply a final scoring rubric to sample student work. Go through the following process to assure interrater reliability before the team of scorers undertakes the formal scoring process:

   a. Ask raters to independently score a set of student samples that reflect the range of texts students produce in response to a direct method.

   b. Bring raters together to review their responses to identify patterns of consistent and inconsistent responses.

   c. Discuss and then reconcile inconsistent responses.

   d. Repeat the process of independent scoring on a new set of student samples.

   e. Again, bring all scorers together to review their responses to identify patterns of consistent and inconsistent responses.

   f. Discuss and then reconcile inconsistent responses.

5. *Interrater Reliability.* Use the following chart to identify discrepancies in scorers' responses and to discuss areas of disagreement before another scoring session is scheduled. After each round of scoring, use this sheet to continue to identify and then resolve discrepancies among scorers before they formally assess student work. In a formal process, establishing a resolution panel to address discrepancies will be important to assure consistency in the application of criteria and scales of achievement.

	Rater Score	Rater Score	Area of Disagreement	Agreement Reached? (Yes/No) Final Resolution of Difference
Criterion 1				
Criterion 2				
Criterion 3				
Criterion 4				
Criterion 5				
Criterion 6				

6. *Student Assessment.* If you find the following format useful, develop a version of it to provide feedback to students at the end of their first year of study in a discipline. You may wish to create additional versions of this format to reflect increasingly more complex expectations as you conduct formative and summative assessment of students.

FRESHMAN YEAR PORTFOLIO REVIEW

This review is designed to evaluate and provide feedback to students during their freshman year. The review is marked on a scale from 1 to 5. A mark of 1 to 2 indicates below average progress, 3 is average. A mark of 4 to 5 indicates above average progress.

The Student's Work in General: 1 2 3 4 5

1. Is the body of work well rounded and grounded in the fundamentals of art?   1 2 3 4 5

2. Does the body of work form both a technical and an expressive base for
   the student's success in future studies?   1 2 3 4 5

3. What level of problem-solving skills does the student demonstrate?   1 2 3 4 5

4. Has the student developed his/her powers of observation?   1 2 3 4 5

5. Does the student demonstrate the ability to make expressive/sensitive
   choices in his/her creative work?   1 2 3 4 5

6. Does the student have the ability to critically and verbally analyze his/her own work?   1 2 3 4 5

7. Does the student have the ability to make reference to philosophy/art history?   1 2 3 4 5

8. Does the student have a professional attitude?   1 2 3 4 5

9. Is the student well organized for the presentation?   1 2 3 4 5

The Student's Specific Skills: 1 2 3 4 5

1. Does the work show knowledge in the use of perspective?   1 2 3 4 5

2. Does the work demonstrate abilities in 2-D design principles?   1 2 3 4 5

3. Does the work demonstrate abilities in 3-D design principles?   1 2 3 4 5

4. Does the work employ sensitive/expressive use of materials?   1 2 3 4 5

5. Does the work show knowledge of color theory?   1 2 3 4 5

6. Does the work demonstrate the abilities to draw

   a. animate objects?   1 2 3 4 5

   b. inanimate objects?   1 2 3 4 5

7. Does the work demonstrate the abilities to draw the human figure?   1 2 3 4 5

Comments

Student Name _____

Major _____

Faculty Reviewer _____

Date _____

Freshman Portfolio Review

Source: Contributed by Julie Stewart-Pollack, Rocky Mountain College of Art & Design. Reproduced with permission.

APPENDIX 5.1 INSTITUTIONAL EXAMPLE: *New Jersey City University Quantitative Reasoning Scoring Rubric*

Student Name: _____ **Date:** _____

Course Title: _____ **Reference #:** _____

Students must be able to use the knowledge, skills, and attitudes of mathematics and the sciences for effective quantitative reasoning.

Assessment Criteria	N/A*	N/E**	Developing	Proficient	Accomplished
1. Results and conclusions:					
A. Reasonableness of results	☐	☐	☐ Results often unreasonable	☐ Results usually reasonable	☐ Results almost always reasonable
B. Checks results for correctness	☐	☐	☐ Very seldom checks	☐ Usually checks	☐ Almost always checks
C. Justifies conclusions	☐	☐	☐ Very little justification	☐ Some justification but incomplete	☐ Extensive justification
2. Uses the language and methods of mathematics in other contexts					
A. Correctly	☐	☐	☐ Many errors	☐ Some errors	☐ Very few errors
B. Independently	☐	☐	☐ Requires much help	☐ Requires some help	☐ Very seldom needs help
3. Uses the language and methods of the sciences in other contexts					
A. Correctly	☐	☐	☐ Many errors	☐ Some errors	☐ Very few errors
B. Independently	☐	☐	☐ Requires much help	☐ Requires some help	☐ Very seldom needs help
4. Uses scientific methods of analysis and experimentation					
A. Appropriately	☐	☐	☐ Applications often inappropriate	☐ Applications seldom inappropriate	☐ Applications never inappropriate
B. Accurately	☐	☐	☐ Many errors	☐ Some errors	☐ Very few errors

Levels

Continued

APPENDIX 5.1   (CONTINUED)

Assessment Criteria	N/A*	N/E**	Developing	Proficient	Accomplished
				Levels	
C. With insight and knowledge	❑	❑	❑ Exhibits little knowledge or insight	❑ Exhibits considerable knowledge and insight	❑ Exhibits full knowledge and insight
D. With complete documentation	❑	❑	❑ Very little documentation	❑ Some documentation but incomplete	❑ Complete documentation
5. Uses examples, counter-examples and mathematical proof					
A. With understanding and insight	❑	❑	❑ Exhibits almost no understanding or insight	❑ Exhibits considerable understanding and insight	❑ Exhibits complete understanding and insight
B. Correctly	❑	❑	❑ Makes many errors	❑ Makes some errors	❑ Makes very few errors
6. Uses conjecture and testing, mathematical modeling, computer simulation, and statistical techniques for realistic and relevant real-world applications	❑	❑	❑ Requires considerable guidance and explanation	❑ Requires some guidance and explanation	❑ Requires very little guidance and explanation
7. Uses various measure-ments, data-gathering techniques, sampling, probability, and descriptive and inferential statistics to support or reject claims of size, relationship, or relative accuracy					
A. With understanding and insight	❑	❑	❑ Exhibits almost no understanding or insight	❑ Exhibits considerable understanding and insight	❑ Exhibits complete understanding and insight
B. Correctly	❑	❑	❑ Makes many errors	❑ Makes some errors	❑ Makes very few errors

APPENDIX 5.1 (CONTINUED)

	*	**			
8. Uses a variety of graphical, tabular, numerical, algebraic, verbal, schematic, and experimental techniques to represent, interpret, and draw inferences from data or function values					
A. Correctly	□	□	□ Many errors	□ Some errors	□ Very few errors
B. Independently	□	□	□ Requires much help	□ Requires some help	□ Very seldom needs help
C. With understanding	□	□	□ Can represent but cannot interpret or draw inferences	□ Can represent and interpret but not draw inferences	□ Can represent, interpret, and draw inferences with much understanding
9. Creates generalizations from observed patterns and develops specific examples from general statements	□	□	□ Requires much assistance	□ Requires some assistance	□ Requires very little assistance
10. Engages in self-assessment	□	□	□ Synthesizes feedback with assistance	□ Synthesizes feedback and integrates with self-analysis	□ Utilizes self-assessment and feedback to modify performance

*Not Applicable
**No Evidence

Source: Contributed by Dr. Richard Riggs, Professor and Chairperson, Mathematics Department, New Jersey City University. Reproduced with permission.

Assessment Criteria

	Novice	Developing	Proficient	Accomplished	Not Applicable
Extent of Information					
1. Defines and articulates the need for information	☐ Cannot develop a thesis statement	☐ Develops a clear thesis statement, formulates a question based on information needed	☐ Defines or modifies information to achieve a manageable focus and can identify key concepts and terms	☐ Combines existing information and original thought, experimentation and/or analysis to produce new information	☐
2. Identifies a variety of types and formats of potential sources	☐ Does not recognize that knowledge is organized into disciplines and cannot locate information beyond local and print resources	☐ Recognizes that knowledge is organized into disciplines and identifies the value differences of potential resources	☐ Identifies the purpose and audience of potential resources, reevaluates the nature and extent of information needed, and differentiates between primary and secondary sources	☐ Recognizes the use and importance of primary and secondary sources and realizes that information may need to be constructed with raw data from primary sources ☐ Knows how information is formally and informally produced, organized, and disseminated	☐
Access to Information					
1. Selects the most appropriate investigative methods of information retrieval systems	☐ Cannot select appropriate investigative methods for information retrieval	☐ Identifies appropriate methods and investigates the benefits and applicability	☐ Investigates the scope, content and organization of information retrieval systems	☐ Selects efficient and effective approaches from the investigative method or information retrieval system	☐

2. Constructs and implements effectively designed search strategies	❑ Cannot construct or implement search strategies	❑ Identifies key words, synonyms and related terms	❑ Constructs a search strategy appropriate to the information retrieval system	❑ Selects discipline-specific search vocabulary and develops an appropriate research plan
3. Retrieves information using a variety of methods	❑ Cannot retrieve information effectively from any source	❑ Uses various search systems in a variety of formats	❑ Uses various classification schemes and other systems to locate information resources and identifies specific sites for exploration	❑ Uses specialized services (on site or online) as well as surveys, letters, interviews, and other forms of inquiry to retrieve primary information
4. Refines the search strategy	❑ Cannot assess the quantity, quality, and relevance of search results	❑ Revises and repeats searches effectively	❑ Identifies gaps in retrieved information and determines if search strategy should be revised	❑ Assesses quantity, quality, and relevant search results to determine whether alternative information retrieval systems or investigative method should be used
5. Extracts, records, and manages the information and its sources	❑ Cannot select appropriate information technologies to gather information	❑ Selects appropriate sources and can create a system for organizing the information	❑ Differentiates between types of sources and understands the elements and syntax of citations	❑ Uses various technologies to manage information and can record all pertinent citation information for a wide range of resources
Evaluation of Information				
1. Summarizes main ideas	❑ Cannot select main ideas from text information gathered	❑ Selects data accurately	❑ Identifies verbatim material and appropriately quotes it	❑ Summarizes main ideas from information sources and can restate textual concepts in own words

Continued

APPENDIX 5.2   (CONTINUED)

Assessment Criteria

	Novice	Developing	Proficient	Accomplished	Not Applicable
2. Articulates and applies initial criteria for information and its sources	☐ Cannot evaluate information	☐ Examines and compares information from various sources to evaluate reliability, validity and timeliness, authority, and point of view or bias	☐ Analyzes the structure and logic supporting arguments or methods ☐ Recognizes prejudice, deception, or manipulation	☐ Recognizes the cultural, physical, or other contexts within which the information was created and understands the impact of context on information	☐
3. Synthesizes main ideas to construct new concepts	☐ Cannot synthesize main ideas	☐ Uses computer and other technologies for studying the interaction of ideas and other phenomena	☐ Recognizes interrelationships among concepts and combines them into potentially useful primary statements with supporting evidence	☐ Extends initial synthesis to construct new hypotheses that may require additional information	☐
4. Compares new knowledge with prior knowledge to determine the value added, contradictions, or other unique characteristics of information	☐ Cannot determine whether information satisfies the information need	☐ Tests theories with discipline-appropriate techniques	☐ Uses consciously selected criteria to evaluate information from other sources and draw conclusions based upon information gathered	☐ Integrates new information with previous knowledge, can select information that provides evidence for the topic ☐ Determines probable accuracy by questioning the source, the limitations of gathering information, and the reasonableness of the conclusions	☐ ☐

APPENDIX 5.2 (CONTINUED)

5. Determines whether new knowledge has an impact on the individual's value system and takes steps to reconcile differences	❑ Cannot determine whether new knowledge has an impact on one's value system	❑ Investigates differing viewpoints	❑ Investigates differing viewpoints to determine whether to reject viewpoints encountered	❑ Determines whether to incorporate viewpoints encountered into one's own value system
6. Validates understanding and interpretation of information through discourse with others, including experts and/or practitioners	❑ Cannot effectively participate in discussions	❑ Participates effectively in classroom and other discussions	❑ Effectively uses class-sponsored electronic communications forums	❑ Seeks appropriate expert opinions through a variety of mechanisms
7. Determines whether the initial query should be revised	❑ Cannot determine if information needs have been satisfied	❑ Determines if original information need has been satisfied or if added information is needed	❑ Reviews search strategy and incorporates additional concepts as necessary	❑ Reviews information retrieval sources and search strategies used to revise initial queries
Use of Information				
1. Applies new and prior information to the planning and creation of a particular product or performance	❑ Cannot organize content in a meaningful way	❑ Manipulates digital text, images, and data from original locations to format a new context	❑ Organizes content in support of purposes and format and articulates knowledge and skills from prior experiences	❑ Integrates new and prior information, including quotations and paraphrasing, in a manner that supports the product or performance
2. Revises the development process for the product or performance	❑ Cannot effectively revise work	❑ Maintains a journal or log of activities	❑ Maintains a log that includes an evaluation of information relevant to the data found	❑ Reflects on past successes and failures and develops alternative strategies in searching, evaluating, and communicating

Continued

APPENDIX 5.2   (CONTINUED)

Assessment Criteria

	Novice	Developing	Proficient	Accomplished	Not Applicable
3. Communicates the product or performance effectively	❑ Cannot communicate effectively	❑ Uses a limited range of information technology	❑ Uses a range of information technology ❑ Chooses communication medium/format that best supports the purposes of the product or performance and the intended audience	❑ Incorporates principles of design and communication and communicates clearly to the intended audience	❑
Ethical and Legal Issues 1. Understands ethical, legal, and socioeconomic issues surrounding information and information technology	❑ Does not understand the ethical, legal, and socioeconomic issues surrounding information and information technology	❑ Identifies and discusses issues related to free versus fee-based access in print and electronic environments	❑ Identifies and discusses issues of privacy, security, censorship, and freedom of speech	❑ Demonstrates an understanding of intellectual property, copyright, and fair use of copyrighted material	❑
2. Follows copyright and other laws, regulations, institutional policies, and etiquette related to the access and use of information resources	❑ Does not follow appropriate laws, policies, and "netiquette"	❑ Uses appropriate passwords, ID, and "netiquette" in the collection of information ❑ Understands what plagiarism is and does not plagiarize	❑ Complies with institutional policies on information resources and preserves the integrity of information sources, equipment, systems, and facilities	❑ Obtains, stores, and disseminates text, data, images, and sounds within legal guidelines ❑ Understands relevant institutional policies including those on human subject research	❑

	Does not acknowledge sources	Inappropriately acknowledges sources	Usually acknowledges sources in an appropriate style	Consistently cites sources in an appropriate style and posts permission-granted notices for copyrighted material, where applicable
3. Acknowledges the use of information sources	❑	❑	❑	❑
Self-Assessment	Identifies major weaknesses and strengths	Synthesizes feedback and integrates with self-analysis	Synthesizes feedback and integrates with self-analysis	Utilizes self-assessment and feedback to determine means of modifying performance
1. Self-regulates and sets goals	❑	❑	❑	❑

Source: The Association of College and Research Libraries (2000). *Information Literacy Competency Standards for Higher Education*. Chicago, IL: ACRL. Rubric developed by G. Bulaong, Library Director; Dr. H. Hoch, Chair, Biology; Prof. R. Matthews, Business Administration; New Jersey City University. 3/4/03. Reproduced with permission.

APPENDIX 5.3 INSTITUTIONAL EXAMPLE: *Rocky Mountain College of Art & Design*

INTERIOR DESIGN STUDIO FINAL PROJECT CRITERIA

DESIGN CONCEPT

Excellent: Concept is clear, well defined, and skillfully and appropriately applied throughout the project.

Good: Concept is clear, well defined, and applied throughout the project.

Needs Improvement: Concept needs development and is applied inconsistently in the project.

Unsatisfactory: Concept is poorly developed and defined. There is little evidence of application of concept in the project.

PROGRAMMING

Excellent: All steps of the programming process are thorough, consistent, and complete and address all required areas of the design in the standard format.

Good: All steps of the programming process are complete and address all required areas of the design.

Needs Improvement: Program has gaps in information and does not address all required areas of the design.

Unsatisfactory: Program is poorly written, excludes essential information, and does not address all required areas of the design.

SPACE PLANNING

Excellent: Space planning is highly functional; reflects major client and user needs; is ergonomically correct; and is appropriate for all intended purposes.

Good: Space planning is functional, reflects major client and user needs, is ergonomically correct, and is appropriate for most intended purposes.

Needs Improvement: Space planning needs development for function and ergonomics; reflects some client and user needs; and is appropriate for some intended purposes.

Unsatisfactory: Space planning does not function; shows little or no consideration of client and user needs; and is inappropriate for the intended purpose.

FURNITURE, FIXTURES, AND EQUIPMENT SELECTION

Excellent: Selections reflect a thorough understanding of the project and design requirements; function well for their intended purposes; reflect a high level of product knowledge; and are appropriate in scale and proportion.

Good: Selections reflect understanding of the project and design requirements; function for their intended purposes; reflect a developing level of product knowledge; and are appropriate in scale and proportion.

Needs Improvement: In most cases selections reflect an understanding of the project and design requirements; need better considerations for function; reflect need for product knowledge development; and are appropriate in scale and proportion.

Unsatisfactory: Selections do not reflect understanding of the project and design requirements; do not function well for their intended purposes; reflect little or no development of product knowledge; and are inconsistent in scale and proportion.

COLOR PALETTE

Excellent: Color palette is functionally and aesthetically appropriate for the established design concept; is creatively and appropriately applied; and reflects depth of understanding of human psychological and physical responses to color.

Good: Color palette is functionally and aesthetically appropriate for the established design concept; shows a developing level of creativity; and is applied with some understanding of human psychological and physical responses to color.

Needs Improvement: Color palette is not entirely functionally or aesthetically appropriate for the established design concept; reflects minimum levels of creativity; and is applied with a minor understanding of human psychological and physical responses to color.

Unsatisfactory: Color palette is not appropriate; lacks creativity; and indicates little or no understanding of human psychological and physical responses to color.

MATERIAL SELECTION

Excellent: Materials are very well chosen for function, aesthetics, pattern and textural relationships, and scale, and are very appropriate for the established design concept. Selections reflect a strong understanding of the characteristics indicative of quality, wearability, and maintenance.

Good: Materials are appropriate for function, aesthetics, pattern and textural relationships, scale, and the established design concept. Selections reflect a developing understanding of the characteristics of quality, wearability, and maintenance.

Needs Improvement: Materials are not entirely appropriate for function, aesthetics, pattern and textural relationships, scale, and the established design concept. Selections reflect limited understanding of the characteristics of quality, wearability, and maintenance.

Unsatisfactory: Materials are inappropriate and reflect little or no understanding of the characteristics of quality, wearability, and maintenance.

LIGHTING PLAN AND APPLICATION

Excellent: Lighting plan is technically accurate and demonstrates a high level of understanding of lighting principles and application.

Good: Lighting plan is technically accurate and demonstrates a developing understanding of lighting principles and application.

Needs Improvement: Lighting plan has minor technical problems and demonstrates a need for greater understanding of lighting principles and application.

Unsatisfactory: Lighting plan has major technical problems and demonstrates little or no understanding of lighting principles and application.

CODE COMPLIANCE (NOTE: THERE ARE ONLY THREE RATINGS FOR THIS CRITERION.)

Excellent: All national, state, and local codes and standards applicable to this project are met consistently and without exception.

Needs Improvement: Some minor code and standard violations are noted.

Unsatisfactory: Major code and standards violations are noted.

QUALITY OF DRAWINGS

Excellent: Drawings are clean, precise, easy to read, consistent, and technically correct, and meet all project requirements.

Good: Drawings are clean, consistent, and technically correct, and meet all project requirements.

Needs Improvement: Drawings need development, are inconsistent, and have minor technical problems.

Unsatisfactory: Drawings are difficult to read, imprecise, and inconsistent, and have major technical problems.

VISUAL PRESENTATION

Excellent: Format is consistent and aesthetically and technically appropriate for the project; conveys the visual information neatly and clearly; is very well organized; is correctly labeled; and shows a high level of creativity.

Good: Format is consistent and aesthetically and technically appropriate for the project; conveys the visual information clearly; shows developing skills of organization; is correctly labeled; and shows a developing level of creativity.

Needs Improvement: Format is not entirely appropriate for the project; shows some inconsistencies; needs work on neatness, creativity, and organization; and labeling is inconsistent.

Unsatisfactory: Format is not entirely appropriate for the project; is inconsistent, messy, disorganized, and incorrectly labeled; and lacks creativity.

VERBAL PRESENTATION

Excellent: Presentation is professionally organized and presented, beginning with introductions, orientation, and explanation of design concept, followed by a well-described overall walk-thru of the space, thorough explanation of design details, and a conclusion. Reasoning and rationale for design decisions are well described. Client and user requirements are well referenced. Presentation is made with enthusiasm, and responses to questions/comments/criticisms are mature and professional.

Good: Organization and presentation follow logical, professional format. Reasoning and rationale for design decisions and client and user requirements are occasionally referenced. Responses to questions/comments/criticisms are mature and professional.

Needs Improvement: Presentation needs work on organization and development of the professional format. Reasoning and rationale are unclear. Client and user requirements are rarely referenced, and responses to questions/comments/criticisms are often defensive and lack maturity.

Unsatisfactory: Presentation lacks organization and professional format. Reasoning and rationale are unexplained. Client and user requirements are never referenced, and responses to questions/comments/criticisms are inappropriate.

Source: Contributed by Julie Steward-Pollack, Rocky Mountain College of Art & Design. Reproduced with permission.

APPENDIX 5.4   INSTITUTIONAL EXAMPLE: *Hampden-Sydney College, Department of Psychology*

PRIMARY TRAIT SCORING SHEET FOR SENIOR THESIS

TITLE

5   Is appropriate in tone, structure, and length for psychology journals; fully explanatory of the study; identifies actual variables or theoretical issues of study; allows reader to anticipate design.

4   Is appropriate in tone, structure, and length; generally explanatory of the study; identifies some variables or theoretical issues of study; suggests design.

3   Suggests nature of the study; may identify only one variable of the study; does not allow reader to anticipate design; may contain superfluous information.

2   Identifies only one variable of the study; contains superfluous information; lacks design information or is misleading.

1   Patterned after another discipline or is missing.

ABSTRACT

5   Is appropriate in tone, structure, and length; fully descriptive of the study; identifies the problem, subjects, methods, findings, and conclusions or implications of the study.

4   Is appropriate in tone, structure, and length; generally descriptive of the study; identifies most but not all of the elements of the study; may contain some superfluous information.

3   May be lacking in tone, structure, or length; identifies only some elements of the study; does not summarize the article so that the reader understands what was done; contains superfluous information.

2   Inappropriate in tone, structure, and length; is not descriptive of the study; contains irrelevant, inappropriate, or incorrect information.

1   Inappropriate for the discipline or is missing.

INTRODUCTION: PROBLEM

5   Clear statement of problem under investigation; identifies the major construct or conceptual IV(s) and the behavior or conceptual DV(s) of interest; clearly states goal(s) of the study; problem identified in introductory paragraph.

4   Problem under investigation stated in general terms; identifies only some of the conceptual IV(s) and DV(s) of interest; goals of the study stated less clearly; problem identified in introductory paragraph.

3   Introductory paragraph may not identify problem under investigation; nature of problem being studied is not clear to the reader; conceptual IV(s) and DV(s) may not be identified; the reader has to find the goals of the study.

2   Problem not identified in introductory paragraph; reader may be unable to determine the problem being investigated; the purpose and/or goals of the study are not apparent to the reader.

1   Fails to identify purpose of the research.

INTRODUCTION: LITERATURE REVIEW

5   Articles reviewed are relevant to the problem being investigated; coverage of previous empirical and theoretical studies is thorough; issues are clearly explained; issues related to the problem are discussed in a logical progression; the number of articles cited is fully sufficient for the task.

4   Articles reviewed are relevant to the problem; coverage of previous empirical and theoretical studies may not be complete; some confusion over concepts or issues may be present; issues related to the problem may not be presented in a logical order; the number of articles is adequate for the task.

3   Some articles reviewed are irrelevant to the problem, or relevant articles from the literature are not reviewed; important information about articles being reviewed may be left out, and/or irrelevant information may be included; confusion about some concepts or issues being discussed; issues related to the problem are not organized in a way which effectively supports the argument, are arranged chronologically, or are arranged article by article; the number of articles is fewer than necessary for the task.

2 Articles reviewed are not directly related to the problem, though they may be in the same general conceptual area; important information from articles is ignored, and irrelevant information is included; lack of understanding of concepts or issues being discussed; presentation of previous research and theory not organized in a logical manner; inadequate number of articles reviewed.

1 Research and theory related to current problem is not reviewed or discussed.

INTRODUCTION: HYPOTHESIS

5 Clear statement of expectation(s) for outcome of study, relating IV(s) and DV(s) as identified in statement of problem; is or can be stated in "if . . . then" format.

4 Expectation for outcome(s) of study is stated, but not entirely clearly; one or more IV(s) or DV(s) may be left out of statement of hypothesis; is or can be stated in "if . . . then" format.

3 Expectation for outcome(s) of study not clear; one or more IV(s) or DV(s) are left out; is not or cannot be stated in "if . . . then" format.

2 Confusion about expected outcome of study; IV(s) and DV(s) are not identified; cannot be stated in "if . . . then" format.

1 No statement of hypothesis or expected outcome of study.

METHODS: DESCRIPTION

5 Contains effective, quantifiable, concisely organized information that allows the experiment to be replicated; is written so that all information inherent to the document can be related back to this section; identifies sources of all data to be collected; identifies sequential information in an appropriate chronology; does not contain unnecessary, wordy descriptions of procedures.

4 As in 5, but contains unnecessary or superfluous information or wordy descriptions within the section.

3 Presents a study that is definitely replicable; all information in document may be related to this section but fails to identify some sources of data or presents sequential information in a disorganized, difficult way; may contain unnecessary or superfluous information.

2 Presents a study that is marginally replicable; parts of the basic design must be inferred by the reader; procedures not quantitatively described; some information in Results or Discussion cannot be anticipated by reading the Methods section.

1 Describes the study so poorly or in such a nonscientific way that it cannot be replicated.

METHODS: EXPERIMENTAL DESIGN

5 Student selects experimental factors that are appropriate to the research purpose and audience; measures adequate aspects of these selected factors; establishes discrete subgroups for which data significance may vary; student demonstrates an ability to eliminate bias from the design and bias-ridden statements from the research; student selects appropriate sample size, equivalent groups, and statistics; student designs an elegant study.

4 As in 5, student designs an adequate study; choice of subgroups may exclude conditions that would make the study more complete, or may include conditions that are not necessary for answering the question.

3 Student selects experimental factors that are appropriate to the research purpose and audience; measures adequate aspects of these selected factors; establishes discrete subgroups for which data significance may vary; research is weakened by bias or by sample size of less than 10.

2 As above, but research is weakened by bias and inappropriate sample size.

1 Student designs a poor study.

METHODS: OPERATIONAL DEFINITIONS

5 Each of the independent (where appropriate) and dependent variables is stated in terms of clear and precise operational definitions.

4 Major independent (where appropriate) and dependent variables are stated in terms of clear and precise operational definitions; some variables may not be defined operationally, or operational definitions are not sufficiently precise and clear.

3 Only some of the variables are operationally defined, and the definitions given are not sufficiently precise and clear.

2 Major independent (where appropriate) and dependent variables are not operationally defined, and other variables are not defined in terms that are sufficiently clear and precise.

1 Variables are not operationally defined.

RESULTS: CHOICE OF STATISTICAL ANALYSIS

5 Student chooses methods of summarizing and analyzing data which are ideal for the dependent variable(s) (DVs), and for answering the research question given the parameters of the study (e.g., experimental or correlational study; number of IVs; number of levels of IVs; between- or within-subjects IVs; independent or matched treatment conditions; level of measurement of DV); data analysis is complete and thorough; statistical analyses are performed properly.

4 Choice of methods of summarizing and analyzing data is appropriate for the DV(s), and for answering the fundamental research question; statistical analyses are performed properly; data analysis may be incomplete: basic analyses are done, but not all follow-up or post hoc analyses are performed; analyses, though correct, are lacking in thoroughness.

3 As for 4, but some analyses may not be appropriate for the research question or analyses may not have been properly performed; descriptive statistics may be adequate, but inferential statistics are inadequate.

2 Data are not analyzed beyond the descriptive level; inferential statistics are not performed or are performed incorrectly.

1 There is no attempt to summarize or evaluate the data and only raw data are reported.

RESULTS: REPORTING STATISTICAL ANALYSES

5 Student has reported results of all statistical analyses using proper format; all information that is necessary to validate statistical findings is reported.

3 Results of statistical analyses are not completely reported, or are reported in incorrect format.

1 Results of statistical analyses are not reported.

RESULTS: GRAPHS AND TABLES

5 Choice and format of tables and graphs are appropriate for the data; the correct type of graph, where used, is used for each type of DV;

tables, where used, are clear and effectively represent the findings of the study; the graphs/tables are effectively captioned and labeled and have descriptive legends; graphs are visually "appealing" and do not have wasted space; one graph or table is presented per page.

4 As for 5, but with graphs or tables which do not present results as clearly; captions, labels, or legends are not completely descriptive of what is displayed in graph/table; graphs/tables may be more difficult to interpret; graphs may be lacking some visual "appeal."

3 Graphs/tables are not as clear as for 4; captions, labels, or legends may be inadequate or missing; an inappropriate type of graph may be used for the specific type of variable used; graphs may be too "busy," or have too much wasted space; size of graph as prepared is inappropriate (too small or large) for the circumstances; graph is lacking visual "appeal."

2 Graphs/tables do not clearly or effectively present the results; captions, labels, or legends are missing or inappropriate; too much or too little information is presented in the graphs or tables; graphs/tables are sloppy and appear to have been prepared in a haphazard manner.

1 Graphs/tables are missing or wholly inadequate for purposes of presenting the findings of the study; if present, graphs/tables have been prepared or drawn by hand.

DISCUSSION: INTERPRETATION

5 Student has summarized the purpose and findings of the research; has drawn inferences that are consistent with the data and scientific reasoning and relates these to the reader and intended audience; has identified whether findings are consistent or inconsistent with research hypothesis; has related results to previous research and theory; explains expected results and offers explanations for unexpected results; distinguishes between fact and implication.

4 As in 5, but may not adequately explain unexpected findings, or thoroughly relate findings to previous research or theory.

3 As in 4, but student overinterprets findings and draws conclusions from the data which may not be justified, or fails to draw conclusions which may reasonably be deduced from the findings.

2 Student summarizes the purpose and findings of the research; does not fully explain expected results, and ignores unexpected results.

1 Student does not relate findings to original hypothesis; results may or may not be summarized, but student fails to interpret their significance for the reader and the intended audience.

Discussion: Applications/Extensions of Findings

5 Student discusses possible applications of findings to contexts outside that of the study (e.g., outside of the laboratory); methods of the study are critically evaluated; student identifies questions that are unanswered as a result of current study; suggestions for further research or follow-up studies are identified and described.

4 As in 5, but student does not discuss possible applications to contexts outside that of the study.

3 As in 4, but the methods of the study are not critically evaluated.

2 Applications and extensions of research findings do not follow logically from the original research question or are not made in the context of a stated theoretical framework.

1 Student does not discuss applications or extensions of the research findings or suggest further research or follow-up studies.

References

5 List of reference citations is complete; all works cited in the body of the paper are listed, but only those works; references are listed in alphabetical order; proper APA reference citation format is followed.

4 As in 5, but references are listed that were not cited in the paper; minor errors in APA reference format may be present.

3 As in 4; student has not followed proper APA format for reference citations.

2 Student has failed to include all references cited in body of the paper; information in the references is incorrect or incomplete; references do not follow APA reference citation format.

1 Reference list is wholly inadequate, incomplete, or missing.

APA Format

5 Student has followed all conventions for proper format of a research report as described in *APA Publication Manual* (current edition).

4 Student has made minor deviations in APA format: e.g., incorrect form of page headers, improper section headings, or incorrect citation format of references.

3 As in 4, but more serious and consistent errors in APA format: e.g., subsections (e.g., *Subjects* or *Apparatus*) are omitted, absence of page headers or numbers, non–APA-style citation format, improper tense or voice for the paper, figures/tables inserted in incorrect location of paper, incorrect information included on title page or critical information omitted, incorrect references to figures and/or tables.

2 Major errors in APA format: e.g., major sections of paper omitted, absence of title page, information presented in incorrect sections, critical information omitted, figures or tables left out.

1 Paper does not follow APA format.

Writing Quality

5 Student has written elegantly and cogently, using proper grammar, syntax, punctuation, spelling; the paper has a neat appearance and is free of typographical errors; wording is appropriate to the context; paragraphs are well constructed; paper exhibits a logical "flow" from section to section; student used proper voice for the paper.

4 As in 5, but with occasional uncorrected typographical errors, or a very few minor errors in spelling, grammar, syntax, or punctuation; however, errors do not detract from the overall ability to convey meaning; the paper is not as elegant as in 5.

3 The paper exhibits numerous typographical errors and repeated errors in basic elements of writing; the student has not expressed ideas with clarity and precision; transitions between paragraphs are awkward; wording of sentences tends to be simplistic in style and content.

2 The student has displayed serious and consistent problems in basic writing skill; the ability to express ideas is compromised by the poor writing quality.

1 The paper is seriously deficient in quality of writing.

SENIOR THESIS PRIMARY TRAIT ANALYSIS—SCORING SHEET

Student name_____

Rater name _____

Category	Weight	Rating	Score
Title	1	_____	_____
Abstract	1	_____	_____
Introduction: Problem	1	_____	_____
Introduction: Literature Review	2	_____	_____
Introduction: Hypothesis	1	_____	_____
Methods: Description	1	_____	_____
Methods: Experimental Design	2	_____	_____
Methods: Operational Definitions	1	_____	_____
Results: Choice of Statistical Analyses	1	_____	_____
Results: Reporting Statistical Analyses	1	_____	_____
Results: Graphs and Tables	1	_____	_____
Discussion: Interpretation	2	_____	_____
Discussion: Applications/Extensions . . .	2	_____	_____
References	1	_____	_____
APA Format	1	_____	_____
Writing Quality	3	_____	_____
Total	**22**		_____

Letter grade conversion:

Letter Grade	Total Score	Average Rating			
			A	99–110	
A	93–110	4.25–5	A−	93–98	
B	75–92	3.4–4.2	B+	87–92	
C	57–74	2.6–3.35	B	81–86	
D	39–56	1.75–2.55	B−	75–80	
F	22–38	1.0–1.7	C+	69–74	
			C	63–68	
			C−	57–62	
			D+	51–56	
			D	39–50	
			F	22–38	

Source: Contributed by Robert T. Herdegen III, Hampden-Sydney College. Reproduced with permission.

Chapter 6

DESIGNING A CYCLE OF INQUIRY

It is reasonable to expect a college student to be able to apply in a new context a law of physics, or a proof in geometry, or a concept in history of which she just demonstrated mastery in her class. If when the circumstances of testing are slightly altered, the sought-after competence can no longer be documented, then understanding—in any reasonable sense of the term—has simply not been achieved.

—John Gardner, 1991

OVERVIEW: Designed to assist institution- and program-level assessment committees or working groups orchestrate and then move through one cycle of assessment, this chapter describes strategies for collecting evidence of student learning, scoring student responses, analyzing, representing, and interpreting results to make decisions about educational practices, and then re-entering the assessment cycle. Use this chapter to develop and implement a plan to assess one institution- or program-level outcome based on collectively agreed-upon assessment methods. Progressing through one cycle of inquiry helps an institution and its programs and services determine how to position assessment as a core institutional process—how to adapt existing processes, structures, and channels of communication or how to create new ones. The Worksheets, Guides, and Exercises at the end of this chapter are designed to guide two processes: (1) an institution- or a program-level cycle of inquiry and (2) the development of periodic reports that chronicle the assessment process, results, and next steps for each cycle of inquiry. These reports build institution- and program-level knowledge about student learning; they also become a way for colleges and universities to document their achievements, as well as their continuous learning.

A DESIGN FOR INSTITUTIONAL LEARNING

Executing a plan to derive and use evidence of student learning is more than a calendared sequence of tasks leading to a report of percentile results. Without reaching consensus about what we want to learn about our student population at the institution or program levels, information gathering can become a sterile act leading to broad brushstroke generalizations about student achievement. These generalizations may not take into account representative student populations and their learning chronologies, such as

what they knew or were able to demonstrate upon matriculation. Collective development of learning outcome statements, assessment methods, and standards and criteria clarify *what* members of an academic community want to learn about students' progression and eventual achievement. But to learn more specifically about students' learning in relation to educational practices we need to ask: *Whom* do we want to assess—all or samples of our students? And *how*, *where*, and *when* do we want to derive evidence—in what kinds of contexts? Answering these questions leads to a plan to collect, score, analyze, and interpret results of student achievement, processes that lead to institutional learning about the efficacy of educational practices.

Specifically, this chapter describes the primary tasks involved in collecting evidence of student learning and using the results to inform educational practices. These tasks include

- reaching consensus about methods to sample an institution's student population based on what an institution and its programs want to learn;

- identifying contexts and occasions for collecting evidence of student learning through direct and indirect assessment methods;

- scoring student projects, products, work, or responses;

- analyzing results and representing results in ways that promote collective interpretation;

- collectively interpreting and making decisions based on results, such as adapting, modifying, or innovating new ways of teaching and learning or developing new approaches to services or support programs;

- re-entering the assessment cycle to determine the efficacy of adaptations, modifications, and innovations.

METHODS OF SAMPLING

Who our student populations are and what we want to learn about them affect how we go about gathering evidence about their achievement. Establishing the goal of collective inquiry is important before launching into evidence gathering; otherwise, the process of collection may not produce the kinds of results that members of the educational community will find useful. Early identification of the guiding question or questions that lead inquiry also helps to identify other sources of information that may contribute to collaborative interpretation of results (see also page 160). Questions such as the following help to guide consensus about what an institution and its programs want to learn about their students:

- What do we want to know about achievement levels within our representative populations and their learning histories?

- What is the story we want to tell at the end of our inquiry?

- Are members of an academic community interested in making large-scale interpretations or targeted interpretations based on results? For example, is an institution or a program interested in pursuing the progress and attainment levels of students who place into college-level preparatory courses? How well do these students progress toward and eventually achieve institution- and program-level outcomes, especially as they transition out of those courses?

- Is an institution or a program interested in tracking students' achievement under different dominant pedagogies or curricular designs?

- Is an institution interested in tracking students according to their declared majors, areas of concentration, or areas of specialization to learn how well students integrate core curricular learning into their field of study?

Answering these kinds of questions lays the groundwork for actually assessing student learning.

Some Key Institutional Contributors

Answering these questions involves engaging the expertise of several key institutional contributors who also typically serve on groups that design or select assessment methods:

1. Institutional researchers
2. Registrars
3. Representatives from academic support services

These individuals are especially essential in guiding the actual collection, analysis, and interpretation of assessment results. Institutional researchers contribute expertise in the types and logistics of population sampling and in analyzing results that promote community interpretation. Registrars contribute in a variety of ways: they are able to identify and track student cohorts, such as students enrolled in different delivery methods of the same program—for example, online versus face-to-face versions of a program; they are able to identify students' course-taking patterns and information about student progression; and they are able to identify students' placement starting points. At both the front and back ends of the actual process of assessing student learning, they provide, then, valuable information about students' contexts for learning that assist collective interpretation. Individuals from student support services, including student tutors, contribute information about students' persistence in support services or the patterns of difficulty students experience. These kinds of information may well correlate with levels of achievement and, thus, provide guidance to collective interpretation of results. Multiple experts work together, then, to prepare for the collection of students' evidence of learning and to provide information that will enrich collective interpretation of student results.

Sampling

The size of an institution's student body may well prohibit assessing all students at both the institution and program levels. There are, however, opportunities in most institutions for assessing the student population as a whole. Examples include building in a common time for assessment at the end of a required course—for example, at the end of a program or service—or during a required assessment period integrated into a college or university's semester schedule. Sampling members of an institution- or program-level population may, however, be a more realistic and feasible option upon which to make inferences about student learning. Three of the most commonly used methods are the following:

1. *Simple random sampling:* This method draws a representative selection of students from the whole student population in such a way that each student has an equal chance of being selected. Key to this sampling is developing a way to reduce bias of selection by using random number tables, for example.

2. *Stratified random sampling:* This method first categorizes students within the larger institutional population and then draws an independent random sampling within each category. Possible categories within an institution might be based on the following:

- Educational background
- Professional and life experiences
- First-generation populations
- International populations
- Age (traditional- versus nontraditional-aged students)
- Learning disabled populations
- Historically underrepresented populations
- Levels of academic readiness
- Levels of initial placement upon matriculation
- Major program of study

3. *Cluster sampling:* In this method, heterogeneous groups or clusters are defined, representative of the institution- or program-level student population. Simple random sampling identifies students in each cluster; observers then sample students from each cluster (Levy & Lemeshow, 1999).

Whether an institution and its programs assess all students or sample representative populations, reaching early consensus about the focus of inquiry within or across the student population helps to target collective interpretation of results. The institutional example in Box 6.1 illustrates the way in which a community college is tracking student

---

BOX 6.1   INSTITUTIONAL EXAMPLE: Florida Community College at Jacksonville

Florida Community College at Jacksonville, consisting of multiple campuses enrolling 21,000 students, is longitudinally assessing cohorts of students based on their placement in college-level preparatory courses to more specifically learn about their achievement based on their initial course or courses. This cohort model consists of eight groups of students placed in the following preparatory courses:

- Language only
- Mathematics only
- Reading only
- Language and mathematics
- Language and reading

(Continued)

BOX 6.1   (Continued)

- Mathematics and reading
- Language, mathematics, and reading (all three areas)
- Language, mathematics, or reading, but students chose not to matriculate after they received their entry-level placement scores

The last category represents the college's focus on advancing local students' education so that increasing numbers are qualified for work within the surrounding communities.

As Figure 6.1 represents, each cohort includes a student advocate who represents the needs and issues of students in a cohort. Broad institutional participation is also a hallmark of this project, as represented in the seventeen project teams; the direct involvement of campus presidents; and participating groups, such as the faculty senate. Of great significance in this project is the early decision to assess student learning along different cohort compositions, as well as across a range of different needs, such as special needs, remedial instruction, or particular learning resources. This model of inquiry, then, shapes how the college learns about the efficacy of its educational practices in relation to clearly defined cohorts. Institutional learning is enhanced through sampling tightly defined cohorts as they progress through their education.

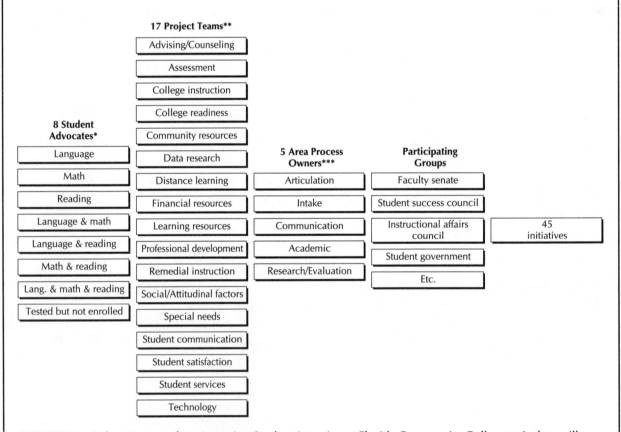

FIGURE 6.1   Cohort Approach to Assessing Student Learning at Florida Community College at Jacksonville.
* Serve throughout the plan as student advocates for each community
** Generated innovations that have led to five major areas and forty-five specific initiatives
*** Led by campus presidents and comprehensive college-wide teams

Source: Contributed by Florida Community College at Jacksonville. Reproduced with permission.

learning beginning with students' placement. What the college wants to explore about its students' learning shapes the resulting data that community members will receive. These results, in turn, shape community interpretations about what, how, and how well students learn. Using a multipronged approach involving interdisciplinary teams across its campuses, this project is designed to explore the efficacy of pedagogy; design of the curriculum, co-curriculum, and instruction; support services; other educational practices; and institutional structures.

TIMES AND CONTEXTS FOR COLLECTING EVIDENCE

The kinds of collective discussions described in Chapter 2 about the design of curriculum, instruction, the co-curriculum, and educational practices promote consensus about appropriate times to assess students' attainment. Building those times into a plan is a next step: when is it appropriate to assess for a particular outcome or sets of outcomes along the continuum of students' learning? After each course? After a certain number of courses? After a set of courses and related experiential opportunities? Selecting and designing assessment methods actually establish the backbone of a chronology: commercially designed standardized tests, for example, are usually designed to be administered during a defined time period, such as at the end of a program of study, as is the case with Educational Testing Services' Major Field Tests. Locally designed formative assessment methods, developed to assess students' learning after each course or across courses, require a different timetable that builds in faculty and staff time to assess student work at these points along students' studies. Establishing a midpoint project designed to ascertain how well students integrate core curricular learning and other institutional learning outcomes into a major field of study requires setting up yet another timetable. Building in a long-term collaborative project designed to ascertain how well groups develop and test a new product requires yet another timetable and set of responsibilities for faculty and staff.

Decisions about ways to collect evidence of student learning through direct and indirect assessment methods follow closely on the heels of establishing an assessment time line. Within what kinds of contexts will students demonstrate or represent their learning—in classes or programs, online, off campus, within the local external community, or in Web-based simulations? The following list represents some ways to collect evidence within that range of contexts:

1. Embed assessment methods into existing courses or services. This method of collection requires that designated faculty, staff, and others who contribute to students' learning reserve time for students to respond to a prompt or task. In some cases an assignment can be woven into a course, service, or educational experience: students may, for instance, hand in their response to an assignment in duplicate. One response is returned to students with faculty or staff comments; the other is turned over to outside scorers for institution- or program-level assessment purposes. Integrating a case study into specific courses across a major program of study provides evidence of how well students are integrating, transferring, and applying new learning. This case study might also be in the form of a simulation that provides observers with an opportunity to assess how well students integrate knowledge, behaviors and attitudes. If an institution asserts that its students reason quantitatively, regardless of their majors, then embedding an appropriate problem for them to solve in an otherwise nonquantitatively based course that students take midpoint and endpoint in their studies would provide evidence of that sustained ability. Arranging for videotaping or observations of students' emerging abilities at various points along their studies—such as their ability to deliver oral presentations to a range of audiences with different knowledge backgrounds and needs—is another way to embed assessment within students' sequence of courses.

2. Extract samples of student work along the continuum of their studies, based on agreed-upon assignments designed to prompt students to represent learning described in outcome statements, so that there is a consistent kind of text to assess. One way to assess students' learning over time is to collect their work at designated points in their studies: upon matriculation into the institution or their acceptance into a program or their entry into a particular service; or at a midpoint in their

studies or during participation in a service; or at the end of their studies or participation in a service. The results of applying scoring rubrics to these chronological samples provide evidence of students' patterns of progress.

3. Establish a common institutional time—days or even a week—to assess student learning. Campuses are increasingly scheduling annual assessment weeks in their institutional calendars as opportunities to assess at the institution and program levels. This scheduled period may be the best time to administer standardized instruments if the week or days are built into students' lives. More important, these times may also serve as celebrations of student achievement, during which students select work they believe represents their learning—performances, artwork, research projects, collaborative projects, or local community projects—and share it with both internal and external audiences.

4. Sample student portfolios that have been designed to include work that represents students' learning and responds to institution- and program-level learning outcome statements. Holding students responsible for submitting certain kinds of work over the duration of their studies provides a rich set of evidence for an institution or program to assess. Furthermore, if students learn upon matriculation that they are responsible for chronicling their learning, they are positioned early on to become themselves assessors of their own work, represented through the texts they produce. Web-based portfolios facilitate sampling across representative student populations and provide evidence of students' learning progression. (Chapter 7 addresses the issue of students' consent to use or access their work for institution- or program-level assessment.)

5. Develop inquiry groups consisting of faculty, staff, administrators, alumni, students, and members of advisory boards, for example, that track a cohort of students over time, using multiple and often concurrent methods to learn more deeply about students' learning, such as assessing portfolios or embedded assignments and then conducting focus groups or interviews about the work.

6. Build in integrative projects, such as midpoint capstone projects, along the continuum of students' learning to assess how well students transfer and make meaning. These projects may become a component of existing courses or services, may become modules attached to courses, or become themselves credit-bearing or required courses.

7. Conduct interviews or focus group discussions designed to complement direct methods. That is, use these indirect methods as ways to probe issues about what and how students believe they learn.

8. Allow students to identify work they believe represents their progress toward and achievement of learning outcomes, providing them with the opportunity to select their own texts. That is, they take ownership of their learning and chronicle that learning through key works. Peer and self-assessment, self-reflection, and students' analyses of how they developed a work might also accompany each piece.

9. Identify opportunities off campus, such as in internships, experiential learning opportunities, students' performances within the local community, or participation in community service projects, that also provide evidence of their learning applied in more public contexts.

SCORING

A plan for assessment also incorporates time to score students' text, assemble responses from a survey or interview, and analyze the results. Actual scoring of student texts or responses can occur in multiple contexts based on the sample strategies discussed in earlier chapters. Testing services that develop commercially designed instruments build in scoring and analysis of results as part of the design of their instruments, using either automated scoring systems or using scorers who have gone through calibration together to prepare to grade student responses, such as writing samples. Developments in technology have even led to automated scoring of writing samples that may also be used on campus (Shermis & Daniels, 2002, pp. 159–160).

Typically, however, internal or external scorers or combinations of these scorers will blindscore student texts using rubrics so that results can be analyzed according to students' performance under each criterion. Specific teams may be formed to observe student interactions, such as in a simulation, or to score written or visual texts. Using two raters to blindscore student work is another common method after those raters have gone through calibration sessions scoring sample student work. If there is a discrepancy between the two scorers, a third scorer may be brought in or a panel may be established to resolve discrepancies. The possible composition of scorers is variable; among those possibilities are the following:

- Internal scorers—faculty, staff, administrators, teaching assistants, graduate students, or other internal contributors to students' education

- External scorers—members of advisory boards, internship advisors, alumni, representatives from professional organizations, faculty from nearby institutions, or professionals from the local community

The institutional example in Box 6.2 illustrates the practice of embedding a direct assessment method into courses along the continuum of students' learning. Interdisciplinary teams score students' writing to assess for three learning outcomes. One of these teams consists of students.

BOX 6.2 INSTITUTIONAL EXAMPLE: University of South Florida

At the University of South Florida, the institution's General Education Assessment Advisory Team, consisting of associate deans from the colleges of arts and sciences and undergraduate studies, faculty representatives, the vice president of student affairs, representatives from career services and advising, and students, establishes multidisciplinary teams to assess (1) students' writing, (2) intellectual development, and (3) key general education knowledge and understanding based on students' writing.

The Writing Assessment Committee, consisting of teaching assistants from English, philosophy, communications, and sociology, scores student essays to assess writing proficiency. Another team, the Intellectual Development Committee, consisting of five faculty, one associate dean, and two assessment directors, evaluates the intellectual development level exhibited in students' papers using the Measure of Intellectual Development (Moore, 1990). A third team composed of students analyzes the content of students' papers to identify characteristics valued in the classroom and to assess students' understanding of issues and attitudes emphasized in the general education curriculum. Writing skills and intellectual development, as defined by William Perry (1970), are assessed by two additional faculty teams at three points in the curriculum:

1. Upon entry into Composition I
2. After the completion of Composition II
3. During junior- and senior-level capstone courses

A student team analyzes the content of the first and third essays.

Because of the nature of the university's general education curriculum and its desire for students to take assessment seriously, all students write essays as part of their courses. Serving two purposes of assessment, these essays also enable the English department to use the initial essays in Composition I and final essays in Composition II to assess students' progress in the composition program. The final essay, written in capstone courses after students have achieved junior or senior status, also serves as a culminating example of students' progress in writing. A tripartite focus on intellectual development, writing, and content, in relationship to general education curricular goals, provides assessment results that are shared with students, programs, departments, and even colleges within the university. The content analysis, conducted by student teams, provides valuable information about what students have learned within the institution's educational context.

Source: Contributed by Teresa L. Flateby, University of South Florida. Reproduced with permission.

ANALYSIS AND PRESENTATION OF RESULTS

The ability to make targeted interpretations about student learning is the direct result of achieving consensus about the most useful ways to present assessment results. Involving institutional researchers early on in decisions about what an institution and its programs want to learn helps these professionals, in collaboration with assessment teams or core working groups, to identify ways to present results that will promote targeted interpretations about pedagogy and the design of curriculum, co-curriculum, instruction, educational practices, and services. What formats for presenting results will prompt those kinds of conversations? How will reporting formats help to answer the major question about assessment results: "Why?" Why are certain cohorts of students unable to reason quantitatively, solve certain kinds of problems, or develop higher-order thinking and problem-solving abilities?

Just as multiple assessment methods provide more comprehensive evidence of student learning, multiple reporting formats assist understanding and appeal to different ways in which audiences make meaning. Analyzed results presented through digital diagrams, tables, charts, graphs, spreadsheets, or maps help many viewers visualize information (Tufte, 1990, 1997a, 1997b, 2001; Harris, 1996). Results of observing group interaction or simulations, for example, or results of focus group exchanges may best be presented in a narrative format that represents results in terms of chronological observations or cause-and-effect relationships. Results presented narratively accompanied by quantitative analyses of student performance based on scoring rubrics provide two ways for groups to identify patterns of strong and weak performance. Plotting students' achievement along agreed-upon criteria and standards of judgment targets attention on patterns of strengths and weaknesses. Visually presented in comparative tables, these patterns might also be presented for different cohorts—nontraditional-aged and traditional-aged students, international students, commuter and residential students, or major field of study—promoting targeted interpretations about why some cohorts do well while others do not.

Other kinds of institutional data that help to answer the question "Why?" may also target interpretations. For example, students' course-taking patterns could, in fact, explain why certain groups of students perform well while others do not. Students' predisposition to navigate the curriculum to avoid taking certain kinds of courses, such as those that integrate writing or quantitative reasoning, may explain their weak performance in these areas. Looking at connections among students' participation in academic support services or programs and services offered through the co-curriculum may help explain results within cohorts.

Comparing students' achievement within the context of *baseline data* may become another interpretive strand. Information about student learning collected at the time of placement or matriculation into an institution or its programs provides baseline data—placement tests, portfolio reviews, samples of students' work, or results of early assessment methods woven into courses constitute baseline data. For example, results of the Force Concept Inventory (see page 114 in Chapter 4), used to assess students' working knowledge of physics before they take introductory physics courses, establishes a baseline against which to assess how well students develop a more coherent understanding of the concept of force in relation to pedagogy and curricular design. In the absence of baseline information, we assume that our curriculum and educational practices advance all students' learning. Such an assumption would have the effect of obscuring or disguising critical considerations:

- How and what did students know, understand, or believe when they entered the institution or a program?
- What practices along the way revised or changed their conceptual understanding in a field of study?
- What practices challenged and even changed their long-held beliefs, attitudes, values, or interpretations? And what practices did not?

We can provide answers to those questions through baseline data that give us a beginning point to track what, how, and how well students learn within the context of educational practices.

COLLECTIVE INTERPRETATION OF ANALYZED RESULTS

Drawing upon multiple analyzed results—results of assessment methods, course-taking patterns, or initial placement, for example—adds both depth and breadth to collective institution- and program-level interpretation. A community process involving both formal and informal occasions for dialogue and collective interpretation educates members of an educational community about the efficacy of its collective practices translated into student work. To deepen a shared commitment to assessment, an institution and its programs build occasions for dialogue into institutional rhythms. Chronologically, common institution- and program-level times to interpret and act on analyzed results unfold as follows:

- Initial time to hear and see analyzed results and ask questions about results
- Team-based time following an initial presentation to interpret those results (What interpretations emerge from teams of faculty, staff, students, and other members of the larger community? These teams may form around interdisciplinary perspectives of faculty, staff, and others who contribute to students' education or around focused perspectives, such as a team of students, a team of librarians, a team of student affairs staff, or a team of teaching assistants. Altogether these teams' interpretations contribute to collective institutional learning.)
- Time to share and discuss team-based interpretations
- Time to reach consensus about adaptations, modifications, or innovations to improve student performance
- Time to learn about the efficacy of changes once they have been implemented and student learning has been reassessed

Institution-level times also include opportunities for the larger community to hear about program-level results and interpretations. What a program learns about its students' achievement informs institution-level discussions; what an institution learns about its students' achievement informs program-level discussions. Establishing reciprocal channels of communication increases awareness about patterns of student achievement and opens up the possibility for greater focus on improving areas of weak performance. That is, these channels promote opportunities for revisions, changes, or innovations in pedagogy and the design of the curriculum, co-curriculum, and educational practices. Collective community dialogue based on results and interpretations of results is not designed to point fingers; rather, it is designed to determine how members in an educational community can work together to improve student learning.

A NARRATED CYCLE

How collaborative tasks and decisions come together to launch a cycle of inquiry is well represented in Box 6.3, the institutional example from Mesa Community College. This narrative chronicles how a core working group of faculty, in collaboration with representatives from the college's office of research and planning, designed, validated, and pilot tested an assessment method it now uses to assess learning outcomes in the arts and humanities. The office of research and planning continues annually to compare results across years to assure the integrity of the assessment method and the way in which it is annually administered. The internally designed assessment method is embedded in non–arts and humanities courses to determine how well students transfer and apply valued ways of

---

BOX 6.3   INSTITUTIONAL EXAMPLE: Mesa Community College

Arts and Humanities is one of seven college-wide general education areas at Mesa Community College. For five of the seven outcome areas, including Arts and Humanities, the faculty have developed their own assessment tools.

Arts and Humanities Student Learning Outcomes

Cross-disciplinary faculty clusters developed specific student learning outcome statements for each of the seven general education areas defined by the college community. Faculty members representing several arts and humanities disciplines defined the learning outcomes for Arts and Humanities to ensure balanced input across the disciplines. Staff from the Office of Research and Planning provided guidance by providing definitions and examples of good outcome statements

(Continued)

BOX 6.3   (Continued)

and guiding the group to write outcomes that are measurable and independent of one another. The Arts and Humanities outcomes describe what students should be able to demonstrate:

1. Knowledge of human creations

2. Awareness that different contexts and/or worldviews produce different human creations

3. An understanding and awareness of the impact that a piece (artifact) has on the relationship and perspective of the audience

4. An ability to evaluate human creations

Arts and Humanities Assessment Tool

After the outcomes were written, the Arts and Humanities faculty cluster met to determine the most appropriate assessment tool. The research office provided support during this process by conducting searches for possible appropriate tools, reviewing items, and helping faculty align items to outcomes. Faculty decided to design their own instrument to assess the Arts and Humanities outcomes.

Faculty made all content decisions related to the development of the instrument; the research office provided structured feedback and technical support. The Arts and Humanities assessment is a four-part multimedia presentation that includes a photograph of an art exhibit, a videotape of a Shakespeare soliloquy, a musical composition, and a story-telling performance. Faculty selected the presentations and produced the CD-ROM. Students write responses to a series of questions about each presentation; the questions are aligned with the learning outcomes. Students are asked to write personal reactions to each piece, to interpret the piece in terms of its historical or social context, and to examine and evaluate artistic aspects of each.

A scoring rubric was developed by the faculty cluster to measure a set of common constructs across all of the presentations. The rubric consists of a five-point scale describing elements that should be present in the responses. The scale rates the responses from lowest (1 = response is completely undeveloped) to highest (5 = response shows a high level of understanding in a broader view and illustrates coherent integrated thinking about the work).

Validity and Reliability

Faculty conducted face and content validity measures to assure that the content was relevant and inclusive. The office of research and planning conducted other validity measures, as well as correlated students' GPA, course enrollment patterns, and overall student performance on the method. Reliability analysis and factor analysis were conducted to explore and improve the alignment of items to outcomes, such as measures of internal consistency among a group of items combined to form a single scale.

Consistency in rater scoring was also built into this process to determine how well evaluators agreed in their responses.

Sampling and Scoring

A cross-sectional research design was chosen for the assessment program. Beginning students who had completed zero to nine hours (pre-group) were compared to completing students who had completed a core of at least 30 hours of general education coursework distributed across the core curricular areas (post-group). The sampling was selected to represent the general population of the campus. Demographic characteristics of participating and nonparticipating students were also compared by cohort and overall. The proportion of students of color and the

(Continued)

BOX 6.3   (CONTINUED)

male/female ratio were compared between groups to determine if there were significant differences in the samples.

Arts and Humanities response booklets were blindscored by a group of faculty using the scoring rubric; each response was scored by two raters. At the beginning of the scoring session, a norming session was held during which raters scored several sample student responses and discussed the elements that comprise excellent, average, and poor responses. Statistical tests were used to compare the total scores and the scale scores for the learning outcomes to determine if there were significant differences between the two groups of students.

Administration of the Assessment

The Arts and Humanities assessment is currently administered to students during the college's annual assessment week; assessments are assigned across general education departments from a pool of more than 200 volunteered sections. In Spring 2003, 537 students took the Arts and Humanities assessment during a seventy-five-minute scheduled class period. In order to ensure that the general education program, and not a particular department, is being assessed, measures that relate to particular disciplines are not administered in those disciplines (e.g., the Arts and Humanities assessment is not administered in art classes). Annually, faculty attend an orientation and follow standard administration procedures. At the end of the assessment cycle, faculty provide feedback concerning the assessment process.

Assessment results are also compared over time. Although different student populations are assessed each year, results are compared between years to determine if the patterns and overall performance are similar.

Source: Contributed by Mesa Community College. Reproduced with permission.

knowing, understanding, and interpreting in contexts outside of arts and humanities courses.

BEYOND A CYCLE

Based on lessons learned from going through one cycle, an institution and its programs develop and periodically update assessment plans that build in cycles of inquiry. Each cycle includes assessing one to two student learning outcome statements, interpreting results, making changes to improve patterns of weakness, implementing those changes, and reassessing how well students improve based on implemented changes. Box 6.4 illustrates Providence College's assessment plan, consisting of cycles of inquiry that stretch across academic majors, administrative and educational support services, academic minors, and the institution's core curriculum.

A sample of interpretations that are now leading to changed practices at the college is shown in

Box 6.5. In the Department of Marketing, the adoption of a case study helped the department target students' weaknesses in solving representative problems. In three other departments, collective interpretations have led to establishing and applying clearer criteria and standards of judgment to student work.

The institutional process Mesa Community College developed and uses to determine and validate its design methods provides a close-up view of the interrelated decisions, tasks, and processes that define a cycle of inquiry into student learning (see Box 6.3). As colleges and universities refine and mature their practices and processes, campus-wide assessment committees establish an institutional timetable, such as Providence College's schedule (Box 6.4). These cycles begin and end with a focus on educational practices—the purpose of our collective inquiry. A final view of how a core institutional process becomes embedded in the life of an institution, illustrated through several institutional examples, is the subject of the final chapter.

BOX 6.4   INSTITUTIONAL EXAMPLE: Implementation of the Assessment Process at Providence College, 1999–2005: Overview

Cycle I: **Academic Majors**
✓ Phase I: Spring 1999   . . . .   *Develop outcomes.*
✓ Phase II: Fall 1999   . . . .   *Develop measures for outcomes.*
✓ Phase III: Spring 2000   . . . .   *Conduct an actual assessment.*
✓ Phase IV: Summer/Fall 2000   . . . .   *Report results/Discuss necessary improvements.*
✓ Phase V: 2001–   . . . .   *Repeat Phases III and IV annually.*

Cycle II: **Administrative and Educational Support Service Departments**
✓ Phase I: Spring/Summer 2000 . . . .   *Develop outcomes.*
✓ Phase II: Fall 2000   . . . .   *Develop measures for outcomes.*
✓ Phase III: Spring 2001   . . . .   *Conduct an actual assessment.*
✓ Phase IV: Summer/Fall 2001   . . . .   *Report results/Discuss necessary improvements.*
✓ Phase V: 2002–   . . . .   *Repeat Phases III and IV annually.*

Cycle III: **Academic Minors**
✓ Phase I: Spring/Summer 2002 . . . .   *Develop outcomes.*
✓ Phase II: Fall 2002   . . . .   *Develop measures for outcomes.*
✓ Phase III: Spring 2003   . . . .   *Conduct an actual assessment.*
✓ Phase IV: Summer/Fall 2003   . . . .   *Report results/Discuss necessary improvements.*
✓ Phase V: 2003–   . . . .   *Repeat Phases III and IV annually.*

Cycle IV: **Core Curriculum**
✓ Phase I: Fall/Spring 2002–3 . . . .   *Review and revise original core objectives.*
✓ Phase II: Fall 2003   . . . .   *Develop outcomes.*
✓ Phase III: Spring/Summer 2004 . . . .   *Develop measures for outcomes.*
✓ Phase IV: Fall 2004   . . . .   *Conduct an actual assessment.*
✓ Phase V: Spring/Summer 2005 . . . .   *Report results/Discuss necessary improvements.*
✓ Phase VI: 2005–   . . . .   *Repeat Phases III and IV annually.*

Source: Contributed by Brian Bartolini, and Ray Sickinger, Providence College. Reproduced with permission.

BOX 6.5   INSTITUTIONAL EXAMPLE: Providence College

1. The Department of Marketing is considering developing a Marketing Management course to help students identify and solve problems as part of the Marketing curriculum. This decision was reached based on interpreting the results of a case study designed to determine students' abilities to identify key marketing problems.

2. The Department of Finance findings have resulted in the department's establishing clearer information technology standards in all required finance courses.

3. The Department of Engineering/Physics/Systems has begun to formalize the evaluation process in its courses when students give oral and written presentations to improve consistency in assessing students' work.

4. The Department of Studio Art has decided to develop a standard set of criteria for reviewing student work to ensure uniformity and fairness in evaluation.

Source: Contributed by Brian J. Bartolini, Ed.D., and Raymond L. Sickinger, Ph.D., Providence College. Reproduced with permission.

WORKS CITED

Gardner, J. (1991). *The unschooled mind: How children think and how schools should teach* (p. 6). New York: Basic Books.

Harris, R. L. (1996). *Information graphics: A comprehensive illustrated reference: Visual tools for analyzing, managing, and communicating.* New York: Oxford University Press.

Levy, P. S., & Lemeshow, S. (1999). *Sampling of populations: Methods and applications* (3rd ed.). New York: John Wiley & Sons.

Moore, W. S. (1990). *The Measure of Intellectual Development: An instrument manual.* Olympia, WA: Center for the Study of Intellectual Development & Perry Network: *www.perrynetwork.org.*

Perry, W. G. (1970). *Forms of intellectual and ethical development in the college years: A scheme.* New York: Holt, Rinehart, and Winston.

Shermis, M. D., & Daniels, K. E. (2002). Web applications in assessment. In T. W. Banta & Associates, *Building a scholarship of assessment* (pp. 148–166). San Francisco: Jossey-Bass.

Tufte, E. (1990). *Envisioning information.* Cheshire, CT: Graphics Press.

Tufte, E. (1997a). *Visual explanations: Images and quantities, evidence and narrative.* Cheshire, CT: Graphics Press.

Tufte, E. (1997b). *Visual and statistical thinking: Displays of evidence for decision making.* Cheshire, CT: Graphics Press.

Tufte, E. (2001). *The visual display of quantitative information* (2nd ed.). Cheshire, CT: Graphics Press.

ADDITIONAL RESOURCES

Analyzing and Presenting Results

Bounford, T., & Campbell, A. (2000). *Digital diagrams: How to design and present statistical information effectively.* New York: Watson-Guptill.

Cleveland, W. S. (1985). *The elements of graphing data.* Boston: Duxbury.

Cleveland, W. S. (1993). *Visualizing data.* Murray Hill, NJ: Hobart Press.

Dey, I. (1993). *Qualitative data analysis: A user-friendly guide for social scientists.* London: Routledge.

Fitz-Gibbon, C., & Morris, L. (1987). *How to analyze data.* Newbury Park, CA: Sage.

Frantz, R., Jr. (2003). *Graphs done right vs. graphs done wrong.* Cheshire, CT: Graphics Press.

Harris, J., & Samson, D. (2000). *Discerning is more than counting* (p. 3). Washington, DC: The American Academy for Liberal Education.

Hartley, J. (1992). Presenting visual information orally. *Information Design Journal, 6,* 211–220.

Hartley, J. (1992, June–July). A postscript to Wine's "Understanding graphs and tables." *Educational Researcher, 21*(5), 25–26.

Henry, G. T. (1994). *Graphing data: Techniques for display and analysis.* Thousand Oaks, CA: Sage.

Howard, R. D., Borland, K. W., Jr. (Eds.). (2001). *Balancing qualitative and quantitative information for effective decision support.* San Francisco: Jossey-Bass.

Kelle, U. (Ed.). (1995). *Computer-aided qualitative research.* Thousand Oaks, CA: Sage.

Morris, L. L., Fitz-Gibbon, C. T., & Freeman, M. E. (1987). *How to communicate evaluation findings.* Newbury Park, CA: Sage.

Richardson, L. (1990). *Writing strategies: Reaching diverse audiences.* Newbury Park, CA: Sage.

Silverman, D. (1993). *Interpreting qualitative data: Methods for analyzing talk, text, and interaction.* Thousand Oaks, CA: Sage.

Stiles, W. (1992). *Describing talk.* Newbury Park, CA: Sage.

Tufte, E. R. (2003). *The cognitive style of Powerpoint.* Cheshire, CT: Graphics Press.

Wainer, H. (1992, January–February). Understanding graphs and tables. *Educational Researcher, 21*(1), 14–23.

Ware, C. (2000). *Information visualization.* San Francisco: Morgan Kaufmann.

Wolcott, H. F. (1990). *Writing up qualitative research.* Newbury Park, CA: Sage.

Wolcott, H. F. (1994). *Transforming qualitative data: Description, analysis, and interpretation.* Thousand Oaks, CA: Sage.

Automated Scoring

Burstein, J., Marcu, D., & Knight, K. (2003, January–February). *Finding the WRITE stuff: Automatic identification of discourse structure in student essays* (pp. 32–39). IEEE Intelligent Systems.

Shermis, M. D., & Barrera, F. D. (2002). Facing off on automated essay scoring. *Assessment Update, 15*(2), 4–5.

Shermis, M. D., & Barrera, F. D. (2002). Automated essay scoring for electronic portfolios. *Assessment Update, 14*(4), 1–2, 10.

Shermis, M. D., & Burstein, J. (Eds.). (2003). *Automated essay scoring*: A *cross-disciplinary approach*. Mahwah, NJ: Erlbaum.

Computer-assisted Assessment

Brown, S., Race, P., & Bull, J. (1999). *Computer-assisted assessment in higher education*. London, Kogan Page.

Interpreting Results

Strain, S. S. (2003, March–April). Keeping the faces of the students in the data. *Assessment Update*, 15(2), 1–2, 14–15.

Sampling

American Statistical Association: *www.amstat.org*.

Federal Committee on Statistical Methodology. Statistical Policy Working Papers: *www.fcsm.gov*.

Healey, J. (2004). *Statistics*: *Tools for social research*. 7th ed. Kentucky: Wadsworth.

Judd, C. M., & McClelland, G. H. (1990). *Data analysis*: A *model-comparison approach*. San Diego, CA: Harcourt Brace Jovanovich.

Sirkin, R. M. (1994). *Statistics for the social sciences*. Thousand Oaks, CA: Sage.

Sudman, S. (1976). *Applied sampling*. New York: Academic Press.

Yancey, B. D. (Ed.). (1988). Applying statistics in institutional research. *New Directions for Institutional Research*, 58. San Francisco: Jossey-Bass.

Resources on Methods in Evaluation and Social Research

Meta-site: *gsociology.icaap.org/methods*.

WORKSHEETS, GUIDES, AND EXERCISES

1. *Progressing through a Cycle.* The following worksheet is designed to guide a cycle of inquiry that begins with collective articulation of a learning outcome statement and ends with collective interpretation of results. This sheet guides either an institution- or a program-level cycle.

Worksheet to Guide a Cycle of Inquiry

a. List institution- or program-level learning outcome statement(s) that align with what and how students have learned.

b. Identify the direct and indirect methods you will use that align with these outcome statements.

c. Identify the kinds of inferences you intend to make based on these methods.

d. Identify the times and contexts within which you will assess students' responses to these methods—for example, formative and summative assessment of entries into portfolios, formative and summative assessment of case studies, or formative and summative assessment of students' responses to representative disciplinary problems included in a final examination.

e. Describe how you will test a method's properties of validity and reliability.

f. Identify how you will score students' work or responses.

g. If you develop your own scoring rubrics, describe how you will develop standards and criteria for judgment, that is, how you will assure you have developed quality standards.

h. Describe how you will calibrate raters to score student work or responses.

i. Determine whom you will assess (sampling method); what, specifically, you want to learn through your inquiry; and how you will derive samples.

j. Identify who will score the samples—for example, teams within the institution or external reviewers.

k. Identify who will analyze the results and how results could most effectively be presented for collective interpretation.

l. Schedule institution- and program-level times to interpret results, make decisions about changes, and develop a timetable to reassess students' learning after changes have been implemented.

2. *Developing a Report.* As your institution and its programs complete cycles of inquiry, maintaining a history of this work is important in building knowledge about practices within a program as well as across the institution. For institutional purposes, campus-wide committees may develop a format that requires documentation of cycles of inquiry into institution- and program-level learning outcome statements. This information, in turn, should move into the processes of institutional decision making, planning, and budgeting. Increasingly, external bodies, such as accreditors, are seeking evidence of institution- and program-level commitment to assessing students' learning as an indicator of institutional effectiveness. Maintaining a history of your assessment cycles, findings, interpretations, and implemented changes should become, then, one of the rhythms of this core process at both the institution and program levels. Use the following format to build an institution- and program-level chronology as you complete each cycle of inquiry.

Report Format

a. State the institution- or program-level outcome(s) statements that directed your inquiry and how you collectively developed those statements.

b. Describe the direct and indirect methods you selected or designed to assess the learning described in those outcome statements and the ways in which these methods align with what and how students learn and with the kinds of inferences you wanted to make.

c. Describe how you determined these methods' properties of validity and reliability.

d. Describe the times and contexts in which students responded to your methods and who scored their work.

e. If you designed your own methods, describe how you arrived at criteria and standards of quality and how you pilot tested your scoring rubric.

f. Describe how you selected samples of student work (sampling) and who scored them.

g.　Describe how results were collected, analyzed, and presented.

h.　Describe how results were collectively interpreted; that is, what conclusions did you reach based on your expectations?

i.　List the agreed-upon changes, revisions, adaptations, and innovations that emerged from collective interpretations, such as changes in pedagogy, curricular and co-curricular design, use of educational tools, and increased opportunities for students to represent their abilities to build on previous learning or transfer learning into new contexts.

j.　Provide a timetable to implement changes and then to reassess students' learning.

Chapter 7

BUILDING A CORE INSTITUTIONAL PROCESS OF INQUIRY OVER TIME

Good-to-great transformations often look like dramatic, revolutionary events to those observing from the outside, but they feel like organic, cumulative processes to people on the inside. The confusion of end outcomes (dramatic results) with process (organic and cumulative) skews our perception of what really works over the long haul. No matter how dramatic the end result, the good-to-great transformations never happened in one fell swoop. There was no single beginning action, no grand program, no one killer innovation, no solitary lucky break, no miracle moment.

—Jim Collins, 2001

OVERVIEW: The preceding chapters focused on the decisions and tasks that characterize progression through one cycle of inquiry. This final chapter explores how this initiative matures over time to become embedded into institutional life as a core institutional process. The maturational process occurs by establishing intentional links or connections with other campus structures, processes, decisions, and channels of communication, oftentimes resulting in complementary or new relationships or new institutional behaviors. Further, it advances through a commitment of human, financial, and technological support; and it manifests itself through new campus practices that publicly and intentionally recognize the enduring value of this work in advancing both institutional and student learning. Representative campuses included in this chapter illustrate some of the ways that institutions are strengthening their commitment. The Worksheets, Guides, and Exercises at the end of this chapter are designed (1) to promote institutional self-reflection about a campus's current commitment to assessing for learning and (2) to stimulate collective discussion about ways in which that current commitment might deepen or expand into a core institutional process focused on advancing institutional and student learning.

A VIEW OF THE WHOLE

"We were doing fine until our provost left." "Our director of assessment left so we haven't been able to sustain our commitment." "We are waiting to hire a new president." When assessment rests on the belief that one person sustains an institutional commitment, chances are that the commitment has not been deeply embedded into institutional life. It may be ingrained in some programs or services but not necessarily deeply rooted in campus life. Some members of the academic community may understand assessment's integral relationship to teaching and learning and its contribution to collective learning. Others may not share that understanding at all.

An institutional commitment to assessing for learning builds over time as a campus or system learns how to develop, integrate, or adapt practices, structures, processes, and channels of communication that support and value a collective commitment to institutional learning. Further, as members of an academic community become themselves more knowledgeable about the interdependent tasks that characterize a collective commitment, expertise grows as well.

Institutional size and resources may shape the practices, structures, processes, and channels of communication that support a collective commitment to assessment. Describing an absolute model that suits all institutions ignores issues of size and capacity and the ways in which a college or university operates to achieve its mission and purposes. In some institutions, a collective commitment to assessment may be achieved by expanding the responsibilities of existing bodies, such as an office of institutional research and planning, or the curriculum committee that might expand its work to include ownership of assessing institution-level outcomes. In other institutions a collective commitment may initiate new practices and structures, such as the creation of a campus assessment committee. How assessment translates into institutional life and rhythms, that is, how it becomes visible, is the focus of this chapter. Seeding and growing a commitment to this process is dependent on numerous variables, not the least of which is identifying previous institutional strategies that contributed to and fostered successful campus change. Thus, rather than prescribing an absolute model, this chapter describes representative ways colleges and universities manifest and value a collective commitment to assessing for learning. Specifically, it describes

1. Structures, processes, decisions, and channels and forms of communication;

2. Resources and support: human, financial, and technological;

3. Campus practices that manifest an institutional commitment.

SOME REPRESENTATIVE STRUCTURES, PROCESSES, DECISIONS, AND CHANNELS AND FORMS OF COMMUNICATION

Some Representative Structures

Often beginning as an ad hoc committee or a task force, over time an institutional assessment committee evolves into a formal committee that develops a mission and purpose statement, describes its roles and responsibilities, and establishes rotational membership from across a campus to build a collective commitment to and advance understanding about the process of assessment. In collaboration with institutional constituencies, such as division chairs from across the institution, it schedules and oversees cycles of inquiry and receives the results and interpretations of those cycles. Assessment committees channel these results and interpretations into annual budgeting cycles and into the larger institutional plans developed by the office of research and planning. Absent an institutional research and planning office on campus, an assessment committee may channel its annually collected results and interpretations into the institution's vice president's or provost's annual planning.

As the committee matures, it sustains inquiry into institution- and program-level inquiry through the following ways:

- Establishing, making public within the institution, and periodically revising a campus plan to improve student learning through assessment at the institution and program levels

- Coordinating assessment efforts across an institution to establish cycles of inquiry

- Informing the larger education community about results and interpretations as well as establishing formal institutional times for collective discussion and interpretation of results to distribute learning across the institution

- Providing guidance to the larger educational community through in-house, Web-based, and online resources about assessment practices and methods

- Providing peer or mentor assistance to support working groups as they progress through assessment cycles

- Periodically reviewing the efficacy of its role in improving student learning

As you have read throughout this book, assessment committees, often named student learning committees, to capture the goal of assessment, may also create core working groups or arms to carry out specific assessment tasks (see Box 7.1). A core working group consisting of faculty, staff, administrators, students, local professionals, and alumni, for example, might develop an institution-level outcome statement that describes how students would

---

BOX 7.1   INSTITUTIONAL EXAMPLE: *Portland State University*

Portland State University's deepened commitment to assessing student learning is reflected in the various arms of support that are available to the larger educational community:

1. Implementation teams for each school or division, led by a dean, associate dean, a lead faculty, faculty teams, and one graduate assistant

2. A cadre of graduate students who have taken the university's Academic Assessment Course designed for graduate students and assist in school or division assessment projects

3. A network of resources on assessment practices

4. Professional development opportunities that are organized based on the needs that faculty express

That is, the university has expanded its institutional commitment to support and sustain collective work.

Source: Contributed by Terrel L. Rhodes, Portland State University. Reproduced with permission.

demonstrate or represent civic responsibility. Another group might be formed to analyze results of direct and indirect assessment methods and present them to the educational community that, in turn, forms cross-disciplinary or specialized groups to interpret results and determine ways to improve student learning. Or, assessment committees may create inquiry circles—groups of faculty, staff, and even students—who track students' learning over time through multiple methods of assessment.

Building in times for its own self-assessment, an assessment committee periodically evaluates its practices for several purposes:

- To assure that faculty, staff, and administrators use and act on interpretations of assessment results to improve student learning

- To assure that interpretations of assessment results are channeled into short-term and long-term institutional planning and budgeting to focus institutional decision making and planning on student learning

- To ascertain how well institution- and program-level educational practices are evolving based on the learning emerging from cycles of inquiry (that is, how do members of an academic community learn, share, and build on that learning?)

Over time, assessment committees will link with other institutional bodies or infuse assessment into their work. Curriculum committees may begin to

assume increased responsibility for reviewing course and program proposals or reviewing current courses and programs within agreed-upon institution- and program-level outcomes. Viewing courses and proposals within this larger context they may seek, for example, to understand how components of a course or a program contribute to both institution- and program-level outcomes, that is, how they contribute to curricular coherence. Increasingly, teaching and learning centers—sometimes called teaching, learning, and assessment centers or teaching excellence centers—are integrating assessment practices and methods into their work and developing workshops to assist faculty and staff as they develop assessment methods and embed them along the continuum of student's learning. Faculty and staff development committees also recognize the significance of awarding funding to individuals or groups interested in designing an assessment project. Representatives from faculty governance committees often serve on assessment committees, and some governance committees now are embedding assessment into their routine discussions and decisions to position assessment as a core focus of their work, as illustrated in Figure 7.1.

Figure 7.1 represents the structure and process of assessment at the United States Naval Academy (USNA). As you will read in the institutional example in Box 7.2, the USNA's original assessment task force emerged as part of the institution's strategic planning and is now evolving into several central agencies that will assume responsibility for sustaining various

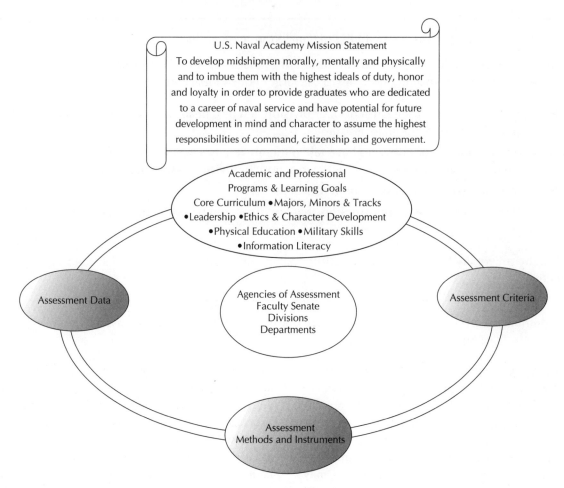

FIGURE 7.1   Assessment Structure and Process at the United States Naval Academy. *Source:* Contributed by Peter Gray, United States Naval Academy. Reproduced with permission.

inquiry cycles. These cycles focus on determining how well midshipmen achieve institution- and program-level learning outcomes. Significant in this model are channels of communication between the agencies and three working groups focused on specific aspects of assessment: developing criteria based on learning outcomes, developing methods, or using instruments to assess those outcomes, and developing ways to analyze results. In addition, the agencies of assessment receive analyses and interpretations of assessment data and channel analyses and community interpretations back into programs that then assume responsibility for improving and reassessing student learning.

Within an institution, individual schools, programs, and divisions, such as the Division of Student Services, also establish assessment committees, microcosms of an institution-level committee. These committees establish individual assessment plans that develop cycles of inquiry to assess several levels of outcomes: institution-level outcomes

expected of all undergraduate and graduate students, those particular to the division itself, and those particular to the programs and services that are housed in student services. Similarly, academic divisions or schools within a university develop cycles of inquiry to assess similar levels of outcomes:

- Those expected of all undergraduate or graduate students

- Those particular to a school, for example, a school of design

- Those particular to a specific area of concentration, such as interior design

Similar to the various working groups that are established in institution-wide committees, these units may also form separate working groups or constitute themselves as a working group. Members might serve on an assessment committee for a two- to three-year period after which a new member of a division or school would join the group. Just as an

---

BOX 7.2 INSTITUTIONAL EXAMPLE: *United States Naval Academy*

In spring 1999, the United States Naval Academy completed a strategic plan that incorporates a list of eleven capabilities and attributes to be attained by graduates in support of the USNA mission *to develop midshipmen morally, mentally, and physically and to imbue them with the highest ideals of duty, honor, and loyalty in order to provide graduates who are dedicated to a career of naval service and have potential for future development in mind and character to assume the highest responsibilities of command, citizenship, and government.*

The various mission-related expectations for graduates are that they should be highly effective communicators, exhibiting high moral and ethical behavior; exemplars of academic, technical, and tactical competence; and able to understand and integrate geopolitical complexities in their decision making. In addition, one of the goals under the Strategic Plan Focus Area of Academic Excellence is to foster an educational environment that supports and encourages midshipman learning and critical thinking. The rationales for assessment at the Naval Academy are, first, to validate the Academy's achievement of these capabilities and attributes in its graduates and, second, to guide continuous improvement.

Assessment at the USNA is designed to address the academy's full range of academic and professional programs as shown at the top of the loop [see Figure 7.1]. These areas define the learning goals and educational experiences that comprise the USNA learning environment and form the starting point of assessment. The agencies responsible for assessment include the Academy-wide Assessment Task Force that will be transformed into the newly established Faculty Senate Committee on Academic Assessment, the academic and professional development divisions, and other departments and centers with responsibility for student learning (listed in the center of the assessment loop).

Moving to the right from the Academic and Professional Programs and Learning Goals, the first step is to develop learning outcomes. The next step is to develop instruments and other methods for collecting and evaluating evidence of student learning. The third step is to analyze and interpret the results and feed them back into the program(s) responsible for the learning goals, that is, close the loop. Of course, it is possible to start at any point in the loop. For example, one could begin with data already collected to determine if the desired learning has occurred or even if the most reliable and valid methods were used. Or, developing assessment criteria might help to focus one's goals and to develop or select appropriate assessment methods.

The USNA implemented this model first by looking at institution-wide goals that are supported by the core curriculum and academic programs. The development of assessment plans by academic departments related to the goals associated with majors, minors, and tracks quickly followed. Recently, leadership assessment and the assessment of midshipman ethics and character development have begun. Planning for the assessment of the core curriculum will begin in 2004.

This model provides a common language and process for communicating, coordinating, and integrating assessment at the United States Naval Academy and, ultimately, for validating graduates' achievement of these capabilities and attributes and guiding continuous improvement.

Source: Contributed by Peter Gray, United States Naval Academy. Reproduced with permission.

institution-wide assessment committee calendars cycles of inquiry, these program-level committees develop cycles that become a part of the campus's plan. That is, they present results and interpretations to the institution's assessment committee, as well as share them in more formal institutional occasions.

Offices of Institutional Research and Planning

Offices of institutional research and planning or offices of institutional effectiveness often work with campus assessment committees as they establish an assessment plan or help to support or coordinate their efforts. In addition, these offices provide

---

BOX 7.3   INSTITUTIONAL EXAMPLE: *Rose-Hulman Institute of Technology*

At Rose-Hulman Institute of Technology, the college's Committee on the Assessment of Student Outcomes is co-chaired by a faculty member and the Director of Institutional Research, Planning, and Assessment. The director's role is to relieve committee members of the administrative aspects of assessment and to serve as a resource. That is, the committee focuses on developing learning outcomes, methods of assessment, rubrics, scoring processes and scorer training, and the review of results. The director focuses on ways to assist the decisions committee members make, thus enabling them to focus primarily on how to capture and score student learning and unburdening them from additional responsibility for the logistics of the process.

Source: Contributed by Gloria Rogers, Rose-Hulman Institute of Technology. Reproduced with permission.

assistance to core working teams as they select or design methods of assessment; develop rubrics; and collect, analyze, and interpret results. (See also pages 154 and 161 in Chapter 6.) Given their role of collecting data on numerous institutional fronts and for numerous purposes and given their expertise in assessment design, selection, and methods of collecting and analyzing results, offices of institutional research and planning support institutional assessment committees (see Box 7.3):

- They offer expertise on both the selection and administration of methods of assessment.
- They provide additional institutional data that may deepen community-based interpretations.
- They become a means to channel assessment results and interpretations into institutional decision making, planning, and budgeting.

Processes and Decisions

Institutional processes and decisions, such as those involved in annual professional reviews, may include criteria focused on an individual's contribution to program- or institution-level assessment. Promotion and tenure criteria may be revised to place value on a commitment to assessment as a form of scholarship. Decisions about program- and institution-level budgeting may focus on ways to deepen an institutional commitment through allocation of human, financial, and technological support. Further, developing an institutional annual and long-range planning calendar that synchronizes assessment results and interpretations with the timing of deliberations and decisions about planning and budgeting represents an institutional

commitment. This scheduling recognizes that information about student learning and ways to improve it should systematically guide decision making at the highest level. Other institutional decisions and processes may eventually contribute to strengthening and deepening the commitment: decisions about hiring individuals who have experience in or a willingness to learn about assessment methods; decisions about release time; decisions about resource allocation that reflect assessment as an institutional priority; and decisions that incorporate the contributions of undergraduate and graduate students to this institutional effort and even those in the local community who serve on working groups or as raters of student work.

Channels and Forms of Communication

Expanding or developing channels and forms of communication also characterizes an institutional commitment to assessment as a core institutional process. These channels build upon and distribute learning to

- share information in order to promote discussions about teaching and learning at the institution and program levels;
- engage members of the community in interpretive dialogue that leads to change or innovation and builds on institutional learning;
- inform institutional decision making, planning, and budgeting focused on improving student learning.

At both the institution and program levels, building in formal times to focus on teaching and learning and the development of methods to assess learning becomes a hallmark of an institutional commitment to assessment. These times also provide professional opportunity for educators not only to share educational practices but also to design sequences of practices that foster desired learning. Results of assessment provide evidence of the efficacy of those designs. These results contribute to institutional learning. Over time, educators

- build on this learning,
- develop and share innovative practices or redesign the curriculum and co-curriculum,
- more intentionally align the curriculum and co-curriculum,
- expand educational opportunities and ways of learning.

Another channel of communication can be developed by bringing together members of a campus community to share and interpret institution- and program-level assessment results in formal campus-wide forums designed to learn about institutional practices, explore new practices, learn about assessment results, and build institutional learning based on those results. Based on assessment results, how is it that programs intentionally contribute to or build on institution-wide learning outcomes? Similarly, how does an institution's core curriculum contribute to learning outcomes within programs, such as students' abilities to bring multiple perspectives to solving problems? Program-level assessment results, such as patterns of students' inability to reflect and act on the ethical dimensions of disciplinary problems, need to come forward to the educational community at large, especially when those results reflect institutional intentions. Bringing program-level results to the larger community triggers collective interpretation and discussion about ways the institution and its programs and services can more intentionally foster desired learning. Breaking an educational community into groups that explore assessment results and then develop complementary approaches to improving student learning develops a collective commitment to learning. Public forums provide an opportunity for that kind of community dialogue.

Further, communication channels are needed to funnel new initiatives into institutional decision making, planning, and budgeting. Assessment committees, institutional research and planning offices, and annual program- and institution-level budgets can serve as those channels. They can earmark support for financial or human resources or support that advances an institution's commitment to improving learning, such as opportunities for faculty and staff to learn about research on learning, developments in assessment practices, or developments in disciplinary pedagogy. For example, based on evidence of students' lower-than-expected quantitative reasoning abilities, an annual institutional budget might propose developing or providing workshops for faculty, staff, and administrators that identify additional ways to integrate quantitative reasoning across the curriculum so that students' continuum of learning includes multiple opportunities to develop this way of reasoning. Offices of institutional research and planning become a major communication channel that synthesizes interpretations and decisions to improve learning and transmits that information into annual and longer-range institutional planning and decision making.

Multiple forms of communication also reflect an institution's commitment to assessing for learning. Catalogues, recruitment materials, public documents, and an institution's Web site reflect this focus for external audiences. Internally, newsletters, resource Web sites, access to student data that informs interpretations, forms of recognition of assessment projects or leaders of these projects, and documents that help students map their learning exemplify some of the ways this focus translates into institutional life.

Institutional knowledge leads to change when it is distributed over multiple channels of communication. Both the institutional example in Box 7.4 and Figure 7.2 illustrate how institutional learning and change occur when a systematic and systemic process of assessment evolves. Institutional rhythms move information into institutional planning and decision making that support proposed changes.

RESOURCES AND SUPPORT: HUMAN, FINANCIAL, AND TECHNOLOGICAL

As is the case with other core institutional processes, commitment of human, financial and technological support underlies the start-up as well as sustainability of assessing for learning. Initially, a start-up assessment committee may be the expression of an institution's support, receiving some

BOX 7.4   INSTITUTIONAL EXAMPLE: *Indiana University–Purdue University Indianapolis*

Indiana University–Purdue University Indianapolis (IUPUI) is building a culture based on evidence (see Figure 7.2). Coordinated by the Office of Planning and Institutional Improvement (PAII), assessment begins with a planning phase in which the campus vision, mission, and goals are established and unit goals are aligned. In academic programs and individual courses, faculty set learning outcomes for students—some discipline-specific and all integrating IUPUI's six Principles of Undergraduate Learning (PULs). Developed over years of discussion involving faculty, students, and staff and approved by the Faculty Council in 1998, the PULs describe the intellectual competence and cultural awareness that every baccalaureate recipient should attain. They include Core Communication and Quantitative Skills; Critical Thinking; Integration and Application of Knowledge; Intellectual Depth, Breadth, and Adaptiveness; Understanding Society and Culture; and Values and Ethics.

Each year deans and vice chancellors use a Web-based template organized according to campus goals (www.imir.iupui.edu/annualplan) to report progress on their goals and objectives. They draw on data the institution has assembled at the campus level (e.g., student enrollment and retention data, survey findings, financial ratios) as well as information gathered on their own. Members of the Program Review and Assessment Committee—faculty from each school, librarians, and student affairs staff—use a matrix format to report annual progress on learning outcomes as well as improvement actions taken on the basis of assessment findings (www.planning.iupui.edu/prac/prac.html). Using this top-down, bottom-up iterative approach over the past decade, PAII staff have created performance indicators that demonstrate campus progress on ten mission-critical goals (www.iport.iupui.edu/performance).

Currently IUPUI is developing an electronic portfolio that will enable students to demonstrate their learning in connection with each of the PULs. Competence at introductory and intermediate levels is being defined by multidisciplinary campus groups, while competence at advanced levels is defined by faculty in each discipline. Planned assessment of the electronic portfolios by faculty will yield evidence for evaluating progress as a campus in advancing student learning of the PULs.

While work on the student electronic portfolio is just two years old, comprehensive academic program reviews involving external disciplinary and community peers in campus visits have been underway since 1994. The university's first locally developed surveys for students were administered by PAII staff that same year. And since then the institution has developed companion surveys containing a core of similar items for IUPUI alumni, faculty, and staff. PAII maintains a rich array of management information to meet the needs of deans and vice chancellors and conduct detailed analyses for both academic and administrative units. Economic modeling services offered by PAII staff link budgets with unit planning and evaluation initiatives. Having become leaders in the development of Web-based assessment tools such as placement tests, course evaluations, and surveys, in 2002 IUPUI became the first institution in the North Central region to use an electronic institutional portfolio to present its self-study for regional accreditation (www.iport.iupui.edu).

Institutional improvement is embedded in the PAII title and is always a paramount goal in collecting and using evidence. For example, enrollment data showing an increasingly younger student body on this urban commuter campus, coupled with disappointing retention statistics and student survey responses indicating the need for more campus programs and services, led to the creation in 1997 of University College. UC is the point of entry for all undergraduates and provides a variety of programs designed to enhance learning and increase retention, including freshman learning communities, peer mentoring, and Supplemental Instruction in reading and mathematics as well as other introductory courses. Assessment focused on each of UC's initiatives has led to refinements in the learning community model, a Gateway initiative providing student support and engaging instructors of our largest introductory courses in faculty development experiences, and modification of Supplemental Instruction to institute a Structured Learning Assistance model. Survey data

(Continued)

BOX 7.4 (Continued)

have been used to suggest improvements and to monitor their impact in such areas as advising, registration, placement testing, and even campus parking! Program reviews, the university's most comprehensive assessment vehicles, have shaped faculty hiring, curricula and degree programs, departmental planning processes, and cross-disciplinary collaboration. Finally, IUPUI's ability to document claims of program progress and distinction using data and other forms of evidence has helped to garner awards and recognition from the American Productivity and Quality Center, the Association of American Colleges and Universities, the American Association of State Colleges and Universities, and the Policy Center on the First Year of College. In addition, in 2002 IUPUI received a Theodore M. Hesburgh Certificate of Excellence for its Gateway initiative.

Source: Contributed by Trudy W. Banta, Professor of Higher Education and Vice Chancellor for Planning and Institutional Improvement. Reproduced with permission.

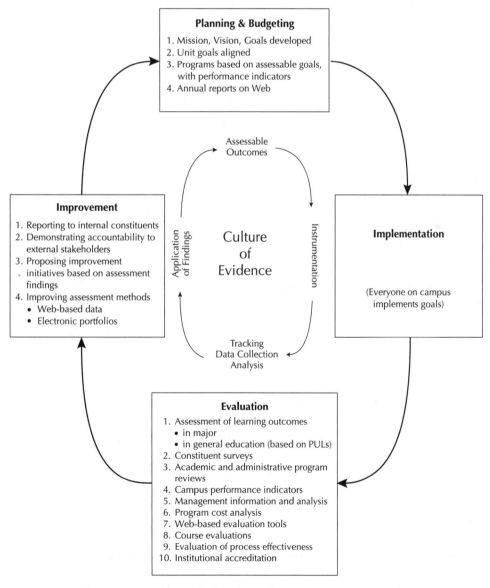

FIGURE 7.2   Planning, Evaluation, and Improvement at IUPUI.

Source: Contributed by Trudy W. Banta, Professor of Higher Education and Vice Chancellor for Planning and Institutional Improvement. Reproduced with permission.

institutional allocation of finances to perform the following tasks:

- Set up a Web site or an in-house center that provides resources on assessment practices and methods.

- Offer, often in conjunction with teaching and learning centers, workshops focused on assessment practices.

- Establish a cadre of faculty and staff who mentor and help colleagues through various assessment-related tasks, such as developing outcome statements, designing or selecting assessment methods that align with what and how students learn, developing and pilot testing scoring rubrics, or designing a research-based project.

- Support faculty and staff to attend assessment-related conferences or convenings, including disciplinary and professional meetings.

Eventually, resources come from multiple institutional contributors, reflecting the depth and pervasiveness of a campus commitment, such as from institution- and program-level budgets, faculty and staff development budgets, teaching center budgets, and grants to support the following:

- Design or initiation of an institution- or program-level assessment project

- Personnel necessary to carry out a project

- Technological assistance such as in creating an institution- or a program-level portfolio that documents efforts across the campus and builds institutional knowledge about practices, results, and innovations to improve learning

- Faculty and staff participation in conferences that contribute to their learning about assessment practices or that they contribute to

- Development of online or in-house resources

- Development of workshops that educate about new practices or bring together faculty and staff to share their practices

As the Portland State University example in Box 7.1 illustrates, a core institutional process requires not only physical resources to sustain the commitment but also human support, such as through the assistance of graduate students. Human support may be needed for other purposes as well, such as for the following tasks:

- Collecting students' responses or work
- Pilot testing a rubric or methods with colleagues
- Developing a research project, for example, to compare student achievement across different pedagogical approaches
- Deriving samples of student work
- Scoring student work or responses
- Analyzing results
- Preparing results for the educational community to interpret, leading to consensus about necessary institution- and program-level changes or innovations

Guam Community College's chronological commitment to assessment, represented at the end of this chapter in Appendix 7.1 and Figure 7.3, illustrates how one institution has expanded its institutional commitment through allocation of human and financial resources. Columns 3 and 4 in Appendix 7.1 trace that commitment over a three-year period. What is significant about this chronology is the institution's dedication of not only human but also financial resources to deepen and mature its commitment to assessment.

Financial commitments take different forms based on institutional resources and capacity. For some institutions, offering release time to pilot or develop a project might be one form of financial commitment. For others, providing release time to spearhead a program-level assessment process that eventually will become a collective protocol may be another form of financial commitment. A commitment also translates itself into annual institution- and program-level budgets that include a line item focused on financial support to build and sustain assessment practices, such as in hiring a graduate student, paying an honorarium to outside reviewers, or purchasing a commercially designed standardized instrument.

Figure 7.2 and Appendix 7.1 both represent another emerging form of support—technology—a way to capture, store, track, and represent student learning. Increasingly, offices of institutional research and planning are establishing databases that store multiple kinds of information that institutional constituencies can access and use to help interpret assessment results (Wierschem, McBroom, & McMillen, 2003). In addition, constituencies can disaggregate populations to look more closely, for example, at sets of educational experiences students have had that may contribute to their levels of achievement. Commercially designed programs also provide a systematic way to record and track student learning, as well as provide the flexibility to disaggregate and aggregate data. Web-based systems such as that developed at Indiana University–Purdue University Indiana (Box 7.4) provide a shared way for educators to post or store information that others can access as well, promoting a collective institutional commitment to assessment. Not only student electronic portfolios but also institutional electronic portfolios store and provide access to undergraduate and graduate work, representing levels of achievement along institution- and program-level outcomes. These portfolios provide not only internal but also multiple external audiences with diverse kinds of longitudinal evidence of student learning accessible through multiple paths of inquiry (see Figure 7.2).

CAMPUS PRACTICES THAT MANIFEST AN INSTITUTIONAL COMMITMENT

A commitment to assessing for learning translates itself into institutional practices that visibly represent an institution's level of commitment. These practices or norms of behavior range from the ways in which institutions and programs orient students toward their education to the ways in which institutions value faculty and staff commitment. The following practices represent some of the major ways that manifest an institutional commitment to assessment:

1. Orientation of students to assessing for learning beginning with their matriculation into the institution, that is, integration of this focus into students' first-year experiences or orientation seminars to prepare them to chronologically assess their achievement, as well as to inform them about institution- and program-level assessment practices designed to improve student learning (See Appendix 7.2 at the end of this chapter about the ethics of inquiry in relation to students.)

2. Periods of formal and informal self-reflection built into institutional life focused on improving learning through collective interpretation of assessment results

3. Recognition of a commitment to assessment as professional and scholarly work through criteria established for promotion, tenure, or periodic review (These criteria recognize that this commitment contributes not only to institution- and program-level earning but also to advancing practices in higher education through national, professional, and disciplinary projects and forums.)

4. Faculty and staff development opportunities dedicated to learning about research on learning and developments in educational practices that advance campus or disciplinary practices or build on current practices

5. Orientation of new faculty and staff to the institutional commitment with opportunity to shadow a current effort

6. Creation of common institution- and program-level times to focus on teaching, learning, and assessment, as well as to collaboratively interpret assessment results that promote dialogue about educational practices

7. Assessment days, weeks, or events that provide opportunities to calendar in assessment of student work through both direct and indirect methods (These times may also provide opportunities for students to present their work for public assessment by faculty, staff, administrators, peers, professional members of the community, members of advisory boards, and alumni, for example. That is, students represent their learning for multiple audiences who, in turn, assess their work.)

The institutional example in Box 7.5 represents how an institution schedules an event that brings together members of an educational community.

SIGNS OF MATURATION

A collective institutional commitment to assessing for learning emerges from intellectual curiosity about the efficacy of institutional practices in promoting student learning. Compelling questions, then, drive a process of discovery that brings a campus community together to gain knowledge about

---

BOX 7.5   INSTITUTIONAL EXAMPLE: *University of Wisconsin–River Falls*

Patterned after a professional meeting poster session, the Assessment Fair is an opportunity for academic and co-curricular programs as well as individual faculty and staff members to showcase their assessment efforts to the entire university community. The poster session format allows participants to display their assessment efforts and share ideas, successes, and difficulties with others on campus.

Departments, committees or teams, and individuals are encouraged to present posters describing assessment activities they are involved in. Participants at all stages of developing and implementing assessment plans are sought. *A fully developed assessment plan is not necessary for participation.* Student organizations and others in the campus community involved in assessment are also encouraged to present their efforts.

The fair helps focus attention on assessment and is an excellent opportunity for all shareholders, whether faculty or students, to become more involved in continuing assessment efforts on campus. It is also an informal and nonthreatening means to gauge the progress the campus community is making toward a culture of effective assessment practices.

Source: Contributed by the Faculty Assessment Committee, University of Wisconsin–River Falls, Dr. Michael Middleton, Chair. Reproduced with permission.

its students' learning and thereby build upon, adapt, or innovate new practices designed to enhance learning. As assessment becomes incorporated into institutional life, relationships among learning outcome statements; the design of the curriculum, co-curriculum, instruction, pedagogy, and educational practices; and methods of assessment become a focus of collaborative work, creating new opportunities for institutional learning. Occasions for dialogue about teaching, learning, and assessment among all contributors to students' education, including students themselves, mark this collaboration.

As this collaboration deepens and becomes both systemic and systematic, the following developments will likely characterize this working relationship:

- Development of institutional forums designed to share research on learning or to discuss how to apply research on learning to pedagogy; the design of instruction, curriculum, and the co-curriculum; educational practices; or the use of educational tools

- Increased focus on how components of students' education build on each other to contribute to institution- and program-level learning outcomes

- Widened recognition of assessment as a field of scholarship that advances institution- and program-level knowledge that, in turn,

advances educational practices within an institution and across the larger higher-education community

- Increased responsiveness to the ways individuals learn over time that prompts the development of varied educational practices and educational pathways

- Collaboration in the design of educational practices among members of an academic community, including instructional designers, and those outside of the community who bring professional expertise to higher education, such as representatives from professional and disciplinary bodies that contribute national perspectives and knowledge about developments in research and educational practices

- Collaboration with professional and national organizations, public audiences, alumni, professionals from the local community, or faculty from neighboring institutions to articulate criteria and quality standards of judgment

- Leadership from campus teaching and learning centers focused on integrating assessment into the processes of teaching and learning; developing conversations about philosophies or models of teaching and learning and the ways in which students progressively learn; and helping to design methods that align with what and how students learn

- Institution- and program-level representations of students' educational journey through curricular/co-curricular maps that assist students in visualizing how courses and educational experiences contribute to their learning (These maps will also help students identify experiences that they believe will benefit them, encouraging them to take responsibility for their learning.)

- Integration of students into a culture of inquiry upon matriculation so they become profilers of their own learning and self-reflective about how their learning builds over time

- Expansion of systematic ways to store and sample student work that can be aggregated and disaggregated for various internal and external audiences and purposes while at the same time illustrating student achievement within institutional contexts for learning

- Intentional collaborations with public audiences to help them understand the complex outcomes higher education aims its students to achieve, as well as to provide them with multiple forms of evidence that capture and represent that learning

Actualizing a professional philosophy, repositioning oneself in relation to a concept, integrating disciplinary learning that shapes decision making, and solving murky problems—these are among the complex issues that colleges and universities prepare students to address. Simplistic assessment methods by themselves cannot capture that complexity. Multiple assessment methods that align with what and how students learn can document the depth and breadth of students' achievement, representing the diverse ways in which students construct meaning.

WORKS CITED

Collins, J. (2001). *From good to great* (p. 186). New York: HarperCollins.

Wierschem, D., McBroom, R., & McMillen, J. (2003, Summer). Methodology for developing an institutional data warehouse. AIR *Professional File*, 88, 1–11.

ADDITIONAL RESOURCES

Nichols, J. O., & Nichols, K.W. (2000). *The departmental guide and record book for student outcomes assessment and institutional effectiveness* (3rd ed.). New York: Agathon Press.

Nichols, J. O., et al. (1995). A *practitioner's handbook for institutional effectiveness and student learning outcomes assessment implementation* (3rd ed.). Edison, NJ: Agathon Press.

Palomba, C. A., & Banta, T. W. (1999). *Assessment essentials: Planning, implementing, improving.* San Francisco: Jossey-Bass.

Pet-Armacost, J., & Armacost, R. L. (2002, April). Creating an effective assessment organization and environment. NASPA *NetResults*: *www.naspa.org/netresults/PrinterFriendly.cfm?ID=622.*

Rogers, G. M., & Sando, J. K. (1996). *Stepping ahead*: An *assessment plan development guide.* Terre Haute, IN: Rose-Hulman Institute of Technology.

Case Studies

Banta, T. W., Lund, L. P., Black, K. E., & Oblander, F. W. (1996). *Assessment in practice: Putting principles to work on college campuses.* San Francisco: Jossey-Bass.

Nichols, J. O. (1995). *Assessment case studies: Common issues in implementation with various campus approaches to resolution.* Edison, NJ: Agathon Press.

Schwartz, P., & Webb, G. (Eds.). (2002). *Assessment: Case studies, experiences and practice from higher education.* London: Kogan Page.

Ethical Considerations in Assessment

American Educational Research Association: *www.aera.net/about/policy/ethics.htm.*

American Psychological Association: *www.apa.org/ethics/code.html.*

American Sociological Association: *www.asanet.org/ecoderev.htm.*

Hutchings, P. (Ed.). (2002). *The ethics of inquiry: Issues in the scholarship of teaching and learning.* Menlo Park, CA: The Carnegie Foundation for the Advancement of Teaching. Includes an annotated bibliography on issues of ethics related to the scholarship of teaching and learning, as well as to ethics within disciplines.

Hutchings, P. (2003, September/October). Competing goods: Ethical issues in the scholarship of teaching and learning. *Change*, 35 (5), 27–33.

National Council on Measurement in Education: *www.ncme.org/about.*

National Research Council. (2002). *Scientific research in education* (pp. 154–157). Washington, DC: Author.

Meta-site: Outcomes assessment resources on the Web: *www.tamu.edu/marshome/assess/oabooks.html*.

Includes a listing of institutional Web sites that contain manuals, guides, and descriptions of college and university assessment processes and procedures.

WORKSHEETS, GUIDES, AND EXERCISES

1. *An Overview of Your Current Institutional Commitment.* Periodically, developing collaborative perspectives on ways in which assessment is rooted in an institution's culture enables members of an academic community to appreciate the types and levels of commitment. Collaborative perspectives, then, lead the way to determining how to deepen or strengthen the commitment. Designed for campus leaders to work with constituencies across an institution, this worksheet asks those constituencies to identify ways in which assessment is already embedded into an institution's culture and to provide evidence that supports those perceptions. Asking constituencies who may not have been directly involved in launching or furthering the initiative provides a realistic read on the current institutional climate.

Structures, Processes, Decisions, and Channels and Forms of Communication	
Institutional structures (committees; regularly scheduled retreats; centers, such as teaching and learning centers; regularly scheduled faculty and staff development opportunities; faculty and staff meetings; governance structures; new structures):	Evidence:
Institutional processes (annual personnel reviews, faculty evaluations, approval of programs and courses):	Evidence:
Institutional decisions (awards, forms of recognition, promotion and tenure, budgetary decisions, hiring decisions):	Evidence:

Continued

(CONTINUED)

Channels of communication (with board, decision and planning bodies, wider public, current and future students, faculty and staff):	Evidence:
Forms of communication (public documents, recruitment materials, catalogue, Web site, newsletter):	Evidence:
Support (line item in budgets; use or development of technology to collect, store, or record assessment results and interpretations; grant support focused on assessment; human support to help carry out aspects of the process, such as graduate interns):	Evidence:
Human:	Evidence:
Financial:	Evidence:
Technological:	Evidence:
Campus practices (new student orientation; new faculty orientation; assessment week; celebration of faculty-staff-student work; program- and institution-level times—common times—to focus dialogue on teaching, learning, and assessment and formal institutional times to receive and interpret results of assessment; collaboration across traditional boundaries to explore student learning from multiple lenses):	Evidence:

2. *Ways to Deepen or Strengthen the Commitment.* Using the worksheet under Exercise 1, ask members of the group to identify ways in which the institution can deepen or strengthen its commitment, including changing, revising, or modifying any one of the criteria listed under Exercise 1.	Evidence:

3. *New Practices.* After these two exercises, ask the group to think beyond
   the institutional norms that exist to invent new practices that promote
   campus commitment to teaching, learning, and assessment to improve
   both student and institutional learning. For example, might it be possible
   to develop a cadre of interdisciplinary teams (such as academic and student
   affairs, academic and student support services) that track cohorts of
   students over the continuum of their learning? Might it be possible for such
   teams to develop an entire program together, moving from agreed-upon
   outcomes to the collaborative design of a program, through collaborative
   development of assessment methods designed to track students' emerging
   learning, to collaborative interpretation of results along the way? That is,
   as an institution deepens its focus on learning through multiple avenues,
   can it change the ways in which it currently operates?

Evidence:

4. *Signs of Maturity.* Based on its research on 26 institutions that underwent institutional transformation, the American Council on Education identifies four attributes that mark successful campus transformation: (1) an institution changes its underlying assumptions, as well as overt institutional behaviors, processes, and structures; (2) the transformation itself is deep and pervasive, affecting the whole institution; (3) change is intentional; and (4) change occurs over time.	Evidence:

Source: American Council on Education. (2001). *On change V: Riding the waves of change: Insights from transforming institutions* (p. 5). Washington, DC: American Council on Education.

Using these four attributes, with a core of individuals from across your campus, consider how your institution's current commitment may advance over time under these four attributes. Rather than inserting assessment as an "add on," discuss how the rhythms of institutional life will intentionally incorporate this core institutional process of discovery or how new rhythms will be created to improve both student learning and institutional learning.

APPENDIX 7.1 INSTITUTIONAL EXAMPLE: *Guam Community College's Institutional Commitment to Assessment: An Evolving Story of Dialogue and Ritual*

PRINCIPLES	PROCESSES	STRATEGIES	RESOURCES
Guam Community College's comprehensive assessment initiative is grounded and steeped in the general question, "What do our educational programs amount to?" In order to answer this question, the GCC assessment process systematically explores and examines students' varied and unique experiences at the institution in terms of an estimate of "learning progress" (both quantitatively and qualitatively) for the following: (1) knowledge gained, understanding advanced (what they know); (2) attitudes formed, dispositions developed (what they think); and (3) competencies acquired, skills demonstrated (what they can do)	Prior Years: Sporadic Assessment ------------------------------ **Year 1 (SY 2000–2001):** Beginning the Conversation, Building a Culture/Infrastructure ●	• Committee on College Assessment (CCA) established in the Board of Trustees-Faculty Union contract; 4 administrators, 4 faculty comprise membership • Comprehensive Institutional Assessment Plan disseminated campus-wide • Template and protocol development (assessment plan & report) by CCA • Series of capacity-building workshops; partaking of food to promote "community" and the development of an assessment culture through informal talk • Annual institutional reporting of assessment activities through print and Internet • Leadership by example: survey of college president's end-of-first-year performance	Institutional support given by: • College president (through college newsletter article, convocation remarks, formal and informal talk, "guinea pig" for first campus-wide assessment) • Members of the Board of Trustees (through passage of Policy 306 and active participation in their own board assessment through surveys and focus groups) • Academic Vice President (through CCA ex-officio membership, Faculty governance remarks, formal and informal discussions with CCA chair) • Deans (through discussion of assessment issues in monthly department chair meetings, reminder memos to faculty regarding their assessment requirements) • Faculty governance leaders (through discussion of assessment agenda in governance meetings)

APPENDIX 7.1 (CONTINUED)

PRINCIPLES	PROCESSES	STRATEGIES	RESOURCES
	Year 2 (SY 2001–2002) Formulating Policy, Fueling Dialogue	• BOT Policy 306 (passage of institutional policy that mandates assessment processes and timelines for all programs, student services, and administrative units) • Ritualizing assessment through bi-annual assessment cycle schedule; college assessment taxonomy established (GROUP A: all AS programs; GROUP B: all Certificate programs; GROUP C: student services and administrative units; GROUP D: special programs (includes GE, federal programs, secondary, and skill development milestone course) (See Figure 7.3.) • Campus-wide compliance rates monitored and reported.	Financial support achieved through: • VEA (Carl D. Perkins III) funds; program agreement written each year, with federal reporting requirements • Year 1 (no allocated funds) • Year 2 ($73,546.22) • Year 3 ($84,281.00) • Year 4 ($121,057.47) As stipulated in the Board-Faculty Union contract, faculty members of the Assessment Committee are awarded release time (one class) to fulfill their committee responsibilities; non-teaching faculty are compensated at adjunct faculty rate In terms of human resources, support is provided by the leadership of the following individuals:

Continued

APPENDIX 7.1 (CONTINUED)

PRINCIPLES	PROCESSES	STRATEGIES	RESOURCES
	Year 3 (SY 2002–2003) Making Changes Internally, Modeling Assessment Externally	• Assessment issues integrated in Faculty Governance Meetings (six times/ semester) • Highlights of assessment results disseminated and discussed in annual college convocation • Assessment video produced • Vocational Program Success Day staged (intended as a public dialogue with the community; student artifacts showcased at the Micronesia Mall) • Leadership by example: BOT assessment • Preceded by a spirited campus dialogue, GE core curriculum established (no standard core in prior years) • Program guides revamped; course guides re-written to reflect student learning outcomes • Articulation of courses forged with the University of Guam through memorandum of agreement	• Associate Dean for Assessment & Chair, Committee on College Assessment • Program Specialist, Assessment • Administrative Aide • CCA members: 4 admin, 4 faculty (AVP ex-officio member) In terms of physical facilities and equipment to carry out assessment activities, the following support is available: • Two offices: 208 sq. ft. 160 sq. ft. • Multimedia equipment (for workshop training sessions and presentations) • VCR, scanner, digital camera, portable screen, easel board • Laptop • 2 computers, 2 printers

APPENDIX 7.1 (CONTINUED)

PRINCIPLES	PROCESSES	STRATEGIES	RESOURCES
		• Programs integrated and consolidated	
		• Assessment results utilized by faculty development committee to address training needs of various programs	
		• Utilizing the Community College Student Experiences Questionnaire (CCSEQ), 638 GCC students surveyed regarding their overall educational experience at the college; results widely disseminated through presentations and printed report; guided Student Development Office in creating programs to meet student needs	
		• Leadership at AAHE assessment conference: facilitated special interest group meeting in community college assessment;	
	Year 4 (SY 2003–2004) Aligning Mission and Assessment, Automating the Process	• Monitoring implementation of assessment results at both the program and course levels	

Continued

APPENDIX 7.1 (CONTINUED)

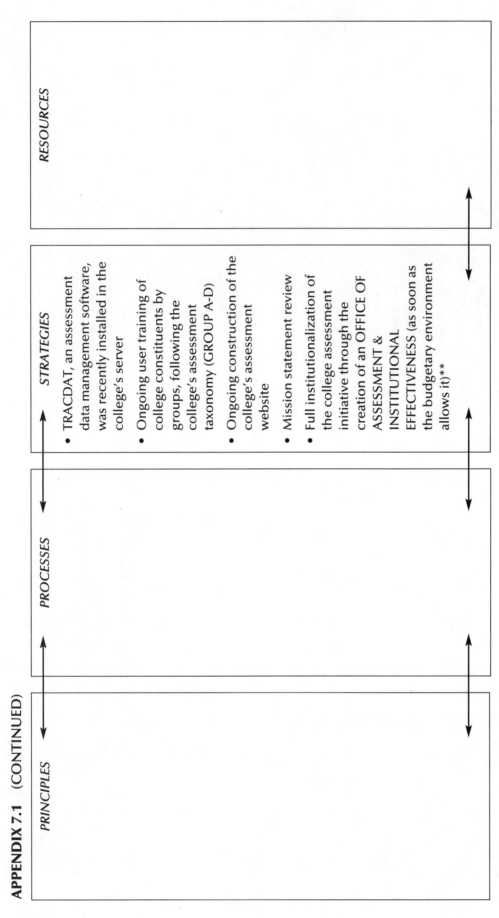

PRINCIPLES	PROCESSES	STRATEGIES	RESOURCES
		• TRACDAT, an assessment data management software, was recently installed in the college's server	
		• Ongoing user training of college constituents by groups, following the college's assessment taxonomy (GROUP A-D)	
		• Ongoing construction of the college's assessment website	
		• Mission statement review	
		• Full institutionalization of the college assessment initiative through the creation of an OFFICE OF ASSESSMENT & INSTITUTIONAL EFFECTIVENESS (as soon as the budgetary environment allows it)**	

**Note: As a two-year public institution, GCC's planning processes have been severely hampered within the last 5 years as a consequence of the Government of Guam's acute budgetary crisis.

Source: Contributed by Ray Somera, Associate Dean and Chair, Committee on College Assessment, John R. Rider, Vice President, Academic Affairs, Guam Community College. Reproduced with permission.

GCC's TWO-YEAR ASSESSMENT CYCLE SCHEDULE
EFFECTIVE SPRING 2004

	GROUP A	GROUP B	GROUP C	GROUP D
	ASSOCIATE DEGREE PROGRAMS	CERTIFICATE PROGRAMS	STUDENT SERVICES & ADMINISTRATIVE UNITS	SPECIAL PROGRAMS
SPRING 2004	Implement use of assessment results; submit implementation memo DEADLINE: MARCH 8, 2004	Prepare and submit assessment report DEADLINE: MARCH 8, 2004	Gather data continuously; submit progress report memo DEADLINE: MARCH 8, 2004	Review existing plan and incorporate modifications; report health indicators DEADLINE: MARCH 8, 2004
FALL 2004	Review existing plan and incorporate modifications; report health indicators DEADLINE: OCTOBER 4, 2004	Implement use of assessment results; submit implementation memo DEADLINE: OCTOBER 4, 2004	Prepare and submit assessment report DEADLINE: OCTOBER 4, 2004	Gather data continuously; submit progress report memo DEADLINE: OCTOBER 4, 2004
SPRING 2005	Gather data continuously; submit progress report memo DEADLINE: MARCH 7, 2005	Review existing plan and incorporate modifications; report health indicators DEADLINE: MARCH 7, 2005	Implement use of assessment results; submit implementation memo DEADLINE: MARCH 7, 2005	Prepare and submit assessment report DEADLINE: MARCH 7, 2005
FALL 2005	Prepare and submit assessment report DEADLINE: OCTOBER 3, 2005	Gather data continuously; submit progress report memo DEADLINE: OCTOBER 3, 2005	Review existing plan and incorporate modifications; report health indicators DEADLINE: OCTOBER 3, 2005	Implement use of assessment results; submit implementation memo DEADLINE: OCTOBER 3, 2005

WASC ACCREDITATION TEAM VISIT: SPRING 2006

FIGURE 7.3 Guam Community College Assessment Cycles. *Source:* Contributed by Ray Somera, Associate Dean and Chair, Committee on College Assessment, John R. Rider, Vice President, Academic Affairs, Guam Community College. Reproduced with permission.

APPENDIX 7.2   CONSENT FORM

Involving students in institution- and program-level assessment efforts carries with it ethical considerations about the use of their work. Beyond informing students that the institution and its programs will assess their work over time, an institution is ethically responsible for providing students with the opportunity to accept or decline the use of their work for institutional learning and improvement. Federal guidelines exempt the following kinds of research from U.S. Regulations Governing Research Ethics Requirements, so long as human subjects cannot be identified or linked to the research:

1. Research conducted in "established or commonly accepted education settings involving normal education practices"

2. Research "involving the use of educational tests . . . procedures, interview procedures, or observation of public behavior"

3. Research involving the "collection or study of existing data, documents, records, pathological specimens, or diagnostic specimens"

Source: Code of Federal Regulations, Title 45, Part 46—Protection of Human Subjects (2001). www.gpoaccess.gov/cfr/index.html.

However, institutional review boards may require approval of any institution- or program-level assessment methods under their human subjects policies, even if students' names are not identified in the results. For that reason institutions should make clear to members of its community the necessary policies and procedures that guide conducting assessment across the campus and within programs.

Viewing assessment as a process of inquiry that advances both student and institutional learning creates a learning partnership between students and the larger educational community. Providing students with opportunities to learn about the institutional commitment during their orientation to the institution, as well as providing them with an opportunity to accept or decline to participate in large-scale institutional efforts, values their role in the assessment process. For that reason many institutions develop student consent forms that explain the process of assessment or the methods of assessment that the institution will use at points in students' studies. Washington State University presents students with the following consent form before students participate in one of the university's institution-level assessment projects. This form provides students with a full understanding of the purposes of the assessment project and their role in this project:

- Explains the purpose of the project within the institution's context

- Acknowledges the value of the project to students

- Describes the process students will be involved in

- Assures confidentiality

- Makes public students' right to participate or decline

- Demonstrates compliance with the institution's review board

CONSENT FORM FOR CRITICAL THINKING STUDY
STUDENT PARTICIPATION AT WASHINGTON STATE UNIVERSITY

Your instructor is participating in a study which is further implementing and developing an assessment instrument, a Critical Thinking Rubric, originally designed at WSU, which would afford a rough measure of student progress in achieving the higher intellectual skills over the course of their college careers. This study is a component of the grant received by General Education, the Center for Teaching, Learning and Technology and the Campus Writing Programs from the Fund for the Improvement of Post-Secondary Education.

The researchers for this project will collect student papers from this class and evaluate them using a group of trained faculty readers to determine the effectiveness of the Critical Thinking Rubric. Your instructor will collect assignments from at least two points in the semester.

Data collected will be strictly confidential and your name will not be recorded. Only the research team will have access to the data. Your performance in your class will have no relation to your participation in this study.

By participating in this project, you will help WSU faculty refine instructional and evaluative methods which will encourage higher intellectual skills over the course of students' college careers. Washington State University and the Center for Teaching, Learning and Technology, Campus Writing Programs and General Education Program support the practice of protection of the rights of research participants. Accordingly, this project was reviewed and approved by the WSU Institutional Review Board. The information in this consent form is provided so that you can decide whether you wish to participate in our study. It is important that you understand that your participation is considered voluntary. This means that even if you agree to participate you are free to withdraw from the experiment at any time, without penalty.

Critical Thinking Study Principal Investigator
Diane Kelly-Riley, Campus Writing Programs

Source: Contributed by Diane Kelly-Riley, WSU. Reproduced with permission.

CONSENT STATEMENT

I have read the above comments and agree to participate in this project. I understand that if I have any questions or concerns regarding this project, I can contact the investigator at the above location or the WSU Institutional Review Board.

Participant's Signature   Date

Print Name   WSU ID Number

Course Name and Number _____

Source: Contributed by Diane Kelly-Riley, WSU. Reproduced with permission.

INDEX

A

AAHE. *See* American Association for Higher Education
Academic affairs, 3
"Academic Librarians and Faculty," institutional example, 108–10
Academic support services, 154
Accountability, 12–13
Accrediting Board for Engineering and Technology (ABET), 13, 15
  North Carolina State University, 65
Accrediting bodies, 13
Accrediting Commission for Community and Junior Colleges of the Western Association of Schools and Colleges, 13, 15
Accrediting Commission for Senior Colleges and Universities of the Western Association of Schools and Colleges, 13, 15
Accreditors, 13, 17
ACRL. *See* Association of College and Research Libraries
Active learning, 43
Administrators in assessment, 7
Advising, 3
Affective domain of learning, 32
Alignment issues in assessment methods, 90–92
Allen, Jo, 27, 112
Alumni, 8
Alverno College, 89, 95–96, 116
American Association for Higher Education, 25
  "Nine Principles of Good Practice for Assessing Student Learning," 23–24
American College Personnel Association, 25
American Council on Education, 15, 189
American Library Association, 65
American Psychological Association (APA), 10, 15, 68
  "Undergraduate Psychology Major Learning Goals and Outcomes: A Report," 65, 68
Analysis and presentation of results in the cycle of inquiry, 160

Analytic scoring rubrics, 123
Anderson, James A., 27
Anderson, L. W., 32, 40, 63, 68
Angelo, T., 25
APA. *See* American Psychological Association
Applying the Science of Learning to University Teaching and Beyond (Halpern and Hakel), 8, 15
Ash, Sarah, 88, 125, 127
Assessment
  collaborative view of, 3–6
  definition, 2
Assessment glossaries, 4, 16
Assessment methods, 85–118
  alignment issues, 90–92
  direct and indirect methods, 88–89, 105, 114–18
  formative and summative assessment, 89–90, 106
  institutional examples
    "Academic Librarians and Faculty," 108–10
    Alverno College, 89, 95–96, 116
    Keystone College, 91
    Marian College, 91
    North Carolina State University, 88
    Stanford University, 87
    "Student Affairs and Academic Affairs," 110–12
    University of Michigan, 88
  multiple methods of assessment, 86–88
  positions of inquiry, 90
  properties of methods, 92–96
    designed methods, 94–95
    reliability, 93, 99
    standardized tests, 93–94, 113
    validity, 93, 99
  range of texts that demonstrate learning, 85–86
Assessment of Student Achievement in Undergraduate Education, National Science Foundation, 10, 16
Association of American Colleges & Universities, 46
Association of College and Research Libraries (ACRL), 108

Information Literacy Competency Standards for Higher Education: Standards, Performance Indicators, and Outcomes, 65, 68
Astin, Alexander W., 24
Athletics, 11
Austin, Connie, 83, 122
Azusa Pacific University, 67, 81–82, 122
  School of Nursing, 67, 81–82

B

Banta, Trudy W., 9, 15, 24, 97, 179
Barr, R. B., 10, 12, 15
Bartolini, Brian J., 164
Baseline data, 160
Bloom, B. S., 32, 40, 63, 68
Bloom's taxonomy, 63
Boards of trustees, 6–7
Book of Professional Standards for Higher Education, The (Miller), 10, 16
Boolean search operators, 108–9
Bowden, D. Vicky, 83, 122
Boyer, E. L., 8–9, 15
Bresciani, Marilee J., 27, 112
Brown, D. G., 41, 46
Bulaong, G., 143
Burros Institute, *Mental Measurements Yearbook Test Reviews Online,* 113

C

Calibration, 126–27
California State Library system, 108
California State University Monterey Bay, 60
Cambridge, B., 97, 116
Campus leaders, 7
Campus practices that manifest an institutional commitment, 181
Campus-wide assessment committees, 33–34, 44
Carnegie Academy for the Scholarship of Teaching and Learning (CASTL), 9
Carnegie Foundation for the Advancement of Teaching, 15
Carnegie Initiative on the Doctorate, 10
Case, J., 92, 97